# THE CLINICAL EXCHANGE

## Techniques Derived from
## Self and Motivational Systems

Psychoanalytic Inquiry Book Series

Volume 16

# Psychoanalytic Inquiry Book Series

# THE CLINICAL EXCHANGE

## Techniques Derived from
## Self and Motivational Systems

*Joseph D. Lichtenberg*

*Frank M. Lachmann*

*James L. Fosshage*

THE ANALYTIC PRESS

1996    Hillsdale, NJ                    London

Published by
The Analytic Press, Inc.
   Editorial Offices:
   101 West Street
   Hillsdale, NJ 07642

Index by Leonard S. Rosenbaum

Library of Congress Cataloging-in-Publication Data

Lichtenberg, Joseph D.
    The clinical exchange : techniques derived from self and
motivational systems / Joseph D. Lichtenberg, Frank M. Lachmann,
James L. Fosshage.
        p.   cm. — (Psychoanalytic inquiry book series ; v. 16)
    Includes bibliographical references and index.
    ISBN 0-88163-220-1
    1. Psychotherapist and patient.   2. Psychoanalysis.
3. Interpersonal communication.   I. Lachmann, Frank M.
II. Fosshage, James L.   III. Title.   IV. Series.
    RC480.8.L534   1996
    616.89—dc20                                          96-28332
                                                             CIP

Printed in the United States of America
   10  9  8  7  6  5  4  3  2  1

*To respond verbally, emotionally, and behaviorally in the therapeutic situation, with a maximal desired effectiveness and minimal untoward consequences, requires an artistic kind of skill which, however, must be based on principles that rest on a firm scientific fundament.*

Ernest Wolf (1995)

# Contents

# Acknowledgments

I am greatly indebted to Frank Lachmann and James Fosshage, my coauthors, for their willingness, actually eagerness, to think and work together with me to carry forward ideas each of us has had independently. I began my series of explorations by reviewing the body of infant research then available and proposing a critique of psychoanalytic developmental theory. I then offered a theory of five motivational systems and a revised theory of affects. I suggested the application of these concepts to a psychology of the self through an empathic mode of perception and the use of model scenes jointly constructed by analyst and patient. Frank Lachmann added his extensive exposure to infant studies derived from his collaborations with Beatrice Beebe and their valuable contributions to communication between infant and mother and to self and mutual regulation. Jim Fosshage brings to our collaboration an extensive knowledge of research on dreams and a careful reconsideration of transference and countertransference. Each of us is a clinician with years of experience in training and teaching, and the author of many contributions to analytic theory and practice. In our presentation we have attempted to speak in a unified voice. Frank's felicitous phrasing and Jim's continuous call for clarity in terminology contribute to each chapter regardless of the principal author.

Each of us has learned from many colleagues and sources as evidenced by our reference list. We want to acknowledge the personal support we receive continuously from Ernest Wolf, Alan Kindler, Beatrice Beebe, Susan Lazar, Robert Stolorow, John Lindon, Rosemary Segalla, Arthur Malin, and Estelle and Morton Shane.

In our effort to draw on recent developments in neurophysiology we received direct help from June Hadley, Fred Levin, and Allan Schore. Similarly we draw on Schore's and Joseph Jones's studies of affects. We have greatly benefited from the many opportunities we have had at meetings and in publications to present our conceptions of model scenes, motivational systems, ten principles of technique, the interpretation of dreams, transference, and the modes of therapeutic action. The questions we have been asked and the criticisms we have received have been a source of invaluable challenge. We are especially indebted to Lawrence Friedmen for his remarkable essay "Main Meaning and Motivation" and to the other contributors to *Psychoanalytic Inquiry,* Volume 15, Number 4: Joseph Weiss and John

Gedo, who raised additional questions; Kay Campbell, Donald Silver, Kerry and Jack Novick, Mary Mittlestaedt, and Ann Walton, who put our assumptions to the test of infant observation; Philip Ringstrom, who applied our approach to brief psychotherapy; and Estelle and Morton Shane, who tested whether our conceptions could explain the feminine dilemma of generativity vs. personal ambition. In a similar vein, Paul Stepansky has been more than our editor, he has been an excellent conceptual critic. The other professionals of The Analytic Press, especially Nancy Liguori and Eleanor Kobrin, have earned our gratitude for their skill. Amy Lichtenberg Vides labored long and patiently to transcribe my scribbles into readable type and convert Frank and Jim's Apple into our PC.

Finally, our book centers on Nancy and her analyst, or on an analyst and his patient, Nancy. Customarily a statement is made to acknowledge our debt to our patients for the opportunity they present us to learn, teach, and advance science. A difficulty with this convention is that the patient is treated as a specimen to be exposed and dissected. If, as in our book, the analyst presents his exact words, interventions, and intentions, he is equally exposed as a specimen for "supervision" and second guessing. Were this objectification (Broucek, 1991) of patient and/or analyst to occur, a major purpose of our book would not be achieved. We hope to present the subjective experience of an analyst and an analysand working together in the special dynamic intersubjective context of a therapeutic exploration. All three of us wish therefore to acknowledge our gratitude to Nancy and her analyst for allowing the authors and you, the reader, to sense into their experience of seeking, finding, losing, and refinding the inner world of the other.

Joseph D. Lichtenberg, M.D.

# 1 Introduction

*The Clinical Exchange* is intended for a readership of practicing psychoanalysts and psychotherapists. We will present our particular perspective on the theory that informs our technique as a stimulus for the reader's reflection, not as a prescription or dogma. We view ourselves in a changing world, accordingly we offer the reader as clear a statement as we can on the major issues that our field of exploratory therapy confronts today. The core of our book is formed by a single case presented as verbatim exchanges in a week's work every two years over a nine-year analysis. We propose ten principles of technique and relate the case material and techniques to the problems of transference, affects, dream interpretation, sexual abuse, and modes of therapeutic action. Our book thus follows in the tradition of case studies and writings on technique.

The saga of psychoanalytic technique is a century old (Breuer and Freud, 1893–1895). The story began with the serendipitous collaboration between Breuer and Anna O. Together they created a method of listener and teller for which they coined the metaphors of "talking cure" and "chimney sweeping." Breuer, the older physician, told Sigmund Freud, his brilliant younger colleague, of the remarkable results of this collaboration between doctor and patient. Without the persistence, dedication, and genius of Freud's inquiring mind, psychoanalysis might easily have ended there as a "countertransference" casualty of an intense erotic transference state. After the puzzlement of his experiences at the Salpêtrière (Jones, 1953), Freud was prepared to welcome a research method that would help to solve the burning problem of hysteria and other psychoneurotic afflictions. The method Breuer and Anna O evolved permitted Freud to discard first hypnosis, then hand pressure on the patient's forehead, and then to adopt "free association." In this method, the patient says what comes into his or her mind, and the analyst listens with free-floating attention and interprets patterns he or she discerns. So simple—and yet so complex that a hundred years later we are still discussing and debating the process.

The lessons from this early period in the history of psychoanalysis still have significance today. Breuer was primarily a physician and his goal was to treat, to cure. His experience tells us that the method he and Anna O discovered can be very difficult for the practitioner, especially one with therapeutic enthusiasm and inadequate preparation. Freud was primarily a discoverer, and his goal was to solve

1

mysteries. To do so he needed a means to gain data to formulate hypotheses, and he needed theories to organize the data and refine the method. Therapy would come as inherent confirmation of method and theory, or theory and method, but it was not to be sought at the expense of either. Thus from the beginning the triad of method, theory, and therapeutic aim has been intertwined. The resulting complexity of this triad has led to a major reconsideration of it every time during the century that a significant change has occurred in each.

Compared to efforts to conceptualize and reconceptualize theory, attempts to describe and codify technique have been sparse and irregular. Both Freud's theory and the psychoanalytic movement were well under way before Freud wrote his justly famous papers on technique (Freud, 1911, 1912a, b, 1913, 1914, 1915). In these papers he described the fundamental rule, the analytic surface, resistance, the unobjectionable positive transference, erotic transferences, working through, and the repetition compulsion (Ellman, 1991). Looking back, we believe that

> Freud's papers on technique were written at a time when he could express supreme confidence in the psychoanalytic process, based on his theory of libido. Freud was far less sanguine about the practices of many contemporary analysts; consequently the papers contain far more don't's than do's. From the vantage point of today, these papers portray a transitional stage in psychoanalysis, an age of innocence, in comparison to the complexities of our current view of the interaction between analyst and analysand [Lichtenberg, 1994, p. 727].

Freud's confidence in the theory that guided the technique papers was rapidly shaken by war neuroses, therapeutic failures, and inconsistencies in the topographic theory—especially with respect to defenses and affects (Gill, 1963). Another decade passed between the technique papers and the postulates of the structural hypothesis (Freud, 1923, 1926). During this interval, the most provocative modifications in technique were the experimental efforts of Ferenczi (1953).

As the implications of the tripartite structure of the mind were being argued and absorbed, a major bifurcation in its significance and application occurred. One group of analysts focused their attention on the aggressive-destructive drive, leading at first to the theory and technical approach of Melanie Klein (Segel, 1974; Spillius, 1995) and subsequently to a major emphasis in various object relational theories (Greenberg and Mitchell, 1983). Another group of analysts focused their attention on the ego and its defensive measures (A. Freud,

1936) and on a functional-structure construct comprising both conflict and adaptation (Hartmann, 1964).

These three approaches—Kleinian, object relational, and ego psychological—came to be called the mainstream of psychoanalysis in that, despite their differences, they all remained within the same international association. We confine our further discussion of works on technique primarily to those that developed from ego psychology and object relations because these are the trends from which we derive the background to our ideas.

Regardless of differences in theory, all of the writings on technique for the next 30 years wrestled with the problem of how to apply or modify Freud's dictums about neutrality, abstinence, the metaphor of the surgeon, and the mirror and the blank screen. Glover (1931), an influential early writer, decried inexact interpretation as a form of suggestion. In light of the recent trend toward relativism in one person's ability to appreciate another, Glover's demand for precision and "thoroughness in uncovering phantasy" (1931, p. 358) is in the tradition of an ideal or pure technique. Within this same tradition, Fenichel (1941) warned against "the Scylla of talking instead of experiencing" and the Charybdis of unsystematic free-floating emotional expression that "is not comprehended by a reasoning power that keeps ulterior aims in view" (p. 6). By the 1950s, the concept of a mainstream approach was sufficiently articulated (in the United States) that Eissler (1953) could define it as "interpretation of defense and conflict aimed at insight" and relegate all other activities of the analyst to the status of "parameters." This view of a basic model technique solidified in psychoanalytic writings the belief in an orthodoxy of theory and method based on a one-person psychology. In response, many other writings followed "revisionist" trends based on criticisms from a number of perspectives. Kardiner (1939) and Erikson (1959) argued that culture was being left out, Sullivan (1953) that interpersonal relationships were necessary to understand development, Racker (1968) that the analyst's contribution was understated, Reik (1949) that intuition was underappreciated, and Deutsch (1944) that female developmental issues were skewed. The need for more attention in technique to relational and humanistic aspects was presented by theorists as diverse as Rogers (1951), Winnicott (1958), Stone (1961), and Guntrip (1969).

Greenson (1967) attempted to pull together many of these trends in an influential text on technique that was richly illustrated with clinical material. Greenson demonstrated the use of his sensitivity to the patient's inner experience and motivation and his ability to apprehend the meaning of the patient's association from the patient's point of view, providing an early example of the empathic mode of perception (see Lichtenberg, 1981). Greenson's book stands out as the richest presentation of clinical material of the period. Most other writings of the time described technique with vignettes—some to delineate the interpretation of conflict within the classical tradition (Arlow and Brenner, 1964; Brenner, 1976) and others to take up specific aspects of more humanistic exchanges (Poland, 1984). Another trend of this period was for analysts to formulate technical modifications that would facilitate treating patients with severe character pathology, such as borderline disorders (Kernberg, 1975, 1976) and preoedipal disturbances (Mahler, 1968; Mahler, Pine, and Bergman, 1975).

The era from which we derive the principles of technique we propose, in fact, the work from which we build a major part of our foundation, began with Kohut's (1971) call for a reconsideration to the whole approach to grandiosity, disillusion, and alienation personified in narcissistic personality disorders. In our previous writings leading up to this exploration of technique (Lichtenberg, 1989; Lichtenberg, Lachmann, and Fosshage, 1992), we have described our debt to Kohut and other self psychologists as well as to the developmental research that coordinates with a theory of the self as a center for experience and motivation (Stern, 1985; Lachmann and Beebe, 1989, 1992). We also include in our theory and clinical practice an emphasis on the theory of intersubjectivity (Atwood and Stolorow, 1984; Stolorow and Atwood, 1992). Looking at other writings of the era on technique, we recognize considerable similarities between our view and social constructivism (Hoffman, 1983; Gill, 1982, 1991) and the approaches of Weiss and Sampson (1986), Jacobs (1991), and Dorpat and Miller (1992). We see more contrast between our view and those that emphasize conflict (Brenner, 1976), defense interpretation (Gray, 1973), aggressive drive, and projective identification (Ogden, 1982). In both the approaches we cite as similar and those we cite as contrasting we find a trend toward an appreciation of the significance of emotion and the moment-to-moment exchange between analyst and patient. Although we evolved our principles of technique independently, we find that they overlap with the models and strategies of Peterfreund (1983).

Our form of presenting our principles is a single case illustration. Thus, our present book is one of a small group of "case" books. In 1978, pioneer self psychologists responded to the request to provide clinical illustrations of the application of Kohut's theories. The case-book (Goldberg, 1978) that resulted described through six examples the placing of interpretive emphasis

> on the periodic unavailability of the self-object, which is what the analyst becomes in a self-object transference . . . whenever the self-object function of the analyst is felt to be unavailable, there follows a period of imbalance and a picture of minor traumatic overstimulation. But correct interpretation will ameliorate such traumatic episodes [p. 9].

The casebook therefore had a strong focus on the interpretation of felt unavailability through physical absence or empathic failure of a presence needed by the patient to maintain or restore self-cohesion. These interpretations included "the reconstruction and inclusion of the genetic context which was precursor to the contemporaneous dynamic" (p. 448). Through our case presentation and discussion, we believe we confirm the essential findings of the 1978 casebook (Goldberg, 1978) while extending the range of interpretation. In the interval between the two casebooks, experience has demonstrated that patients have greater needs than those for mirroring, twinship, and idealizing experiences (Wolf, 1988). We deal with the wide range of needs and patterns that arise by addressing five motivational systems. In addition, the remarkable changes the authors of the casebooks demonstrate (from the relatively restricted repertoire of interpretations they describe) led them to a somewhat false optimism about the thera-peutic power of their interpretive focus. Subsequent clinical experience has demonstrated to us that interpretation (or mutual expanding aware-ness) must cover not only the effect of deficiencies of past and present growth-inducing responses but also the deleterious effect of repetitive conflictual patterns (see Chapter 6). We believe that the combination of attention to a wider range of motivations and to the problematic repetitive patterns of unconsciously organized responses expands the therapeutic scope of our presentation.

Dewald's (1972) case illustration contains richly detailed verbatim notes and commentary. Similar to our intent, Dewald offers a unique opportunity for a reader to experience vicariously the unedited inter-changes between analyst and patient. The two books provide an interesting comparison. Both patients are women, both analysts men, and both patients had experienced sexual seduction as children. Dewald's patient's analysis was completed in the unusually short time of two years, whereas the analysis we report occurred over nine years. In both reports, themes are repeated over and over again, illustrating the elaboration and continuous adding of perspective that characterize a working analysis. The major difference lies in the purpose of the authors. Dewald's (1972) case is presented "to provide primary data illustrating the phenomenology of mental functioning" (p. 7) in order to respond to critics who challenge the status of psychoanalysis as a science and as an effective method. He aims to illustrate the successful application of the technique that followed the line of Freud's papers and the structural hypothesis. The correctness of that technique is assumed and never challenged, but is regarded by Dewald to be "ideally applicable to only a relatively small number of psychiatrically ill patients" (p. 633). In contrast, our book assumes a wider scope of patients for whom psychoanalysis or exploratory psychotherapy is applicable. Rather than illustrate the techniques of either the structural hypothesis or self psychology, we offer a reconceptualization of principles of technique and a theory of motivation. Dorpat and Miller (1992) observed that Dewald gave little significance to "the actualities of his interactions with the patient" (p. 37). This contrasts with our considerable attentiveness to the patient's responses to what the analyst says and does, rather than primarily to what fantasies (distortions) the analyst's interventions evoke. In both books, the case is a record of two people actively engaged. Dewald employs the case to convey his use of ego psychology and adds a brief well-organized discussion at the end. Our book takes up a series of issues that bear on the application of our motivational systems theory and principles of technique to affects, transference, dream interpretation, sexual abuse, and modes of therapeutic action.

We also envision our case material and commentary as providing essential data for clinical research. The usefulness of verbatim material, even sometimes of only an hour, as in the cases of Silverman (1987) and Fosshage (1990), has been confirmed by the repeated reconsideration such material has received in the literature. Besides conceptual discussions derived from brief samples of verbatim material, the whole field of more formal research has grown in the 20-plus years between Dewald's book and ours (Luborsky, 1976; Bucci, 1985, 1992; Weiss and Sampson, 1986; Dahl, Kachele, and Thoma, 1988; Luborsky and Crits-Christoph, 1989; Weiss, 1993). We believe that our book, although primarily directed to those practicing exploratory therapies, responds as well to the call for data to help in the critical examination of our field (Edelson, 1984).

In this book, we present our view of techniques for conducting the clinical exchange. We illustrate our view with the process notes of an analysis, which are accompanied by commentaries on the successes and failures of the analyst's approach. We developed our technique in conjunction with our prior writings. In *Self and Motivational Systems* we addressed the concepts fundamental to psychoanalysis from the vantage point of five motivational systems. The five systems self-organize and self-stabilize in response to an infant's innate needs and response patterns combined with learned responses to the ministrations of caregivers. We took into account fundamental needs for the psychic regulation of physiological requirements, attachment and affiliation, assertion and exploration, sensual pleasure and sexual excitement, and the need to react aversively by using withdrawal or antagonism. We described a sense of self developing as a center for initiating, organizing, and integrating experience and motivation. The sense of self can develop and thrive only with the empathic responsiveness of caregivers.

The implications of our perspective enabled us to revise our understanding of unconscious mentation, distinguishing between fundamental unconscious mentation and the more familiar unconscious symbolic mentation. We recast the topographic preconscious as a path to awareness along which thoughts and feeling will flow when an increased sense of safety is established. We replaced the traditional focus of psychoanalytic therapy on interpreting and removing unconscious defenses with our offering organized responses to aversive experiences and negative emotions. We proposed an alternate theory of conflict based on the dialectic tensions and hierarchical rearrangements between and within systems that occur during the transformations at each stage of development. We questioned a static view of distortion-based transferences superimposed on current figures or relationships, suggesting instead more fluid reconstructions. These new constructions are influenced both by expectations derived from prior lived experiences and by current intersubjective factors. We described the joint construction by analyst and analysand of model scenes. We suggested that each clinical experience can be viewed from three overlapping perspectives: the intrapsychic, the intersubjective, and the assessment of the affective-cognitive state.

At the time we became psychoanalysts, ego psychology dominated the theoretical and therapeutic landscape. Important technical precepts were based on Eissler's (1953) discussion of parameters, Kris's (1956) prescription for the good hour, and Greenson's (1967) emphasis on the therapeutic alliance. The widening scope of psychoanalysis was being hotly debated. The astringent austerity that had come to define classical psychoanalysis in the wake of Glover's (1931) codification of technique was being challenged by analysts within the American classical tradition (Stone, 1961; Greenson, 1967) and by friendly critics such as George Klein (1970).

Looking back, we can apply Robert Kennedy's words to the evolution of psychoanalytic technique, "Some people look at things as they are and ask, why? I dream of things that have never been and ask, why not?" In the past, if analysts asked "why"—for example, why do we use the couch, or see patients four and five times a week, or not answer questions—the answers were derived from a theory of abstinence, neutrality, and optimal frustration. When analysts began to ask "why not"—for example, why not be more affectively responsive, or informative, or flexible in scheduling—a profound shift in the analytic ambiance began. Initially, astringent authority gave way to analytically informed responsiveness. A question might be answered, a fee might be changed, a patient's gift might be accepted without the automatic suspicion that a pathology concealing enactment was being permitted. So far, so good. However, asking "why not?" can easily lead to a hodgepodge of technical misadventures in which efforts to counter the stereotype of the silent, unresponsive analyst result in the use of countertransference confessions and self-disclosures without a well-conceived rationale.

We recognize the shortcomings of a blank screen, reflecting mirror technique, but we also see the dangers in substituting an approach through an interactive relationship construed to be *in itself* the essential source of therapeutic leverage. We aim for a technique that establishes a relationship between analyst and patient that most effectively facilitates an exploration of meanings and motives. As previously stated,

> A unique feature of analysis is that the shifting strains at the junction of the analysand's and analyst's activities create a relational exchange, one that calls for definition and a comprehensible set of emotion-laden meanings. Thus, the relationship between analyst and analysand provides more than the working basis for the analysis, its shifting strains provide crucial data from which the most significant aspects of understanding are derived [Lichtenberg, 1983, pp. 236–237].

In this aspect of our approach we retain continuity with a valued psychoanalytic tradition of enhancing self-reflection. We continue to respect a search for understanding derived from following an associative flow. We consider an analytic frame of regularity of meeting times, fee arrangements, and modes of inquiry to be a prerequisite for the opportunity to explore. It is this frame that has been subjected to the greatest stress. Made so rigid by some that even in skilled hands it was bound to crack, it has been bent out of shape by others under the guise of making up for deficiencies in caregiving. We regard a consistent, well-conceived frame to be an essential support for the development of a relationship of trust and hope. Within well-recognized boundaries, situationally appropriate flexibility adds to the human exchange and provides experiences for self-reflective investigation.

Our elaboration of technique is derived from two sources: self psychology and empirical infant research. From self psychology we derived our central concern with the sense of self and the maintenance of a feeling of cohesion and vitality. From infant research we deduced our theory of five motivational systems and the significance of lived experiences for development and memory. From both self psychology and infant studies, we derived our emphasis on emotions as a principal guide for appreciating self-experience and the desires, wishes, goals, aims, and values that come to be elaborated in symbolic forms. In our experience as patients, therapists, and teacher-supervisors we have been guided by an empirical approach to psychoanalytic propositions. Our practical experience has enabled us to formulate principles that we believe speak to the safety, confidence, and restoration of hope required by therapists and patients in the conduct of treatment.

In the chapters to come, we follow an analyst in direct confrontation with the moment-to-moment dilemmas of comprehending the experience, meanings, and motivations of a patient. We witness the analyst's success and failure in his attempt to sense the patient's lived experience from the patient's point of view. In these clinical exchanges, theory and intuition join in the spontaneous moment—affording us an opportunity to explore the implications of what analyst and analysand say to each other. Implicitly and explicitly, principles of technique serve as guides in the clinical exchange. Subsequent reconsiderations of the choices made help us to define and refine these principles.

A brief description of ten user-friendly principles of technique follows. We then launch the reader into the verbatim case material of the analysis of Nancy. Throughout the book, we use the analysis of Nancy, as well as other clinical experiences, to illustrate technique. The process notes of Nancy's analysis cover a week's analytic work approximately every two years from 1983 to 1990. An explanatory commentary accompanies the associations and interventions. Later, the ten principles are discussed in detail with illustrations drawn from the case, followed by suggested revisions in the theory and technical management of affects, transference, and dream interpretation. Furthermore, the clinical material provides a basis for explicating our use of model scenes to understand and analyze sexuality, affection, and erotization. Finally, we reconsider the modes of therapeutic action: self-righting, joint expanding awareness, and the reorganization of symbolic representational schemas.

We introduce our principles of technique briefly so that the reader will be able to enter into the clinical exchange that follows, aware of the technical considerations that guide the analysis.

As our first principle, we advocate that the *analysis be conducted in a frame of friendliness, consistency, and reliability and an ambience of safety*. Arrangements that promote an atmosphere of safety for both participants will increase the likelihood that the patient can access the relatively inaccessible associations that are barred by shame and fear. The analyst who is stabilized and oriented within a familiar working mode can access the most spontaneous responsiveness. Maintaining and adjusting the frame affects all occurrences of the analysis, usually in the background.

Through the second principle, *systematic application of the empathic mode of perception*, analysts gain information as they listen within the patient's perspective. How a patient senses himself or herself and others, the sources of these affective-cognitive states, and the potential range or flexibility of the patient's response to such states can then be recognized, conceptualized, and interpreted. Thus, when we say we have made a successful interpretation based on our having entered the patient's experience through the empathic mode of perception, we mean that we have grasped the patient's whole experiential state, in an articulated sense. That is, we mean that we have discerned aspects of the patient's relationship of self with other, linked temporal sequences, proposed causal relationships, and assessed affective ranges. Attempting systematically to sense into the patient's state of mind permits the analyst to perceive associations that connect conscious, preconscious, and sometimes unconscious threads.

We proceed with our user-friendly principles, from the general frame and a general stance toward the patient and his or her subjective world to more specific principles. The third principle addresses the requirement that we *discern the patient's specific affect to appreciate his or her experience and we discern the affective experience being sought to appreciate the patient's motivation*. Capturing the patient's affect enables the analyst to appreciate the quality of experience being described. Discerning the selfobject experience sought enables the analyst to appreciate the patient's motivation. From the patient's point of view, is the goal he or she seeks soothing, vitalization, or to have one of a wide range of need fulfillments?

The fourth principle is that *the message contains the message*. We listen to the patient's narrative, the rendering of an event or the explanation of a symptom, for what is stated as well as for what is implied. By attending to what is in or close to awareness, we affirm for the patients the value of their spontaneous associations, of telling the story of their life as it comes to mind. We do not assume and communicate that what is presented is designed to divert from what is not presented, or that what is missing is necessarily of more analytic importance than what is presented. We hear and see the patient's delivered communication, verbal, gestural, and facial, to familiarize ourselves with the patient's intentions as he or she wishes them to be known. As a result of the esteem enhancement of being listened to in this way, patients are encouraged to make previously hidden or unconscious motives and messages more accessible to awareness.

Our fifth principle is *to fill the narrative envelope*—to learn the who, what, where, and when of an event that has come up in the patient's associations or in the analytic exchange. Through our analytic inquiry, we bring a unique perspective to the patient's narrative. As we encourage patients to reveal themselves and their experiences in increasingly explicit ways, we can stimulate and enhance the emotional richness of the events recounted, especially those that transpire in the here and now of the analysis and involve us. In addition, the patient's success in organizing each element of his or her life story helps in the consolidation of a sense of self.

Our user-friendly techniques are designed to increase access to transference communications for the patient and the analyst. To further the joint exploration of the patient's transferences, we propose our sixth principle, that *the analyst wear the attributions of the patient*, thus enabling both analyst and analysand to better see the analyst from the patient's point of view. This refers to the analyst's acceptance and subsequent exploration of the direct and indirect attributions made by the patient. We include here an investigation by analyst and patient of how the analyst knowingly or unknowingly may have triggered the attribution.

Our seventh principle is to *jointly construct model scenes*. When the analyst and patient pool their information to construct model scenes, previously puzzling information becomes clearer, previously acquired understanding becomes integrated, and the exploration of the patient's experience and motivation is furthered. In this process the analyst draws on his or her immediate experience of the patient, on a theory of adaptive and maladaptive development in each of the five motivational systems, and on images and representations drawn from previously revealed schemas of self with others. Model scenes highlight and encapsulate in graphic and metaphoric forms experiences that represent salient motivational themes constructed and reconstructed as unconscious fantasies and pathogenic beliefs.

In delineating the five motivational systems, we placed aggression (antagonism), along with withdrawal, as a response pattern of the aversive system. Just as aggression does not occupy a privileged position among our motivations, neither does resistance, reluctance, or defense occupy a privileged position among our technical recommendations. Our eighth principle is that *aversive motivations are a communicative expression to be explored like any other*. As with any other verbal and nonverbal communication or enactment, we focus on patients' withdrawing, fending off, provoking, denying, and obfuscating from the point of view of what the patient experiences. We believe that only when the patient can bring into awareness aversiveness as a subjective experience in an intersubjective context can the analyst and patient ascertain the patient's motives as he or she construes them.

Our ninth principle describes three ways in which analysts intervene to further the exploratory process. First, the most common interventions are those that address what the analyst has sensed, using the empathic mode of perception to be inside the patient's point of view as the patient would construe it. In these interventions, we communicate our comprehension of what the patient is trying to communicate. We express our grasp of the patient's affect states, and we articulate or illuminate recognizable patterns that organize the patient's life, experience, and transferences. Second, as analysts, we form impressions as we step away from the patient's experience in order to access our own experience during an analytic session. We convey our appraisals, intentions, and feelings, thus offering our point of view. Third, we recognize that occasionally significant interventions deviate from these more customary forms of the analyst's communications. These may be spontaneous, unpremeditated, and yet apt. They convey our intimate attention to and involvement with the patient. We term these "disciplined spontaneous engagements." They signal our readiness to participate authentically in the immediacy of a particular interaction or role enactment without sacrificing the overall structure of the analytic frame.

Our tenth and final principle is again an overarching one. We *follow the sequence of our interventions and the patient's responses to them to evaluate their effect*. We are particularly observant of inevitable disruptions in the optimal level of shared communication. Thus we strive to identify sources of disruptions, particularly those triggered by the patient's perception of an empathic failure. We believe that following a patient's responses to a sequence of interventions is the principal means available to an analyst to assess therapeutic effectiveness. Patients rarely experience the analyst's intervention primarily as "an interpretation," but rather as a *sequence* of involved or uninvolved listening, spoken words, plus hmms and other nonverbal communications. Through a sequence of interventions the analyst conveys a coherent sense of purpose, enabling the successive interventions to have a cumulative effect. Through the identification of disruptions in the analytic process and the triggering moment in the exchanges, the analyst restores affective contact with the patient's experience and maintains an ambiance of safety.

Having outlined our ten principles, we will test them in the crucible of an analysis, and so we proceed to the case summary and process notes from Nancy's treatment.

# 2 Case Summary and Effects of Lived Experiences on the Patient's Self and Motivational Systems

Nancy began her treatment with me when she was in her 30s. She wanted to form a deep and lasting relationship with a man and to marry and have children. She felt that she tended to drift along and hoped that treatment would provide her with someone to light a fire under her. She had had several years of therapy with an analyst in another area of the country. Nancy and her analyst both felt it was a success. The central focus of the analysis had been her disturbed, guilt-ridden relationship with her deceased mother. With the help of the analyst, she ended a relationship that seemed to be unworkable and made a major life decision: She interrupted her career as a medical laboratory supervisor and moved east to enter the graduate department of a university as a Ph.D. candidate in philosophy.

The patient's mother married the patient's father, a man 15 years her senior, when she was 22 years old because she was afraid she would be an old maid. She came from a well-to-do southwestern family of eight daughters. Her mother (Nancy's grandmother) was considered a great beauty, as were the daughters, although Nancy's mother considered herself ugly and dumb in comparison to her mother and sisters. The sisters, who all married men in the oil industry, felt Nancy's mother had married beneath herself. Nancy's father came from an established farm family in an eastern state. He left the farm to work in the oil industry, but during a business recession shortly after his marriage he decided to return to farming, thereby separating his wife from her family. Nancy's mother, who had the reputation of being a "saint," accepted her husband's decision but was never happy with it. Nancy was born three years after her older brother, Matt.

During the last trimester of her pregnancy with Nancy, Nancy's mother was ill with placental previa and spent the time with her

15

family in the Southwest. Nancy weighed just under 5 lb at birth, but was healthy. Her mother was recovering slowly and it was decided that the baby would be taken back to the farm by her father, with her mother to follow her some time later. Thus Nancy received her initial care principally from men—her father and grandfather. Nancy firmly believes that even after her mother's return to the family, the feeling of affection that Nancy noted between her mother and Matt never became established with her. Until the age of five, Nancy ate sitting on her father's lap, and until the age of three, Nancy slept in her parent's bedroom. Nancy was also three years old when her grandfather, whom she loved dearly, died. Nancy was enuretic until she was 11 years old and received frequent enemas for constipation.

As a little girl, Nancy had blond curly hair and a petite body. Everyone thought of her as pretty and this won her favor even with her mother. By age five, when she was removed from father's lap, Nancy's hair had darkened and she believes she had lost her attractiveness. For the next few years, Nancy worked in the fields with her father and brother, refusing to wear a shirt to be like them. As a young teenager, she had a rapid growth spurt and thus was a big, awkward girl, hulking over her classmates.

Nancy's relationship with her brother occupied an important role in her early life. She described an early memory of her grandfather waving his cane at Matt, who was teasing and tormenting her. Matt would attack all her toys, he even dismembered and burned her favorite doll. At an early age, Matt began to rub his penis against her leg, and later he would lie on top of her and masturbate. Despite the abuse, Nancy would follow him around, desperately seeking his company. At age 11, Nancy began to rebel against the sexual activity. Matt threatened to injure her if she told their mother and bribed her with money to continue. After about another year, Nancy insisted that the sexual activity stop and Matt turned to the few girlfriends she had made. She felt doubly betrayed as both her brother and her friends turned from her to each other. (She and her principal girlfriend had played many exploratory sexual games.)

In school, Nancy was a good student. She was serious and showed an interest in religion. She never thought of herself as bright or quick as Matt. However, as a late adolescent she learned that she could trick her father and brother into making dogmatic or bigoted statements and she would then feel superior to and be contemptuous of them. Matt left college, having failed there. Her father then refused to give Nancy money for college, saying that if the boys couldn't make it she certainly couldn't—and that a girl didn't belong in college anyway. An aunt gave Nancy money for her first year in college and she went through the remaining years on scholarship.

## EFFECTS ON THE SELF AND THE MOTIVATIONAL SYSTEMS

Overall, when Nancy's self-organization was at its most cohesive and vital, she was an attractive, bright, competent, caring person. But the problems that existed in each of her motivational systems left her vulnerable to episodes of loss of self-cohesion and a variety of painful dysfunctional states.

### Regulation of Physiological Requirements

Nancy's early history of disturbed regulation of elimination, her enuresis and reliance on enemas, persisted in direct and metaphoric forms. She often had difficulty with constipation and this coincided with withholding, forgetting, ignoring, and "messing around" with her payments to me. She often feared and threatened that she would lose control of her money and have to quit the analysis. She wished I would charge her nothing or take over the whole problem from her. She lived a very marginal economic life, supporting herself largely as a laboratory technician on weekends. She received some money from her parents' estate and as a graduate instructor in philosophy. She also experienced severe anxiety that she would lose control of her urine and her menses and flood or soil the couch. During the analysis she stopped smoking and for a period eating became a problem, but not a serious one. She believes she received very little tactile stimulation from her mother and associates the deprivation with eczema episodes that began when she was very young and continued into adulthood. A model scene that ties together many problems of regulation derived from her memory of going up to bed alone and carrying her potty, which she banged noisily on the stair rails. Each night she failed to get her mother to come up with her, leaving her alone to deal with both potty and sleep. Her noisy banging expressed her anger and rebellious spirit mixed with her submission. As an adult she had a degree of sleep irregularity. She had frequent nightmares marked by intense anxiety and shame over exposure to her loss of bowel and bladder control.

### Attachment and Affiliation

Two of Nancy's memories served as triggers for model scenes (Lichtenberg, 1989), which we worked with repeatedly to expand their meaning. The first is Nancy's memory of tugging at her mother's leg or skirt and sensing the stiffening of her mother's body as she resisted the child's importuning. The second model scene is Nancy's mother's leaning down and picking up Matt, placing him on the kitchen table, and having him sing to her. When Nancy climbed onto the table her mother said "You can't sing." These two model scenes help us to define the nature of Nancy's attachment to her mother. It is attachment to a caregiver who has no spontaneous positive inclination toward the child, but whom the child observes to be quite capable of reaching for, lifting up, affirming, and praising another. Nancy saw her mother as always there to do her duty with a "saintly" but unyielding rigidity. In turn, as seen through her mother's eyes, Nancy was an overdependent nuisance who she thought should get out from under her feet so she could get on with her overburdened life. Alternatively, Nancy found many people—mostly men, but also a paternal aunt—who did welcome her and with whom she could experience intimacy.

Nancy's affiliation with her family was characterized by tight intimacy. Life on the farm was isolated for the children. The nearest neighbors were childless uncles on their farms. Playmates were rare, making the family members especially interdependent. This meant that Nancy was more than ordinarily dependent on her family unit for a sense of pride and worth. However, because of the circumstances of their life, she had great difficulty in sustaining a sense of having someone to admire and respect within her family, and nowhere else to get it. Her father's family were established landowners in what had been valuable farm country. Her father had been successful in the oil industry and had traveled widely. But in her mother's view, Nancy's grandfather was a dirty, smelly old man with a spittoon and Nancy's father was an incompetent farmer who drank too much. Nancy's loyalty was primarily to her father's family and her efforts to feel included by her mother's family were blocked by their assumption of condescending superiority.

Nancy felt some affinity to issues of religion, an interest not encouraged by her parents. As an adult, she decided on an independent affiliation and converted to the Catholic church against the expressed wishes of her evangelical Protestant family. Her involvement with psychoanalytic treatment represents to some degree an "adherence" to an independent affiliation, also in opposition to her family.

### Exploration and assertion

In her childhood, Nancy established patterns of exploration and assertion that continue to the present. To feel comfortable and able to
use her excellent mind to explore and sort out her personal creative
responses, she must be alone. This, I believe, derives from times of
creative play with toys and dolls when she was alone or with a girlfriend. For Nancy, play with her brother, and now study or work
involvement with others, meant intense comparison, competition,
and the expectation of put-downs and humiliation. But even more
of a problem than that is her belief that to feel competent she must
accomplish tasks rapidly—without regard to risk. A model scene for
this belief is the children playing on the roof of a shed and Matt
saying that Nancy would have to jump down with him or he'd leave
her up there. Desperate not to be thought cowardly or to be abandoned, Nancy ignored her fear and the danger of injury to her as
a much smaller child and jumped. The result is that Nancy feels
committed to rapid counterphobic action in decisions at work, taking
exams, or plunging into problems in the analysis. Nancy's goal of
quickness and risk-taking is not only to assure herself of being liked
by her brother but also for her to feel a sense of efficiency and
competence. Any other way feels plodding and boring to Nancy. At
some point during latency, she observed one of her mother's friends
who was unmarried but self-supporting as a medical technician. Nancy
formed a career intention by using this woman as a model.

Although Nancy has had a successful career as a laboratory technician and supervisor, she has felt dissatisfied with the low level of
intellectual challenge. She has a strong desire to explore conceptual
matters and chose to attend graduate school to study philosophy
because it allowed her to pursue the study of ethics and responsibility. These moral questions could be applied to issues of patient
care and to her personal quest to sort out questions of responsibility for what had happened and continued to happen to her.

### Aversiveness

Nancy's general sense of friendliness and warmth provides a strong
indication that her innate predisposition was toward a loving relatedness and that despite the difficulties of her early life, her aversive
system was not organized into rigid patterns of antagonism or withdrawal. The aversiveness she felt toward her mother and feels strongly
that she received from her mother were largely the sense of a cool
stalemate. Her anger was muted by the blanketing of her mother's

dutiful, long-suffering care, which led her mother to be regarded as a saint. Nancy was fully aware of her feelings of hurt and resentment only when she observed her mother's delight with Matt. She quickly turned off her open expressions of protest and instead withdrew into self-doubt. The model scene that expressed this sequence took place when Nancy was chosen by her music teacher to sing a solo in the school chorus. She came home excitedly to tell her mother. Her mother responded by saying, "But you can't sing, your brother is the singer of our family." Nancy dropped out of the chorus, confused as to whether she could sing or not. She then gave up singing.

Another prominent pattern of aversiveness toward her mother turned on Nancy's altruistic efforts to look after others. Nancy sensed early on that her mother wanted her to be a big girl, to look after herself and help her mother. If Nancy threw up or soiled her bed or clothes, she would have to clean herself up because, if her mother tried to, she would gag and throw up too. Without much assistance, Nancy frequently fell or was pushed around by Matt. Nancy would then cry out. Any of these behaviors—making noise, vomiting, soiling, crying when hurt—would disturb Nancy's mother and could bring on a migraine. Nancy was then assigned the task of entering the darkened room, carrying cold towels for her mother's head. She was thus both guilty culprit and needed nurse. In adolescence, Nancy felt that her being a big girl/adult led to another episode of exploitation. She had been delighted when her mother spent time with her in the kitchen teaching her to cook and clean. Then she became completely aversive to her new skills when she discovered that her mother's motive was to go off and get a job, leaving Nancy as housekeeper for the men.

For Nancy, altruism, a significant aspect of her approach to her work as a technician, is heavily contaminated by guilt and resentment and has eventuated into crippling panic attacks. Nancy will take on much more than her share of laboratory duties, because of concern that patients who need test results for their care will not receive it otherwise. She obliterates her anger from awareness as much as she can. As her intense feeling of being exploited breaks through, and with it a flicker of rage, she becomes obsessed with some neglectful or harmful act she may have committed. She withdraws in horror and fear and considers abandoning her work. She often cannot rest or return to her studies until she calls the laboratory and receives reassurance that the test was done correctly. This whole sequence is made more intense if a test or procedure involves the patient's respiration, which draws on another source of Nancy's exploitation, fear, and anger—the sadistic game of Matt coming up behind her and holding her nose and mouth. When she panicked at the feeling of suffocation and began to flail wildly, he would let go. As she cried and protested he would chide her that her reaction was a breach of trust in him, that he would never really hurt her and that she should feel guilty for resisting and for her attack. Nancy's complaints to her mother met with similar counterblaming—Matt was a good boy who wouldn't hurt her, and it is her fault for following him around instead of playing with her dolls. Her brother took full advantage of Nancy's altruistic concern by faking serious injuries, arousing her fright and worry and then laughing at her gullibility. Another source of early fright for Nancy was connected with her father. Her mother would often leave the farm for the afternoon. Nancy, too lonely and frightened to remain alone in the house to play or nap, would seek out her father at work. He would place her up on the tractor next to him. Her initial happiness at this closeness to him would turn to disappointment and shock whenever, as occasionally happened, she became drowsy and fell off. She does not remember being hurt badly but each time reexperienced the fear she would fall and be run over. At the same time, she felt ashamed of bothering her father at work. Because of the intense shame and guilt she felt in conjunction with her fears, she did everything she could to suppress and repress her anxiety. A psychiatrist who had spent a lot of time with her concluded that she was the least hysterical woman he had known. It was only in the analysis with me that she began to reexperience prolonged states of anxiety and panic attacks—especially over weekends.

For Nancy, knowing and not knowing became a weapon she could use as an expression of competitive antagonism. A game of setting another up to seem to be the dumb one was seemingly indulged in by each of the family members. As an adolescent, Nancy learned to set up her father and brother by getting them to express political views that she considered far out and of which she could be contemptuous. She continued this form of antagonism with authorities at the hospital and at graduate school, taking stands that often were highly principled but allowed her to experience both righteous indignation and rebelliousness.

### Sensual enjoyment and sexual excitement

Due to her mother's illness at the time of Nancy's birth, and the ensuing separation of infant from mother, an ordinarily expected level of mutual sensual enjoyment in holding, fondling, cuddling, rocking, and vocalizing seems never to have occurred between Nancy and her mother. Alternatively, Nancy's male caregivers appear to have been at least adequate in engaging the infant in body contact. We can form a hypothesis that Nancy may have been a skin-sensitive infant from the eczema that has been a recurrent experience. Whatever its possible connection to sensual maternal under- or paternal over-stimulation, eczema during adult life has become closely related to sexual activities—heterosexual and masturbatory. Throughout her growing up, the high level of overexcitement in which Nancy was a partici-pant tended to limit her ability to experience sensual enjoyment as a soothing, rest-inducing experience. The quest for soothing and comforting regularly turned, either immediately or after some delay, into excitement states that triggered confusion, shame, embarrass-ment, and guilt. She slept in her parent's bedroom until she was three. This early exposure to sexually exciting sights and sounds seems implicated in her persistent enuresis. Her associations suggest that clamoring to be taken out of the crib to go to the potty may have been in response to parental awakenings and possibly attempts to interrupt their intercourse. Removal to her own bed was explained as letting her get to the bathroom by herself—a responsibility she experiences as an abandonment. This struggle over bed-wetting, with its polymorphous link to sexuality, continued until puberty.

Nancy's core gender identity seems to have been clearly female. She was regarded as the pretty, blond-haired, delicate little girl—a favorite of her father and grandfather. Her loving sensual interest was directed toward men early. Too early—in the sense that it served as a substitute for the missing loving sensual interest in her mother and her mother's body. This interest then was played out with her girlfriend in prepuberty and appears in dreams and fantasies as a preoccupation with women's breasts and bottoms—the soft, caress-able body parts. Until the age of five, Nancy ate her meals while sitting on her father's lap. This sensual experience, which she regarded as a source of comfort and safety, became itself a source of sexual excitement and rejection. A reconstruction based on her self-conscious wriggling on the couch and her preoccupation with what I was doing behind her led us both to the belief that she had become aware of her father's arousal and erections, and that the growing threat of his sexual excitement led him, in her view, to push her away. When she was grown, her father often called her by his wife's name. After his wife's death, he made sexual overtures to two of his sisters-in-law. On an occasion when Nancy was planning to leave to spend a weekend with a boyfriend, he told her angrily that if she was going to go off screwing with somebody else she should stay home and sleep with him.

Nancy has no clear idea of when her brother began to rub his penis against her body. In the beginning, the activity was against her leg. Later he would lie on top of her and masturbate to orgasm. With the expulsion from her father's lap, Nancy's orientation toward her femininity changed. She became a tomboy, working along with her brother and refusing to wear a top. Presenting herself as a tomboy who was able to compete with anyone—male or female—became a highly invested motive. This motive served as a spur to Nancy to do well in school, but also became a source of excitement that hampered her performance in graduate school. The quest for exhibitionistic excitement led her to fight real and imagined battles of wit with other students and professors, leading at times to a serious loss of focus on the problem to be solved and to failures.

As Nancy entered puberty, she insisted that her brother stop his sexual use and abuse of her, but was threatened and bribed to continue. At this time, her mother also bribed her to stop wetting the bed. After a year, Nancy refused her brother's sexual demands and also stopped her enuresis, regarding her mother's bribe of money as something of a gift. She was now actively exploring sexual games with a girl her age. A major effect of all the sensual and sexual under- and overstimulation was that Nancy was as far as she can remember totally without sexual sensation or arousal. This complete absence of pleasurable genital sensation continued into her first treatment, despite many promising relationships with men. During her first therapy, she regained sensation, but "shut down" as her arousal approached orgasm. Nancy had her first orgastic experience during the analysis. She had broken off with a flirtatious, "virtuous" man with whom she indulged in ambiguous mutual come-ons. She began a brief tempestuous affair with a foreign doctor who came at her aggressively with unambiguous seductive intent. With mixed relief and guilt, she "succumbed" and had her first orgastic experience. As this affair ended, she experienced humiliation at the sordidness of it and pleasure in having accomplished an important experience— having full sexual excitement.

During adolescence, Nancy rarely dated. Her maternal grandmother told her she pushed boys away, thinking no one was good enough for her. Nancy believes her grandmother was right. Nancy thought that the boys she liked would never be acceptable to her mother's family, and the boys they approved of were unsatisfactory to her—

usually on idealistic grounds. Behind these more surface reasons lay Nancy's own scale of measurement—none was as handsome, bright, or risk-taking as her beloved brother Matt.

# 3  Clinical Exchange:

## 1983, 1985, 1987, 1989, 1990

The goal of a clinical exchange between an analyst and a patient is to facilitate that particular form of attachment that is required to conduct a joint exploration in depth of both the disturbed self-experience of the patient and the nature, tensions, and meanings of the exchange itself. Each clinical exchange is as unique as the fingerprints of the participants compounded by their ever-changing intersubjective fields, and yet clinical exchanges are similar enough that other analysts should be able to enter the scene as a "fly-on-the-wall." However, only the analyst and the analysand were there to make the exchange happen. The spontaneity of the moment is theirs. You, the reader, enter their interchanges after two years have elapsed. Later in the book we will refer to incidents that preceded this entry point. Both the analyst and Nancy believed they had established a way of being with and talking to each other that constituted the essential features of a working exploratory treatment. The form of our presentation in which we present verbatim exchanges with bracketed reflections and explanations by the analyst offers the reader two choices. You can ignore the analyst's post-session commentaries and initially read the exchanges without explanatory interruptions and then read the commentaries. Or you can read the commentaries as they appear and try to experience the session as it is being viewed by the patient during and the analyst both during and after.

4/21/83 Tuesday

83:1:1  P:  Here we are again and I have this reluctance to get started. I worked at the laboratory but decided to ask off after eight hours instead of twelve. I went home, took a nap, and went to the Easter service. It was awesome. I felt good about being there and what we are doing here. It's not at odds—that I am going to destroy myself by being religious. Coming here brings the problems about it into focus. Particularly about my being a saint. It's come up before [*sigh*]. An important problem can be faced in here without destroying

25

my desire to be religious. The part that was disappointing was the priest who did my conversion was too busy to talk to me, too preoccupied, and I felt hurt. I realize he's got things in his life, he's not just there for me. Another thing—Arthur [a man whom she had dated briefly] went to [the] service with me and his ex-girl-friend. It was more comfortable for me to have her along. Over the weekend I was feeling a lot better, but Saturday I felt enormously depressed. I don't know if I hate the weekend because I'm away from you. That must be involved—although I don't know what it means. I'm not happy [about] how we've understood that.

83:1:2    A:    What you said about the priest could apply?
[The sequence begins with an intervention that picks up the themes in the opening associations—disappointment with and hurt over a priest who was too busy and preoccupied to talk to her—combined with her weekend depression. The timing of the question is geared to respond to her self-reflective interest in meaning, an expression of a shared exploratory motive. The intervention is closely woven to the associations and affect. It is based on the assumption that a similar emotional response was triggered in her relationship with both priest and analyst.]

83:1:3    P:    Yeah. That does apply, but it doesn't help me to not feel it. I'm not unwilling to miss you. I'd like not to feel bone-crushing depression. Then I fell out from under the stress of exams and became sexual and felt it's good to have that feeling even if I'm not happy to direct it at Arthur. Fantasies of being close and making love. I trust I can confide in you and talk about it and feel better. On the news I heard about a psychiatrist who raped his patient. Here I am bringing all this explicit sex stuff in. What kind of person are you to want to hear about it, help me with it? Isn't there something perverse about it? [*challenging, provocative tone*] What in all these cases gets out of control? The potential is there. I sense this is going to get personal in a way it hasn't before. Friday I thought of wanting to look at you. At people naked, too—to see my brother's penis. It occurred to me all my fantasies about Arthur are upside down fantasies about you. I say I won't with you, but I will with someone who's opposite—young, tall, and naive. These are ways to get involved with sex without full realization! [*pause*] How can you do this all day, listen to this?

83:1:4   A:   What you asked before, does it put me at risk for getting out of control?

83:1:5   P:   That's a possibility. I see others. You have these feelings—pleasure, excitement.

83:1:6   A:   That I get stirred up as a result of what you're talking about.

[These two interventions were close together in time and theme—the second following up on Nancy's response to the first. She makes more explicit the nature of her rising fear that I will repeat her "perverse" incestuous experiences and I pick up on her attribution.]

83:1:7   P:   You have to deal with it. If you repress it, it comes out some other way. That's the theory isn't it?

83:1:8   A:   Is your hope that if I'd tell you how I deal with it, then you'd know how to?

[This interpretation is aimed at exposing a desire for learning by example or mentoring—the repair of a regulatory deficit. Although that motive may have been present and bringing it into awareness desirable, the intervention may also have had the disadvantage of moving away from the more heated issue of my presumed sexual arousal.]

83:1:9   P:   I wasn't aware of it—it could be my motive. The big difference between how I deal with it and how you do. I am thinking about you, as opposed to me. I'll put the spotlight on you for a while. It's part avoidance but part sincere concern about how you deal with it. I've known psychiatrists who had no method to help them that I knew of. A void in their life. If I entrust myself to you, I want to know you are able to deal with the stuff I bring up. I'm selfish—you could get out of control. Or get deadened, unable to empathize. [*sigh*] I remember talking to Dr. S [her previous therapist] about his having fantasies. I felt comforted by thinking that whatever happened I had control—so he didn't have to. That's not okay anymore. My relationship with you—I think of you as my dad. I was very close to him. I had to deal with feelings that would creep up. I have to deal with my own feelings about you, regardless of anything else [*sigh*]. I'm aware of strongly stifling my curiosity about your life, desk, car—far removed from you personally. It's not right to invade your privacy. That's opposite to my feeling over the weekend, that it's okay to have fantasies about Arthur. Not you! [*sigh*] You represent a verboten character.

83:1:10  A:  Your father?

[This intervention was a spontaneous reaction. Nancy, after briefly (and probably compliantly) responding to the earlier intervention about mentoring, returned to the sexual fear-wish issue. She makes clear now that she is talking about men either acting on or suppressing and deadening their sexual desires. In the course of her discourse, she refers to her dad. Without reflection, I said "father," totally unaware, until I went over the notes, of the ambiguity and condensation of father-priest, father-dad, and father-analyst—thereby reintroducing the religious theme that she next rephrases as you, Dad, and Christ.]

83:1:11  P:  My dad and God. I can't about any of you.... More precisely—you, Dad, and Christ. [I experience some drowsiness] I'm responsible for any responding you or Dad might have. [My drowsiness when she responds reflects my temporary lack of attunement with my own unconscious double entendre and how it triggered her return to the religious idiom, which I hear as intellectual.] That's what I didn't want to accept! That was the whole point of I'm not allowed to go around not fully dressed. Not being fully clothed all the way is attempting to seduce.

83:1:12  A:  If you keep yourself under tight control you'll do nothing to be seductive, reveal no parts of your body?

[Nancy has made a dramatic shift from a focus on me to her part in the seducer–seduced pairing, and I follow her: I recognize that in her protestation of responsibility, she is repeating what she had been told, really doesn't believe, and is furious about.]

83:1:13  P:  Right. But it doesn't work, still comes out. [I thought of a colleague's question in a clinical presentation about whether I found Nancy seductive and my answering no and wondering why not. At this moment, I became particularly aware of her completely non-revealing style of dressing.] Sally [her housemate] walks around in T-shirt and panties. And she's very verbal about people being fully dressed. So I got mad—the same stuff as Dad—I have to wear clothes to not disturb him. Nobody cares how it disturbs me! It's not fair. [*angry*] Do you? You look—what we said last week, it's interpreted as my problem. Why does it bother me? Why do I want to look and turn away? There's another class of verboten interests. In high school I was particularly curious about women—about breasts, bottoms, legs, and comparing. Am I as attractive? A girl in gym told me not to stare. I was embarrassed and angry. Very. Shit! What's wrong. What's going on. I've become shifty eyed. I can't look at anything.

83:1:14 A:  Are you feeling angry toward me as well?

83:1:15 P:  I feel in all these cases I'm in the wrong and that's not right. What am I angry at you about? I don't know. I feel put upon. One thing that's distressing here—you can see me, my twitches, and I can't see you at all [*calmer*]. If I turn my head back, roll my eyes back, it becomes an "analytical issue." I'm doing something wrong. I remember the first time I rolled by head back and saw you, how reassuring it was. I do it to be reassured.

83:1:16 A:  Reassured in what way?
[Following my inquiry about her anger an affective shift occurred. The sources of her anger move quickly from men who put responsibility for sexual stimulation on her and men who deaden themselves, to a festing of unequal unfair exposure, and back to depression in response to absence— the topic with which the hour began.]

83:1:17 P:  I don't know in what way. That you are there. Not gone. That you're with me. I'm reminded how I felt a year ago. I want to put the spotlight on you. Not only me!


4/22/83 Wed.


83:2:1 P:  I'm tired. I didn't sleep well. Like drugged. I felt thick-headed when I awoke. Slow. I had a vague dream in which I was working on a problem in metaphysics about truth that I was reading about before I went to sleep. No. I was reading Steinbeck's *Travels with Charley*.

In the dream, on a wall were pictures of a brain—
right and left brain, I think. I wish I could keep it
straight but I never can. I was in a class but I couldn't
answer. Somebody answers. There was a dish on the
table. I was saying: Can you take out what you know
and put it in the dish? It was strange, it was unclear
whether it was what you know or part of your brain.
I feel tired, thickheaded, irritable. I'm irritated with
Sally. She and Phil came in at two in the morning.
Phil went in the bathroom. Sally didn't close the door,
and my dog, who's a trained watchdog, bit him and
woke me up. I don't want to work.

83:2:2   A:   Is there some way in which you feel I've disturbed
your rest?

83:2:3   P:   It's stuff I don't want to talk about, deal with, work
at.

83:2:4   A:   Does it go back to yesterday, to your curiosity, your
sexual interest in me?
[These interventions address Nancy's explicit statements of
reluctance to open her dream and her current affect state
to exploration—a paralysis of curiosity. My inquiry is an
attempt to link her disturbed sleep and current affect state
to the previous hour.]

83:2:5   P:   Ultimately, it's what it resolves to. I don't want to face
it. That's the truth!

83:2:6   A:   In your dream you position yourself as unable to deal
with the question before the class.
[This intervention attempts to demonstrate to Nancy how
she has represented the aversive motivation in her dream
and thus to invite associations about her felt opposition or
incapacity for exploration.]

83:2:7   P:   [nods] Now I don't want to. I don't know if I can. I
don't want to get close enough to knowing what the
issues are. I want to escape to the garden. I'd like to
be in a pretty place. One thing I think about is sexual
thoughts. None are right. Never. Some worse than
others. In a strange way its okay to have sexual fantasies
about Christ. He represents perfection and is immaterial, so there's no way to act. It's safe.

83:2:8   A:   As compared to my physical presence, so near?

83:2:9   P:   Yeah. I want to be angry with you. I feel it's wrong.
Perverse. My lying here on a couch talking to you

about sexual fantasies about you. There's no way I can make that okay. I don't know what to do. It can't be okay.

83:2:10  A:  Does it have too much the sense of incestuous feelings?

[The transference situations that had been opened up in the previous hour are now reopened; my first intervention refers to the triggering of excitement, my second to the triggering of guilt.]

83:2:11  P:  Not necessarily. I guess that must be what I think. It wouldn't with someone who would be appropriate. You are specifically not—that's the incestuous part. Not a clear distinction between fantasy and action. I'm being seductive when I don't mean to be and when I mean to be, I'm not. I've reasoned myself into a trap, but my brain has shut down.

83:2:12  A:  Back to your position in your dream?

83:2:13  P:  Yep. Do I mean to be overtly or covertly seductive in here? Trying to seduce you? [sigh] If I say no—me thinks she doth protest too much. I don't want to be overtly but covertly I do. It's a minefield here. Best to not do anything [crossing arms].

83:2:14  A:  Put yourself in a state of empty paralysis?

83:2:15  P:  I feel trapped.

83:2:16  A:  Trapped?

83:2:17  P:  Nothing I can do that will be right and even doing nothing is wrong. There's no way to make it okay. My very being is wrong. Confusing. Labyrinthian. Paradox— trying to be seductive and I'm not, I'm not then I am. Weird. I'm supposed to know what I am doing. Be responsible for it all. My actions, my desires, my responses. Clear I can't control it.

83:2:18  A:  Trying to structure it as a metaphysical question?

[These comments describe the nature of Nancy's aversive withdrawal, inferred from her verbal and gestural communications. The sequence of my interventions oscillates between attempting to invite further content associations and recognizing the aversive response that follows those attempts.]

83:2:19  P:  Keep us as far from the reality as possible.

83:2:20  A:  Focusing on the brain brings it closer to body but still pretty far.

[This intervention constitutes a breach with the previous relatively successful attempts to remain closely attuned to Nancy's immediate affective state. It was a push from me to address the additional meanings of her dream and represented my impatience, that is, my shift from an expectant exploratory motive to an aversive mild frustration.]

83:2:21  P:   Again I feel trapped.

83:2:22  A:   By me, then.

[Nancy's second reference to feeling trapped alerts me to the impact of my pressuring her. In her first expression of feeling trapped, she related it to her internal struggle with guilt, in her second to a struggle with me. I have unconsciously been drawn into an enactment in which seducer-seduced roles become confused, and with this confusion, responsibility becomes actualized as an issue in the analytic relationship.]

83:2:23  P:   Um-hm. You know where that leads—connecting brain to body, the dream to here. What do I want? I want you to take out some part of you and share it with me [*slightly facetiously*]. We immediately have something very explicitly sexual and if you can make it my fantasy—it's my problem. You don't have responsibility. It's all mine. I'm the one who started it. That's what happened with Matt. I'm the one with the secret desire to flirt with you. You don't have to take responsibility. My brother didn't. I seduced him. In here I'm trying to seduce you. If you act, you have no responsibility. Whatever I do, talk, be quiet, squirm—it's always mine. You can do what you want, feel what you want.

83:2:24  A:   Your sense is of being trapped in a situation that seems manifestly unfair?

[This intervention conveys both an empathic understanding of her inner state of feeling unfairly trapped and an ingenuous denial on my part of my responsibility for my participation in the role enactment.]

83:2:25  P:   What do you mean seems? Is! I'm so angry, when I think about it, it frightens me. I don't want to think about it.

83:2:26  A:   How angry you feel toward me is what frightens you.

[Nancy picks up on my ingenuousness, reacts now not with withdrawal but with aversive antagonism, which frightens her. My intervention recognizes her immediate affective state.]

83:2:27  P:  Yes. I want to kiss you. No, castrate you—that would be worse, you'll know what it feels like to be on the other side. My father's favorite story was about Socrates going to the top of Mount Parnassus to praise the gods for not being born a woman. There's nothing worse—being blamed for 99.99% of all the vile acts and being utterly incapable of changing that. So the other half of the world can carry out whatever acts it wishes free of response. It's better to not be bright enough to understand it. [*very animated*] It's a double-edged sword—what my dad was saying about me being a girl wasn't because he didn't like me but because he thought I was the cause of all the sexuality. He treated me like a boy by developing my mind so I was stuck with the notion of [the] way things are for girls clearly enough to understand it. You're the same.

83:2:28  A:  The same double-edged sword?
[This final intervention is intended to indicate I have followed the significant associations in which she has attempted to explore many of the obscure representations of her dreams, the relations between mind and body, male and female, and the inability to integrate the two "edges."]

83:2:29  P:  Exactly. I have to see it and there's nothing I can do about it! [she left crying angrily.]

4/23/83  Thursday

83:3:1  P:  Well, I was pretty mad yesterday. I come back, lay down, and I get mad again. I don't like to be mad. It's so overwhelming. What is going on in here is I take all the responsibility and you get all the fun [*chuckling*]. Getting so mad about taking all the responsibility destroys the possibility of my living at peace with the world. A fundamental injustice between men and women. I have two choices, deny that it's real, or if it's real, I have to accept it. I don't like the feeling of being manipulated, which is how I feel in here. Not only male-female but the way I see things in general. I feel like I have one foot nailed to the ground while I struggle to do things and the rest of the world moves about freely. [*mildly angry*] I had a dreadful thought about you yesterday. My brother would examine things—pull

the wings off a fly and watch it squirm and get pleasure—
that's what you are doing! You're part of it. You can
do nothing about it but make the best of it by making
your living off it. I feel like a real misogynist. Before
this when I got really angry with you I could tie
myself down [*crying*] by reminding myself you seem
to be a decent man. If doesn't help now. You look
benign.

83:3:2   A:   Could that be a part of the problem?

83:3:3   P:   That you look benign.

83:3:4   A:   Yes—if my very presence and my benign appearance
invite your interest and curiosity, that becomes a part
of the problem?

[A temporary minor disruption of Nancy's sense of trust
had been precipitated by the role enactment. Nancy attempts
to deal with "the fundamental injustice" first with humor,
then with anger and an accusation of sadism, and finally,
with distress. My first interventions are aimed at exploring
what I think may be the most promising entry into her
response to my contribution, as she experiences it. I do not
take up her slip, "misogynist," with her implied self-hate.]

83:3:5   P:   [*sobbing*, wiping away tears, getting tissues, returning
to couch] I feel we are back where we were yesterday
when I got mad, feeling trapped. I don't like the feeling.

83:3:6   A:   Such a deep feeling of unfairness it's hard to shake or
move along with?

[This follow-up intervention notes my awareness of the
affect triggered by the previous interpretation.]

83:3:7   P:   It destroys my life. What I was thinking yesterday,
driving home from here, I hate you for being a man
and at the same moment I'm working so hard to be
like you. [Nancy may now be picking up on the misogynist theme] No. I don't want to be like you. I want
to be me! But if I don't try to be like you, I feel I
have to knuckle under. I don't like anybody—you, me,
anybody. The women who don't seem to notice this
problem, and the women who have, haven't dealt with
it any better than I have. Everything I do works against
me. I can't turn to anybody. No one I trust. [*sobbing*]
I look back at the work we've done, it looks like a big
farce. Well, okay, she's following the line.

83:3:8   A:   Following the line?

[Nancy made what appeared to be another slip—or, at the least, used an obscure phrase. I ask for clarification. Does she mean "following the party line"?]

83:3:9  P:  Falling into line—saying okay, I agree—it's all my fault. I should change. I start everything. I have to take the responsibility. I'm responsible for all my feelings and all of yours. I'm responsible if I fall down the stairs, if you get a headache. If I walk into the bathroom and you are there, if you walk in and I'm there. [These are references to memories. The first occurred when her mother reacted to the patient's falling down the stairs by getting a migraine headache at the trouble her "awkward, clumsy" daughter had caused her. Instead of concern for her possible injury, Nancy had to apologize and nurse her mother, applying wet washcloths to her head in a darkened room. The second memory is of Nancy entering the bathroom, which was not allowed to be locked, when her father was there and his shocked anger at her and, that when her brother came in when she was using the toilet she was told to shut up and not make a fuss.] I'm responsible for Matt doing it with me [masturbating] and if I didn't let him anymore I'm responsible for his going off and doing it with my friends [sobbing].

83:3:10  A:  Like it's as though your actions and feelings are the only ones that are factored in?
[My use of the conditional "as though" is rhetorically appropriate in that Nancy, to make her point, has resorted to an exaggerated overstatement. What I did not consider at the time, and therefore could not have worked with, was the likelihood that my failure to acknowledge in either hour that no attempt had been made to consider a more fair distribution of responsibility may have contributed to her use of exaggeration out of desperation to be understood empathically.]

83:3:11  P:  It makes it easy to understand why it is so difficult here—what's going on with me is the only thing factored in.

83:3:12  A:  That it creates for you such a pessimistic view?
[This intervention reflects the patient's affect state within the sequence, but I again fail to pick up on "why it is so difficult here."]

83:3:13 P:   I can only survive. I can't live, love, act. Only insu-
             late myself. May be what I've done so well. I want a
             cigarette. I dreamt about smoking.

83:3:14 A:   Smoking fits both wanting comfort and the hopeless
             death idea? [After a long struggle, Nancy had given
             up smoking in the second year of the analysis. In this
             reference to a desire to reverse a gain pridefully attrib-
             uted to the analysis, I feel intuitively that she has invited
             me to return to the familiar ground of wish and guilt-
             punishment.]

83:3:15 P:   That's right! I might as well. Another strange thing
             is this is all related to your going away. For the last
             24 hours I've been very aware I won't see you for two
             weeks. I had real ambivalent—not ambivalent, I want
             you to go! To not have to come here and talk. Out
             of sight, out of mind. As long as you're here I have
             to deal with whatever my unsuccessfully repressed fantasies
             are.

83:3:16 A:   Absent I'm not an invitation for your fantasies and
             feelings?
             [With the partial restoration of an idealizing transference
             that has taken place, Nancy associates to her preconscious
             concern with my anticipated two-week absence. My inter-
             vention responds to her association by linking absence with
             stimulating presence.]

83:3:17 P:   Right [*pause*] I'm not at all certain you're not just an
             awful human being. Who are you? Am I doing the
             right thing by coming? Can I trust you? Yet I find
             myself not wanting to be separated from you. Whatever
             you are it's better than being alone. I hate myself for
             that. I hate you for not being one or the other—good
             or bad. I seem not to be able to deal with the notion
             you are human, not perfect.

83:3:18 A:   In the imperfections you experience me as having, is
             the one about my going away the most problematic
             at this time?
             [Having addressed one side of her ambivalence about my
             presence in the previous intervention, I now invite her to
             focus on the absence.]

83:3:19 P:   I don't know. I wouldn't have said that was necessarily
             an imperfection—I don't want to admit that's it. I did
             think of it, that's true, but I don't want to admit that

separations are as distressing as they are. I get so angry at you and at me. What is wrong is I feel so dependent. Yet I'm frightened when you go away. I want to hang on so tight. I want to say you aren't worth that allegiance. I'm so mad. It catches up again and again. I'm no better off. You let me be—or don't stop me from being so dependent. I think with a sick feeling in my stomach of what happened in January or February when you were gone. I pointed out the student to my friend, told her she's the girl who cheated.

83:3:20  A:  You're feeling I'm responsible for letting you down.

83:3:21  P:  I'm going to say my problem with your being benign is I try to trust you—things will be okay—and they aren't, and then it's my problem.

83:3:22  A:  We also looked at your feeling I cheated. I tempt you to trust me and then I go away.

[In these two final interpretations, I return to the theme of my share of the responsibility as she experiences it. I respond to her memory of a previous absence during which she acted "irresponsibly" by gossiping about a student of hers who had cheated. The analytic work at the time exposed the view of me as one who cheated—a tempter who takes no responsibility—exactly the type of men she often became involved with. The meaning of "tempter" crosses between her father and brother as sexual tempters and her mother as tempter for dependent attachment. My final interventions are open-ended to invite associations to either sexual or dependent attachment wishes. Nancy's response was to access her strong feeling of anger at her mother who, in the little girl's view, invited and frustrated her attachment needs and whose emotional and physical absence resulted in Nancy's seeking the males for contact without the watchful protective eye of a mother.]

83:3:23  P:  [crying] I'm the one who has to stay and take care of things while you're gone. Make mistakes. I hate you for going away and doing that. [she was crying, then getting tissues.] The same way I hated my mother. I have a vision of getting up and throwing everything in this room at you. A barrage of stuff. That's what I'm doing right now.

83:3:24  A:  Our time is up.

83:3:25  P:   You're out of Kleenex. [Referring to her crying] I hate this. [*smiling sheepishly*] Especially without having my sunglasses.

12/6/85 Wed.

[Nancy entered the room smiling pleasantly and enigmatically.]

85:1:1  P:   Well, Karl finally asked me over for dinner. He did it so diffidently—as if he were merely paying me back for having him over. It was weird. Then I got weird, too, saying, "Well the only time I'm free is next week." I didn't want to be too enthusiastic. He was acting as if he was unsure I'd want to, although I think I made it clear. He was being cool so not to make it a "date."
[Her enigmatic smile referred to the secret—"Karl asked me out." Karl is a fellow student who has shown an interest in Nancy. "Diffident" is a loaded term referring to a transference early in the analysis—I had been so diffident in broaching sexual matters it gave her pause to not shock me or breech some standard of "etiquette," but if I was at all eager or earthy I would scare her off (by being too much like her father and brother), so she knew I couldn't win.]
I know I give the impression that I'm so busy it's hard for anyone to make it into my time. [*pause*] Both of us are being weird about the whole thing. He was saying he was paying me back, so I should say "Okay." I'll accept it as that and let things take their course.

85:1:2  A:   You're saying you have to resist the temptation to get excited?

85:1:3  P:   Yeah. I think that's accurate. On the other hand it's fun to get excited—I wish I didn't have to restrain that. Staying calm and waiting to see is more reasonable. It's a good way to do it, but can't I ever get excited? Maybe I could be a little and still wait and see.

85:1:4  A:   You're saying you could be excited, but temper it?

85:1:5  P:   What's temper. [*pause*] I guess that's it.
[My first intervention is to attempt to tell her how I am sensing into her affect state. I offer an affect descriptor— excited. I was unaware at the time that I had switched from her term—"enthusiastic." My aim is to get her response. If

"excited" is off, I will alter my approach to follow her lead. If it is on, she and I will be aligned to work further. In addition, I understand more than the *latent* affect of excitement by her attempt to "restrain" herself, to protect herself from something that she fears will have an undesired consequence. In my next intervention, "temper" fails to capture her meaning as she is developing it. She is mildly startled, but is compliantly acquiesent and then goes on to make her motivation clearer.]

> What I do is say it means nothing. Just paying me back [*deep, masculine voice*]. Or I could zing off into how it's the first step into marriage [*feminine, flighty voice*].

85:1:6  A:  Do you have any thoughts about your voice when you said "means nothing"? Was it the deep voice of pseudo superreason?

85:1:7  P:  You're hearing my tone as saying it's reasonable to deny that it means anything?

85:1:8  A:  I'm wondering why you would cast it in the deep tone.

85:1:9  P:  It's the opposite of flying off into fantasyland. I'm not sure. My "reasonable" tone? When people are nice to you, it doesn't mean they care about you—they are only exhibiting good manners. It's my mother saying to me: Don't take it personally. Or if someone is rude, it's the same. It's nothing to do with you personally. Don't fly off into fantasyland. People can use an angry tone or a pleasant tone and have no meaning behind it. It's true, but couldn't I have some reason to believe maybe he's interested in me, wants to know me better [*slightly plaintive tone*]?

85:1:10 A:  Do you hear Mother as inclined to eliminate that?
[To better sense into factors affecting her affect state I inquire into her "tonal" affect expression, which was relatively dramatic. She accepts my guidance that she associate to it and identifies its source and meaning. I could then have responded to her "couldn't I believe" as a request for reassurance from me in the immediate exchange between us. I chose to stay with the venue she has picked of hearing her mother's voice actively present.]

85:1:11 P:  I think so. Mother's "Don't take it personally" makes me into a nonentity, as if I have no personal effect on people. I'm not noticeable. Being *affective* is in my

head. Effect? Affect? I'm not sure I arouse affect—
emotion—plus or minus. It reminds me of my mother's
anger at my aunt [paternal relative]. I'd visit—clean
for her. She'd give me money. We'd sit and talk, have
a Coke. Mother would only see it as her using me. I
thought she was being affectionate. As if nothing about
me was worthy of being affectionate about. I end up
feeling very small.

85:1:12  A:  Insignificant?

85:1:13  P:  Yeah, and insecure [*pause*] I can say to you, I do think
there is reason to believe Karl is interested in me and
I in him. It will be interesting to pursue and see what's
going on [*pause*]. If I put myself in the mood of the
deeper voice "means nothing" [*pause*] then I will not
be. I will make myself unavailable, make it hard for
him to get to know me. It's what I did . . . about
time—I'm so busy. I know I can find the time, but he
might not know. I'll make it impossible for him to get
through.

85:1:14  A:  Like an impenetrable wall?
[I offered a paraphrase of an ambiguous body reference—
partly in response to her stiff body posture on the couch,
partly to her ambiguous phrase "impossible to get through,"
and partly to an earlier phrase, "it's hard for anyone to
make it *into* my time."]

85:1:15  P:  All the way, saying to myself: Here I am trying to be
friendly, flirting a little. A double message.

85:1:16  A:  One message to yourself and one to him?

85:1:17  P:  I hadn't thought of it that way. But that's what it ends
up being. Even if I send both messages and he's a
nervous receptor, he'll chose that.

85:1:18  A:  Which gets us back to the inclination you see in him
to be diffident.

85:1:19  P:  Right.
[Nancy does not pick up on the invitation to explore the
body sensual-sexual aspect of the problem but, rather, chooses
to remain in the relational domain. I follow her lead with
another ambiguous word—"diffident."]
It's interesting because it brings to mind how frustrating it was for me when I thought you were diffident.
When I first came here, I felt I couldn't trust you if
you were being so careful in what you say. To trust

you I needed to feel you were in command. Your being careful not to put ideas in my head, not to impose, was very frustrating. I realize now, your not taking things for granted means you do understand in a way that's more truthful about what it is I'm trying to say . . . I guess. It's frustrating because my inclination is to push through things. Take off and go. I don't like to go slowly. My steamroller approach [*emphasizes with a gesture*]—mows down the opposition.

[Nancy is now exploring the meaning of immediacy and impulsivity as contained in the other voice: the first-step-into-marriage flighty tone as it impacts on the fit or match-mismatch experience she has with me; that is, my deliberate manner and cautious expressiveness pointing up a contrast to her desire to rush ahead.]

It's funny, I don't like it that you were right. Because what I like about you is your real sincere gentleness, comfortableness. It's different from my flapping around. I hate to have my way be exhibited as not so good.

85:1:20  A:  You appreciate it in me but you have a reaction when you compare?

85:1:21  P:  It's nice for you, but it's not the way I am. Or the way I want to be. So there! Pugnacious [*with humor*]— I say, I have to leave Washington in a couple of years so we have to get this work done. [*talking fast*] So come on. I realize that if I do the work every day, follow it and let it go where it has to. But it's so unlike me. It's so hard to do. What we were talking about yesterday—whether I'm going to be able to avoid the sexual issues—so my way is to come in every day and immediately talk. It's my wrongheadedness, but I can't ignore it ... as you said yesterday, at least one or two times in therapy I was able to avoid it—me and the therapist too.

85:1:22  A:  And it's a big worry whether I will facilitate your avoiding it here?

85:1:23  P:  I worry if I'm not talking about explicit sexual material I'm avoiding. I go back to last week—talking about John and living with him. I was saying I felt guilt, there's something wrong with it. Strange. I can't remember what I felt but as a result of our talking I feel it's okay— a strange friendship but okay. Oh, I was saying

I was attracted to Jim, but it's wrong because I'm using it to avoid others who are more possible.

[Nancy has three housemates: Jim, who is planning to become a priest; Mike, who is sexually provocative; and Sally, with whom the patient often fights.]

Since then I've stopped feeling attracted. I like him, but I'm not wishing he could be something he's not. What's worrisome is my being attracted physically but not really [*pause*]. It's hard to explain. What I want him to be is an appropriate partner for me—attractive to me, attracted to me. None is the case ... talking about Mike going around the house with no clothes on. How it angered me. Jim was staying in his pajamas too. His are not as revealing, but I think it's funny it didn't bother me the way Mike did. Both were exhibitionistic. Mike was trying to get a response. Sex, anger, something. With Jim, it's a way to test.

85:1:24 A:  Test?

85:1:25 P:  The safety of our friendship. See if these aren't big issues. Brothers and sisters in a house. Sally too—we're not as intimate as brothers and sisters are. Jim is saying: When you're a Christian with strong values, these issues don't come up in the same way.

85:1:26 A:  But there is the overload of brother and sister in your experience.

[Nancy had brought into focus the issue of sexuality in the "home," but was talking diffidently with circumlocution— I opted to be specific as an encouragement, but without pressure as the hour was coming to an end.]

85:1:27 P:  Jim acts as if he's clear about what he believes. He wears pajamas that are not revealing. Not jockey shorts and no shirt.

85:1:28 A:  Like Mike?

85:1:29 P:  And my brother, who didn't act as if there was any distinction.

85:1:30 A:  Hm.

12/7/85 - Thursday

[Nancy arrived four minutes late.]

85:2:1 P:  My washing machine overflowed again and I had to clean it up. [*pause*] When I left yesterday I thought it was a good hour but still something is wrong in the background. Papers of my students were lost. I took care of that. Then, like an idiot, I didn't check the garbage disposal and the washing machine overflowed. The other thing is, I haven't paid my bills. I can, but barely. I don't know what's going on. I left yesterday after a good session. I told myself I have to relax, to take things as they come, to look at them with you, and everything will be okay. Now I'm back in a big panic [*sigh*].

85:2:2  A:  Your sigh?

[Nancy is repeating a familiar pattern of gaining understanding in an hour or in a week's work and then becoming panicky in response to an external or self-instigated stress. We thought of this pattern as sometimes her way of assuring my continuing interest—if she is okay, I'll happily leave her to look after herself. At other times, the panic over money or school work or a laboratory error served to block entry into her sexual problems. I determined to work with her immediate affect—the sigh—and follow her associations to learn which motivational system was dominant.]

85:2:3  P:  I'm so perplexed by the student papers disappearing. It's true it was late when the students handed them in. A lot of people were around me as I gathered them up. I don't think I was careless. One was lost there. Then two others said they put late papers under my door. It's perplexing. Does it have importance?

85:2:4  A:  The importance you're observing is that you feel so disturbed by it, you can't follow the plan you set for yourself yesterday.

85:2:5  P:  I tell myself I can't be responsible for students putting late papers under a door in a dorm. [*sigh*] I told the one student she could either reconstruct her paper or I'd average her other grades. She said she'd redo the paper. She's not aggressive the way the other students were. I made my decision they'd have to turn in new papers. But I can't let it go. I stay worried and insecure [*sigh*]. It's so routine for me to do this stuff. I'm angry I don't not do it. It's a cop-out but I'm aware you'll be gone next Wednesday [I had told her some weeks before I would be away]. It's hard to get into a pattern of working with so many stops and starts.

I have to recognize that's the way it is. You have to
go away. I do too and can't come four times a week.
I have to accept it and work when I can. That sounds
reasonable, doesn't it? [*pause*] But I'm so unsatisfied,
incomplete, anxious.

85:2:6   A:  Would you feel so unsatisfied, incomplete, if you follow
the plan you described?

85:2:7   P:  I would feel more complete.

85:2:8   A:  I would think so.
[From many prior experiences, I recognized Nancy's temptation to respond with such aversive intensity to *any*
separation or mishap that a chaotic affect state would
result in making exploration impossible. After the prior
work, she formed a plan to react emotionally but not
chaotically. We both knew the choice at any moment hung
in the balance and this is what I was addressing, somewhat too indirectly.]

85:2:9   P:  [*pause*] I don't know. Maybe its a cop-out. [*pause*] I
left yesterday and Karl called. We arranged next week.
He said it's okay if you're too busy. I said I know I
seem to be but I don't mean to. We talked. It was nice
but uncomfortable. I realized how hard I make it for
a man to approach me. Michel [the man with whom
she had had her first orgasmic experience] had to grab
me in the hall, I'd ignored him so. I stay so busy. I
think about talking to you. The problem is, it seems
decadent.

85:2:10  A:  Decadent?
[Nancy had opted to resist the plunge into self-pity or
narcissistic rage. She reopens the subject of how she puts
men off, quickly refers to talking to me, and mentions the
enigmatic designator "decadent." Throughout the remainder
of the hour I am puzzled by how talking to me is "decadent."]

85:2:11  P:  Something pleasurable and helpful. It's painful and
good for me—that's not decadent. What if I could
come in my three days and talk about how things are
at home with Jim and Sally [her housemates] and it
would become clear and get worked out. Then it wouldn't
have the onus of being miserable, awful, dirty, uncomfortable. It would be fun and I would have the time
to do what I need. That's *decadent*—too good to be

true. The other term I think of is "mental masturbation." Dr. Moser [an internist] used it when he told me I shouldn't go into analysis. He said "Why buy a Cadillac when you only need a VW, and besides, it's mental masturbation." That's a hip phrase. It applies to the pleasure of talking with you. It's self-arousing and self-satisfying.

85:2:12 A: Um-hm.

85:2:13 P: It's funny. Before I said that, it was as if I were going to say something awful. But it's true. Talking to you is self-arousing and self-satisfying. It's not the same as masturbating because something comes of it. That's what Dr. Moser would deny. [*pause*] I've been noticing a bump on the ceiling, like a nipple. I associate to people's bottoms. I'm not sure why I'm still interested. [*pause*] As farmers we produced milk. I was talking to Jim about how difficult it was for Mother to be generous to me. She was a few times in later years but not before and I had nothing to give back. Every time I talk about women's soft bottoms, I get back to Mother and not being able to cuddle, nestle, or nurse as a baby. Or snuggle. I told Jim I've come to terms with it. I regret it. I hate that she couldn't nurture me. It comes up because what happens here in a decadent way is I talk to you about relationships with people. Without your nurturing me, you are helping me to grow up.

85:2:14 A: And that's, as you said, both pleasurable and helpful.

85:2:15 P: So it's not decadent! But it seems decadent in contrast to what I'm used to.

[Nancy has identified a beneficial experience in the treatment as the source of her feeling of decadence. Symbolically, talk between us provides sensual nurture satisfaction and facilitates her growth. Yet she senses that some shame or guilt evoking moral transgression is being committed—as implied by "decadent" (reminding me of Freud's concept of moral masochism), if she is not plunging herself into suffering.]

I sense there is something wrong with it. It means I'm dependent, weak. The way in which Jim and I take care of each other is nice. He's having end-of-semester terrors, but helped me with the washing machine overflow. That's not building dependence, it's taking care.

85:2:16  A:   You could speak of that as an old-fashioned virtue.
              [This phrase popped out of my mouth so spontaneously
              that both Nancy and I were somewhat startled by it. Obviously,
              I was associating to "decadent" and choosing vocabulary
              attuned to it, which was unlike my usual phrasing.]
85:2:17  P:   Why did you bring that up?! John would think of it
              that way. The way people are—not trying to be virtuous.
85:2:18  A:   Were you bothered by my saying it?
85:2:19  P:   Not at all. It's a term people don't use. A moral term.
              In ill repute. I'm still trying to work through what
              was going on with Jane. I was trying to be an old-
              fashioned virtuous friend, to think of her needs and
              not build dependence and it got confused.

              [Jane is a fellow graduate student whom Nancy frequently
              helped out with her children. Nancy became very critical
              of Jane's handling of (ignoring) the children and the friend-
              ship blew up with Jane accusing Nancy of trying to make
              Jane dependent on her. This was a bitter disappointment
              to Nancy. It had not come up in the analysis in many
              months.]

              It's perplexing how, given my desire to be a good
              friend, what I did would seem so opposite to her—
              developing dependence.
85:2:20  A:   And some of the issues turned on dealing with the
              discipline of the children?
85:2:21  P:   Why is that important? [*wary*] It's true. The most problem
              was my growing sense from Jane that the children
              made her tired, kept her from doing what she wanted
              to do. The only problem with discipline was she couldn't
              put the children to sleep.
85:2:22  A:   It would be better for me to say the problem of living
              with children in a way that would be pleasurable and
              helpful?
85:2:23  P:   Yes. That's it.
              [In her helping me to make a more accurate statement of
              the problem with Jane, we arrive at a clearer association of
              Jane with Nancy's mother.]

12/12/85 - Tuesday

[The beginning of the hour was spent in Nancy's making comments
about her having gotten an insurance payment, being about to pay

me, and being able to make progress in a number of other areas but feeling depressed. If everything is in order, then she has no excuse to avoid problems she needs to deal with here. I indicated the need then to talk with me about her sexual problems, as she had begun to do last week. She became physically limp and still and silent. I asked what she was experiencing.]


85:3:1  P:  Fog. I feel I'm in a fog when I try to think about my sexual problems.

85:3:2  A:  Can you penetrate the fog to sense any of the factors? [I asked a question that was ambiguous, in that she could associate to the fog or to the sexual problems. She chose the latter.]

85:3:3  P:  Being in my parents' bedroom, observing their sex and being confused. Getting enemas. The sexual activity with my brother. Being banished from my dad's lap. Being banished always from Mother. Never being able to snuggle or cuddle with her.

[This had the quality of a recitation of lessons learned, but at the same time of lifting out of repression the results of a great deal of prior analytic work that appears and disappears into the fog. It is noteworthy that her enuresis is omitted.]

It has all taken on the same character—of being bad, naughty. I got the enemas because I was bad—didn't go to the bathroom—and I was bad because the enemas gave me a lot of stimulation I liked. I was banished from Dad's lap over stimulation—my bad response. I couldn't be close to Mother because I was bad—it was put as dependence but I don't know what it was. It wasn't that. [Her tone is a mixture of being troubled and guilty, of being both serious and facetious.] Everything sensual is all bad. Touching, masturbation, looking at myself, hugging Mother, squirming in Dad's lap. All ends up being bad—wanting to stick like glue to Mother. Not going to the bathroom. Teasing Matt, getting into sexual activities with him. All problems. My play with Margaret and the dolls doesn't seem so problematic—it was just 10-year-old stuff. What does it mean that I don't think it was problematic?

85:3:4    A:   Can you describe it?

[I answer a question with a question that is in fact a suggestion—the purpose being to fill the narrative envelope by
moving from the too general to the specific, from the already
said to the new.]

85:3:5    P:   We were playing with our dolls, being mothers trying
to breast-feed, although of course we didn't have breasts.
We were holding the doll against our breasts and feeding
it. Another day we were worried about breast cancer,
checking out our flat chests [*laughing*] at eight or
nine. I don't remember much sensation. I was interested in my body. We had fantasies of being in love
with movie stars—mine was Perry Mason, I was Della
Street. We played doctor. One was sick, the other came
to listen to the patient's chest and stomach. We had
play stethoscopes. We were undressed partially. It had
nothing to do with genitals. It all had to do with our
nonexistent breasts [*pause*]. It was not dirty. It was
clean. There were no secretions. With my brother, it
was his ejaculation that was sick, gross. As you said
before, in the play with Margaret we were equals. My
brother would rub against me. Against my leg, my
stomach, until he had ejaculations. I felt very dirty
and used.

[This added considerable richness of detail. It was stated
with feeling but without a sense of becoming overwhelmed
with revulsion, as in the past.]

85:3:6    A:   You didn't have a sense of being appreciated for yourself but for the purpose you served?

85:3:7    P:   Women often talk about being angry about being receptacles. In a sense, that's what they are—just a place
for men to get rid of their excitement without having
to do with the being of the person. I'm angry at men
for taking women as receptacles. I'm angry at women
for being vulnerable enough to let it be carried out
and, worse, to invite it.

[The patient is airing deeply felt hurt and anger but is
doing so with a circumlocution that removes the issue from
herself.]

85:3:8    A:   And that makes you feel bad about yourself, that you
were inviting it—the alternative of being unnoticed
was such a painful choice.

12/14/85 - Thursday

85:4:1   P:   I'll spend five minutes complaining about the process
              and then get to work. It's like any work. I *have* to talk
              a bit at a time and I hate it. I think I should be able
              to be brilliant and wonderful and not have to work.
              I had dinner with Karl. It was awkward at first. Then
              it was okay and a lot of stuff came up. I don't want
              to deal with it. I like it better when all this is under
              wraps. When I left Tuesday, your last statement made
              me feel bad. It's a deplorable situation when a woman
              lets herself be used as a receptacle. You said what I
              did as a kid. You men blame everything on women [*a
              tone of pseudo-outrage*]. I don't want to be teasing Jim
              or have to think about it. I got over being angry at
              you. It's true to say I invited that response. No. It
              sounds defensive, but it's not true. What you said was
              the alternative was so painful—not teasing. It's hard
              to feel it now, but on Tuesday I could, that I couldn't
              survive the isolation. I couldn't—physically even. It
              was too much. [*pause*] It seemed so real. It was true
              to me at the time. It's no longer true. I don't have to
              be isolated, and if I did, I have the strength to deal
              with it. Then I didn't. It's a sad state of affairs, the
              way things were [*sigh*].
85:4:2   A:   Your sigh is your feeling about the "sad state of affairs"?
85:4:3   P:   I was thinking what could have changed it. A lot of
              things. But they weren't there. My mother wasn't there
              to watch over me. She just wasn't there . . . I was
              thinking on the way home what you said puts it in a
              different light. My anger toward my brother was miti-
              gated. He had no supervision, no rules or guidance.
              We were all there together. [*sigh*] I don't like the way
              he treated me. I really don't like him. I can see he was
              a kid too—a kid supported and maintained to have
              the idea he could do whatever he wanted. . . . After
              dinner with Karl—oh, it came up in a dream about
              Jim. I was nervous how Jim would be. I hadn't told
              him I was going out with Karl, although he knew Karl
              called. Jim came out of the room and I worried he'd
              be jealous. That's how it was in the past with my
              family—jealousy.

85:4:4  A:  On whose part?

85:4:5  P:  My brother's. When I was in high school and college everyone let me know my place was to be with my dad and my brother. Any boy I brought home was not good enough because he was a threat. Once when I was home on a visit, a man I was going with called me and asked me to come back because he was lonely. I wouldn't. He had a bad temper and I was glad to get away. My brother heard me talk and said, "You know where your place is." In a dream I had last night, I was on the floor picking up something. Jim came over. I put my arm around his leg. Only it wasn't his leg, it was his crotch. When I realized it I tried to back off, but he wouldn't let me. I was trying to give him an affectionate gesture, let him know I had not gone, and then it got misplaced from Karl to Jim. But where does it come from. You're suggesting it's from my living with my family—my memories. In the dream one thing was apparent about making mistakes. My first was misconstruing where I placed my cheek. Then his in not letting it go. That is like my brother. I was not trying to get my face near his genitals. I was trying to share affection. That's what I was trying to do in the dream as well.

85:4:6  A:  In the dream, what were you doing to begin with? [Throughout the hour Nancy has been carrying forward her associations with little need for encouragement or focus. I wanted her to remain in touch with the dream imagery and I was curious about the beginning image, which had not been clear to me.]

85:4:7  P:  I don't know. I was down on my knees picking up something. A note card maybe. He comes in. I want to make a gesture of affection, put my arm out and lean my face against—it would be his knee or upper calf. Then the size perspective changed, from child to adult. It's important because that's what gets played out here—feeling childish. [*pause*] I just had a question: Do I understand the importance of what I'm saying? [*sigh*] The answer is no. Like when I say something and you say it back to me and then I see it.

85:4:8  A:  Are you asking me to say it?

85:4:9  P:  Perhaps.

85:3:10  A:  Do you want me to call attention to the longings that were so strong for you as a child?

85:4:11  P:  My immediate response is to say no! Don't. That's stuff I don't want to touch [*playful tone*]. But if I don't, they'll keep coming up misplaced into an adult context, won't they?

85:4:12  A:  Yes.

85:4:13  P:  Okay. So let's start with Number 1. You can go ahead and state it if you want. [*giggling*] I can't.

85:4:14  A:  A longing to have somebody else take the lead and the responsibility?

[The interchange has taken on a playful quality. I was a participant in the mood state but I addressed the issue that seemed to me most immediately manifest in the intersubjective context.]

85:4:15  P:  That's not so bad. Seems pretty normal for a kid, huh? So what's another? One thing that's clear is wanting to be close to people, treated tenderly and affectionately [*pause*] [*sigh*].

[I could easily pick up on the theme of wanting a positive attachment experience—the frustration of her mother's stiffening when Nancy reached for her leg, as in a model scene that had been worked with extensively. The desperate seeking of intimacy with the other available family members—all male—was a natural consequence. Nancy's long silence may have been an expectation of this familiar theme being reactivated.]

Are there worse ones that are more scary? These don't seem so scary.

[I assumed the patient to be saying she was ready to deal with a new problem area.]

85:4:16  A:  One longing might be to explore things that are unknown and scary.

85:4:17  P:  Right. And not to have to do it alone.

85:4:18  A:  Yeah . . . and a man's crotch could be just such an area of curiosity and interest.

85:4:19  P:  It seems reasonable that it would be [*giggle*]. And breasts and bottoms—everything that's covered up I'd want to understand [*sigh*].

85:4:20  A:  Your sigh?

85:4:21  P:  No way to do that that doesn't make me feel depraved. It makes sense. A child wants to see adult bodies and her own body. To do it and get rid of fears. My parents feared an interest in my body and others would lead to depravity. I don't know what it would be.

85:4:22  A:  What form could the depravity take?
[Nancy is using distancing speech forms—"A child wants" rather than "I wanted." I could have commented on this, but I chose not to, assuming she would use more direct speech as she became more comfortable with this "unknown and scary" area of exploration.]

85:4:23  P:  Yeah. I don't know. [*pause*] For Mother and me, being covered always. I never saw my mother's breasts until she was in her 50s. I could say I never saw my father naked but in tight revealing jockey shorts. And the time he got so mad because I walked in on him in the bathroom and stood staring aghast at his genitals. It makes me mad. There was nothing wrong with *his* not locking the door. It was me. And now I have this interest. It has become very important, everything now has a sexual genital flavor.

85:4:24  A:  And seems to retain the flavor of either "it's your fault" or "it's not your fault, it's the fault of someone who won't take responsibility."

85:4:25  P:  That's what it had. What am I supposed to do with that? [*argumentative*] That's the way the messages came across to me.

85:4:26  A:  In your dream, you do parcel it out in a clear fashion.
[Nancy had been associating in a relatively free, open fashion. Then her anger mounted and she became mildly provocative. I had the choice of either directing her attention to her argumentativeness with me as a recrudescence of her anger at her father (something I had done many times in the past) or trying to get more work done in associating to and exploring the meaning of her dream. As the hour was drawing to an end, and a weekend break was coming, I chose the latter.]

85:4:27  P:  Yeah. What are you suggesting? I could have as a kid? Or I could parcel it out now and I'm not?

85:4:28  A:  How does it sit with you?

85:4:29  P:  I don't think I could have as a kid.

85:4:30  A:  Um-hm.

85:4:31  P:  I think I could now. But I get caught in it. I did when I left Tuesday. I started thinking, "it takes two to tango."

Then I lose it, and I'm back to "it's all my problem."
Then I think, "kids need adults to learn." It's a real
problem for that not to be available.

85:4:32 A: Yes.

85:4:33 P: I can take responsibility for wanting to know about
everything.

[Nancy begins to sort out her thinking, how she goes back
and forth with blame. She identifies parental responsibility
in a general sense—"kids need adults." I affirm her recognition of this and she shifts to the personal pronoun in
saying, "*I* can take responsibility (for her curiosity)".]

I was a very curious little girl. But curious isn't perverted.
If it becomes perverted, it's because something is wrong.

85:4:34 A: Our time is up.

85:4:35 P: Let me say one more time I hate this work [*good-
naturedly*]—the work I love to hate.

[Nancy returns to the resentment toward the analyst that
remained unexplored when I chose to return to the dream.]


10/1/87

87:1:1 P: I haven't made any progress on the question, at the
end of the week, of why I feel like I have to face a
sense of moral failure if I can't be friends with Jane. I
know that right now I am very depressed. I don't know
why I feel so bad. Over the past several months I've
gone back to being chronically constipated. I feel I
have to do something, force myself. At Saturday
evening's service, Charles presided as minister with his
friends in a thanksgiving for his ordination. It was very
moving. I felt good to be a part of the group. Charles
made a good decision to become a priest. But I was
also very struck that Jane and her kids took presents
to the altar. They have a special relationship with him.
I got depressed that there's nobody in the world that
I'm special to. Wanting so much to be special was part
of the cause of the trouble with Jane. I'm ashamed.
But I'm not special in an intimate way with anybody.
I'm lonely and depressed to the point of being frightened. [*After starting with a timid tone, she is now speaking
in a full voice*] It's ironic that in the middle of the
service I'd be so aware of feeling alone. I reminded

myself I have lots of friends who love me. [*Her arms are at her sides, held stiffly*] I was overcome with hopelessness nevertheless—a fear I'd never be close, always on the fringe.

87:1:2  A:  Would that feeling pressure you to want to try again with Jane and your aunt?

87:1:3  P:  Perhaps. I do feel a devastating aloneness and I feel it as a consequence of my own actions [*she rubs her eyes at intervals throughout this sequence*]. It's so hard for me to be outgoing, generous, and gregarious. It wasn't always. Only recently. My need to revitalize my attempt to be friends with Jane is part loneliness and part guilt. It's so hard for me to put myself out and I have to do it. What do I mean by that? After the service, I had to work the next two days. It was 8:30. I was tired. I wanted to go home and eat and rest. But I went to the reception for a little while, let people know I care. We talked on Friday about my getting myself paralyzed. I feel bad and get paralyzed. We talked about my wanting to do that to keep myself from doing things that are hard to do.

87:1:4  A:  What are you thinking of that's hard to do?

[I have been listening to Nancy, perplexed as to what she is getting at. I am convinced, that her distress and her feeling of disappointment that she isn't important are authentic, but the references to herself as not being outgoing or generous, her mea culpa, arouses my skepticism. I want to try to follow her as open-mindedly as I can in these early moments of the week's work, until I get my bearings.]

87:1:5  P:  Going to the reception. At the time I felt the warm thing to do was to stay and talk. But I couldn't. I felt guilty when I went home, berating myself for being weak. Later I thought that you and I have talked about my having to have certain of my needs met first before I can feel friendly.

87:1:6  A:  Yes.

87:1:7  P:  And I was tired, hungry, headachy—and I needed to get up early. If I go into a social situation that way I say and do things I'm not happy with. Then I go back to being paralyzed. Not before I go home but after when I feel bad and can't come up with other ways to let people know I care. [*pause*] I feel really uptight.

87:1:8   A:   What you said on Friday was that it was clear to you that Jane and your aunt operate to be one up on you and that's not a friend. Then you stated, "Oh, it's me, what I do," then you became paralyzed.

87:1:9   P:   The paralysis was to avoid drawing the conclusion it's not a friend who does this stuff.

87:1:10  A:   Yes.

[I believed on Friday that Nancy had arrived at a degree of clarity about the nature of these competitive relationships, which were replete with their self-righteous put-downs and her own 1) aversiveness to acknowledge the aggressive contribution of the other and 2) martyr-saint receptiveness. Now her expanded awareness, so difficult to arrive at, was once again scrambled. I chose to remind her of it straightforwardly—in the hope she could self-right and restore the cohesive state she had achieved. Her initial response was hopeful.]

87:1:11  P:   I had breakfast with Jane and concluded she is not a person I *want* to *be friends with*. That's all there is to it! She doesn't bring out the best in me. Just the opposite—gossip and complaints. It's tiresome. I was glad to have it happen, to be reassured. I get it clear, and then it falls apart. Again and again. With my mother, my aunt, Jane. Anyone I think I don't like. [*She places her hand over her mouth*] Them [*her hands explode outward*]! I never said before I don't like my mother. I said it with Jane. But there it is!

87:1:12  A:   As though it should be unsayable?

87:1:13  P:   Is that it? I'm not just saying something about them, but about me too.

87:1:14  A:   Which is?

87:1:15  P:   That I don't like someone.

87:1:16  A:   That you—*you* are capable of *not* liking someone.

87:1:17  P:   It gets thrown back to me. That I'm not capable—a slip—that I am capable, I'm open to criticism, that I'm like the other person. If I don't like Jane's being whiney, then when I'm whiney or critical I'm open to being criticized, and [*said humorously*] we both know how I don't like being criticized. What does it say if I say I'm not capable of not liking? That I'm a saint—and have no mind. I don't want to take the responsibility of saying I don't like someone.

87:1:18  A:   That you could feel that way.

87:1:19  P:   I don't want the consequences. She doesn't like, she criticized, let's criticize her. If it's fair for one, it's fair for the other. I don't want to not like people—my looking-for-sainthood side.

87:1:20  A:   Do you have a saintlike feeling that you value?
[The disruption marked by Nancy's depression and mild fragmentation of thought in the initial part of the hour ended with my clarification about the gains made in the Friday hour. Her difficulty in acknowledging her resentment and her attempt to maintain a saintlike image similar to her mother's was then explored. My question was intended as an invitation to her to go beyond an intellectual recognition of her seeking sainthood and avoiding criticism to sense the probably elevated *feeling* of moral superiority.]

87:1:21  P:   I have an uncomfortable feeling when people—others— are being critical. I don't like it. People at the laboratory criticize the docs and I get into it. Let's call a spade a spade. But what does it say about me? I don't want to say anything then.
[Nancy has ignored my question about the feeling of saintlike superiority and returned to her aversiveness to be seen as critical, suggesting to me this is the issue she is more motivated to explore at this time.]

87:1:22  A:   Back to feeling paralyzed—retentive and paralyzed.

87:1:23  P:   Perhaps the problem with my saying I don't want to not like people is that it's too bald a statement. When I'm being critical of a doctor, it's not that he's a bad person, or a bad doc, but that it takes him such a long time to trust the techs. The way he treated me was menial and he does it to other people. I'm uncomfortable with the inclusiveness of it. Am I backing off now?

87:1:24  A:   Is the difference you're getting at the difference between a total attack on a person's whole self and a specific action?

87:1:25  P:   What I do is a total attack on a person. Others do too. Then it comes back to me as inclusive and we're dead in the water.

87:1:26  A:   The whole friendship is dead in the water.

87:1:27  P:   Yeah. Yeah. That's the whole point. I come home from breakfast with Jane and say she's just critical and whining and I don't want to be her friend.

87:1:28  A:   The difference between not liking her complaining and whining and saying Jane is just a whiner.

87:1:29  P:   But she is just a whiner and complainer most of the time we are together. It's less if other people are around.

87:1:30  A:   Are you experiencing a sense of being criticized by me?

[Her last comment struck me as argumentative and, on reflection, my comment to her sounded sanctimoniously critical—more preachy than empathic.]

87:1:31  P:   Your tone was [*pause*] um [*pause*] I'm not sure how to say it—sarcastic. No, heavy-loaded.

87:1:32  A:   Yes. I loaded one side of it.

[I recognize and accept (wear) her attribution. This has the immediate effect of confirming her "reality" of our inter-subjective context. It is too near the end of the hour to examine any further implications.]

87:1:33  P:   Right. So, I guess I do feel criticized. You were saying something that I was saying, but you loaded it differently, so I do feel criticized.


10/3/87

87:2:1  P:   [*She hands me a check.*]

87:2:2  A:   Thank you.

87:2:3  P:   I balanced my checkbook after paying my bills. I had the wonderful experience of something left. Not much, but it was wonderful. I thought of paying you a higher fee, but it's not really possible in the foreseeable future. I know you have not asked me for more and I appreciate that. What I want to say today is—I won't let it go as an issue. If you need more money, I will leave it to you to tell me. It's like the special attention I get from the dean. I'm aware of it, appreciate it, but I'm not sure I'm worthy of it. It makes me feel uncomfortable. [*Her earnest tone suddenly dissolves into a self-conscious laugh as she says*] Aw shucks. [*We both laugh*] Thanks [*playful.*]

87:2:4  A:   You're welcome [*playful*].

87:2:5  P:   Now on to other stuff. I had a lot of trouble sleeping last night. I ran into Sean. He's being ordained in May. We were chatting and he invited me to go to a play. I told him I'd like to if I can get off. He called last night to tell me the date. Then I started feeling weird. We are just friends, so what's the problem? I wouldn't want to go with him if I didn't find him attractive and interesting. The danger is that I want to be special to someone. I think I can go with Sean if I don't put stuff into it neither of us thinks should be there. I have to be clear—I do want to be special to someone and am trying to be, but Sean is not the one. In the past the way I handled it was to avoid. I wish [*with feeling*] I were going with someone sexually attractive, like Brian, that I could be intimate with. It makes me sad [*sigh*]. It's come up before that I'm attracted to men who are not available. Now it's priests. It used to be others. I can use this to get to a man I could be with. I feel guilty with Brian. Why? I think it's an overstatement, but if I'm not sure about the sexual component I should just walk away. That's why I haven't been able to work it out—I walk away. I don't know how to think about it. I wish you'd help me now. Ask me questions. Help me.

87:2:6   A:   Give you a lead to follow?
[Nancy has been carrying forward on her own, using the understanding we had gained about her difficulties with flirtatious but unavailable men. My impression is that she is primarily asking for affirmation—to know I am here rather than for specific "help."]

87:2:7   P:   Yeah. Yeah. It doesn't seem problematic to be friends with a man or a priest—or that I have to sterilize the relationship by acting like I have no awareness of sex differences. I need to set limits.

87:2:8   A:   We were discussing that you had concluded that the only way to set limits or regulate is on-off.

87:2:9   P:   And that's not true. But you see an infinity between.

87:2:10  A:   Um-hm.

87:2:11  P:   And that's the trouble. It seems to me that I'm confused about what I'm regulating. I think I feel I'm regulating my feelings. You would say, "You don't regulate your feelings." Feelings are your feelings. You look at them. You recognize them. Feelings change. But with any hint of sexual attraction, I say, "Turn everything off, turn the other way."

87:2:12  A:   Lest?

87:2:13  P:   Lest I lose control. Become so attracted, I seduce them.
As I say that, it's not just an issue of Brian and Anthony
[*priests*]. It was with my brother and dad. All men I'm
not supposed to seduce. It extends to all men. For two
different reasons. Dad, my brother, Sean, you—because
it's inappropriate. If I act seductively, it's an attempt
to break that down. With Dad and my brother—they
are unable to withstand that temptation. Seduction
might work! My power to be enormously attractive.
My strength. They are weak, susceptible. The other
side comes from Mom, to want to be attractive in any
form to men is selling your soul. I can't be independent, on my own, without needing a man, not my
own person . . . I was thinking, coming here today,
about what kind of clothes I'm wearing. Jeans and a
baggy shirt say something.

87:2:14  A:   What are you suggesting you're saying?
[We worked with the Eve-seducing-Adam theme (model
scene) extensively in the past. She brings it up now with
an ironic twist that I hear as "I know and you know that
they sold me a pile of crap that they were crafty enough
to believe (in their self-serving way) and that I was fool
enough to accept then and feel guilty about to this day
(it's part of my concern about being a moral failure)."
Alternatively, she was bringing up for the first time a reference to her mother's belief that she was selling her soul in
being attractive. In preadolescence this had to do with chasing
after her brother, in adolescence to how much of her body—
arms, legs, cleavage—she allowed to be exposed. I surmise
she is trying to move toward something particular now and
I ask an open-ended question to encourage her further
associations.]

87:2:15  P:   I'm not sure. If I'm talking about being attractive to
Sean, I don't want you to get aroused. So I'm unattractive. What I wear is important. At times I want
to look good to you. Most of the time. I want you
to think I'm taking care of myself. Besides I want you
to like me, approve of me. That's enhanced if I'm
dressed [*pause*] not femininely [*pause*] that's part of it.
Something we've never talked about is my wanting to
be special to you. I haven't thought about it much.

87:2:16 A:  Can you say more about this feeling?

87:2:17 P:  I see it as theoretical. I'm not aware of feeling it—
like I did Saturday night at mass. Wanting to be
special to someone. I think it's you, but I don't have
a feeling for it. It's just an idea. That's funny, particularly in the light of what we started with—my
appreciating your special treatment of me with money.
Being special [*sigh*] carries a feeling of something
that's a problem. It slides into sexual . . . warmth.
That feels problematic. So I can say I appreciate and
get uncomfortable, make a joke—aw shucks—it's a
way of not being attuned to what it feels like to feel
special.

87:2:18 A:  Umm.

87:2:19 P:  Not that I never feel it. I just don't feel it here. When
I leave a session, I often feel how special you are to
me. How affectionate, how much regard and esteem
I feel for you. My regarding you, not you me—and
not here.

87:2:20 A:  Are you emphasizing both the experience, which is
very important, and your distancing?

87:2:21 P:  When I thought about money last night, I came to
grips with not being able to pay you more. I leave
myself in a position of being beholden to you. Not
that I was special—like with the dean. Part of the
problem we haven't talked about was to be special with
a man is to set up the potential for real problems of
a sexual nature. My grandfather seems right here!

87:2:22 A:  Um-hm.

[This reference to her paternal grandfather brought back
into focus an early idealization experience with a person
whom she felt was her concerned protector. He would chase
her brother away and enjoyed her spending time with him—
unlike her father, who was struggling with the farm and
her mother, who was depressed and often ill. He had not
been mentioned for what seemed to me several years. I was
interested in how she would relate him to this context.]

87:2:23 P:  I was special to him and that was a big problem for
Mother. She thought he was a dirty old man. I thought
it was because he didn't bathe often and spit tobacco.
He was ripe smelling.

87:2:24 A:  Any thoughts beyond that now?

[The dirty old man phrase is obviously ambiguous, raising a question of sexual involvement, even abuse, that had not, it seemed, been suggested in earlier discussions.]

87:2:25 P:  I don't know, there were a group of men—neighbors, a man in the church—who gave me attention. They fussed over me. I thought I was their little friend. The fear in the back of Mother's head. . . . It wasn't completely bizarre, she needed to pay attention. If that's the case [*with rising angry indignation*], why in the name of Hell didn't she pay the same attention to my brother?! Because the men were old? She saw it where it wasn't and didn't where it was [*sigh*].

87:2:26 A:  Your sigh?

[Her anger has faded into a somewhat defeated resignation.]

87:2:27 P:  It was a big mistake.

87:2:28 A:  Yes.

87:2:29 P:  It was reasonable that she paid attention, but what she wanted was for me to think there was something wrong with my being friends with them. And I don't think it was wrong when it was limited to affection.

10/4/87

87:3:1 P:  I realized, after you requested I come at 1 o'clock next Thursday (because you have to be out of town on Friday), my readiness to do it even at the expense of a friend. I asked her and she said fine, but I said yes without thinking would it be a problem for Sue. It came up today with a student who asked if her parents could sit in the class. I said okay and got to class and found other people there too. I was nervous to make a good impression. I did okay, but it pointed up to me.

87:3:2 A:  How almost automatically you tilt in the direction of saying yes?

87:3:3 P:  Yes. You know I'd try to be accommodating, but I know you wouldn't want me to not keep an agreement to do you a favor. I don't like the automaticity of it [*reflectively*]. You're right. Not at all [*with emphasis*]! [*pause*] My sister-in-law called to tell me Aunt Tina is not doing well. She's becoming forgetful.

I'd written to her last week, and I'm glad I did.
[*pause*] It brings up all kinds of feelings. Some I
don't like. If she died, I'd get an inheritance. I don't
really want her to die. I would like things to be
better financially, but they aren't so bad. [*pause*] [I
might have commented on her ambivalence, but I
didn't feel it was either necessary or where her main
feeling was. I thought it better to listen further to
sense the feeling.] I hate it that she's alone. Nothing
I can do.

87:3:4  A: Can you say more about that?

87:3:5  P: When you are old and frail, it's not good to be alone.
I know what it feels like to be alone. I'd hate it if she
died alone. Uncle Henry said he wanted to be in his
own house and die there. When he died, I felt terrible.
I missed him dreadfully—but that's for *me!* The situation with Aunt Tina is different. I won't miss her, I
don't think.

87:3:6  A: Is that hard for you to feel?
[Based on her general feeling that it is necessary to position herself with the morally correct attitude, I want to
acknowledge that she is taking a stand based on her aversive experience and that to do so is difficult—aversive to
her).

87:3:7  P: It's hard for me to say, and it's sad . . . I think about
whether she leaves me money or not, I'm glad I don't
need it. If she doesn't, it will be hurtful in what
others will think. Because she's family. As you said,
I'm her sister's daughter. I used to feel she had an
obligation to me, but I don't think that any more. It
will just be sad and hurtful—another reminder she
has no obligation to me and that she felt none. It's
unfortunate. I keep wanting to make things different,
but I can't.

87:3:8  A: And that's very frustrating.
[I was trying to select out the thread of her dominant affect,
which was on the edge of her awareness.]

87:3:9  P: Yeah. How can I say it's frustrating and that I'm at
peace with it? They don't go together. Am I kidding
myself? I don't think so.

87:3:10  A: Does having written Aunt Tina last week help you to
feel more at peace?

[She has spontaneously recognized her ambivalence toward her aunt—I have previously stressed her underlying antagonism toward her, but now I want to give recognition to her attempt at reconciliation and restoration of a degree of attachment.]

87:3:11 P: Yeah. I did think it was the best I could do in a tough situation. In the past I'd have felt obligated to go there and take care of her. Now I feel it's not appropriate, but I do hate for her to be alone. She's 80 and won't live much longer. It brings up my greediness. Life would be easier for me, but I'm not willing to do something to ensure I get something.

87:3:12 A: And what you may have been willing to do at one time or another for money is a very loaded issue.

[I am aware of a subtheme that touches on a major trend in the work—her withholding her payment to me, her recurrent constipation, her acceptance of her brother's bribes for sexual favors, her acceptance of her mother's bribes to give up her rebellious hold on her mother with her enuresis. I want to offer Nancy the opportunity to open that issue in any form she chooses—or not to—as her trust–aversiveness balance dictates or it is a dominant theme of the moment.]

87:3:13 P: It sure is. Clearly it was strange with Aunt Tina and Mother. Perhaps Dad too, but less so. Money is a tool to get people to do things they wouldn't do otherwise. [*Her speech is becoming freer*] My brother has been better at resisting that with Aunt Tina. Matt would say he was more influenced by Dad, who wouldn't do what he didn't want for money, and I am more like Mother. This summer he said he understood how I let Tina lure me because mother had taken money from her for my college.

87:3:14 A: Did it establish in your mind that by your agreement— that is, yours, your mother's, and your aunt's—your Aunt Tina would serve as your sponsor?

[This is a *new* connection worth noting, but it was stated in a mode of unclear responsibility, as very often happens.]

87:3:15 P: I don't think so. It's what Matt thought. I'm not sure it's what I thought. She only gave me money for one year. Nothing else until I came here. She lent me, gave me money. She's given me clothes. [*pause*].

87:3:16 A: Are you feeling tense?

[Her body posture is stiff, the silence is strained.]

87:3:17  P:  Yeah.

87:3:18  A:  Any sense of what is contributing to it?

87:3:19  P:  I'm groping to figure out what the issues are, or even what I'm feeling. Now that you say that, I'm reminded that you said what I'm willing to do for money has been a problem for a long time. Perhaps I don't like to be reminded of that.

87:3:20  A:  Hmm.

87:3:21  P:  [*less body rigidity*] I'm glad I wrote. I don't want her to be so alone. There's not much else I can do. She is alone in her relationship with me. A distance [*sigh*]. [I hear this as an acknowledgment of an aversive separateness—one not to be bridged by an altruistic surrender. I hear her sigh as an indication of resignation, of mourning.] I don't know. Writing to her is also like saying that's what I will do for money. Write occasionally so she can't cut me out of the will entirely. I don't think I'll feel good about any money I get from her.

87:3:22  A:  I think you've been trying to say something all hour about how moved you feel by the thought of someone being all alone. [Immersed in the line of thought about money—subservience, altruistic surrender, responsibility for greed—I had also been preoccupied with another affect-laden associative path—"alone." One result of her analysis had been her lessening her ties to her family. Suddenly the word "alone" began to resonate in my mind and I spoke almost as soon as the thought crystallized.]

87:3:23  P:  You're right. [*crying*] Maybe that's it. I know that experience. It doesn't feel good [*wiping away her tears*]. [*pause*] Another way of saying I don't like what I did in the past for money is to say I don't like what I did but I can understand it—and the same with Aunt Tina. What she does with money is similar. She's alone and doesn't want to be. Or with people either. [*pause*] I was going to say I'm sure she's lonesome, but maybe not. Like Uncle Henry. He didn't mind.

87:3:24  A:  Is what you're sure of that if you were she, you'd be lonesome?

87:3:25 P: Perhaps . . . I'm not sure about later. I think when I die, I'd like to be like Uncle Henry. Not have people feel manipulated. Guilty. Less feeling alone as feeling abandoned.

[I'm now aware that in keying on her well-recognized sense of feeling alone, I ignored the issue of her pride in trying to be more self-reliant—like Uncle Henry. When she clarifies that her fear is of feeling abandoned, that is, not being alone by choice, I'm free to respond.]

87:3:26 A: Unattended, rejected, uncared for?

87:3:27 P: That's it! Rejected, uncared for. That's why I wrote. To say she's not uncared about.

## 1/5/89

89:1:1 P: [Nancy handed me a check.]

89:1:2 A: Thank you.

89:1:3 P: [*on couch*] Happy New Year.

89:1:4 A: Happy New Year.

89:1:5 P: Business first. I want to start paying you $100.

89:1:6 A: Okay.

89:1:7 P: I got a check from my aunt. Unfortunately, she didn't sign it. But I can manage on my own. It will be tight in June, but you will be away. I had a lot of trouble figuring it out. I couldn't until today. Wednesday we were talking about my being Lady Bountiful. I was doing the same to you as my aunt did to me—debating $105 or $100. Making a big plan and then falling back. I don't like that about myself. I can look at it— that it's you. It's money I have to pay to you. It becomes sticky—is it my money or your money? I'm Lady Bountiful. No, this is the best I can do. [*pause*] Now that I've talked to you, I don't feel so good about it.

[My impression is that her feelings are hurt by my interpretation of her intent to offer more than she felt she could afford. I decided for the moment to listen further (I did keep it in mind as an empathic failure on my part and five months later she brought it up. Then we recognized she felt she wanted credit for acting "justly" by offering to raise the fee—an affirmation of her thoughtfulness that got lost in the analysis of her overgenerous, overquick inclination).]

I felt good when I decided it. It was right after my second job interview. I went home and wanted no stimulus! I worked over the weekend too much—a bad decision—I got sick. I worked three days at Christmas, then went to meetings. And four days at New Year's. Without blinking an eye. I couldn't do it.

89:1:8   A:   An expectation that was hard to live up to. [I had recognized from her tone her inclination to want to dazzle: "without blinking an eye." This was a familiar pattern set by her desire to emulate her brother. My comment was designed to focus on that motivation.]

89:1:9   P:   The old fast stuff! Whatever I can do isn't fast enough, good enough. I should promise more, beat myself to do more. If I stay with my routine, pace, rhythm—but the ethicist's meeting is stiff competition. If I get a job I will be very lucky. That reminds me, I'm leaving here at the end of July. Finishing and going my way. . . . I'm jerky with my talk today. I will have to reexamine that between now and July. When I got sick at the lab I didn't make a big deal, didn't force myself to work. I said I'm sick and have to stay home. It brings up what I'm going to do when I don't have you around. You were here last week and a big help. I'll keep making my plans for July and talk to you. That doesn't sound bad. I was careful to not get caught up in the chaos at the hospital New Year's. I dealt with the problems with a supervisor and it went okay, so why am I in a tizzy? I think it's a good omen that I'm being honest with people. I told my supervisor, who is my friend and is lazy, that I didn't appreciate her assigning me work. My brother called and I told him that I was going to use my remaining money to buy a house. He said, "Yeah, like California." I said, "Wait a minute, you didn't do well with your money then either. I don't like your tone—that you can talk to me like I'm an idiot." He said, "You're right." I said, "I do want to talk seriously about the idea of investing." I was pleased.

89:1:10  A:   Yes.

[Nancy is using clear examples of her hard-won ability to be assertive as reassurance for herself in her anxiety about termination. I offer a simple affirmation.]

89:1:11  P:   I stood up for myself and turned it into something productive [*sigh*].

89:1:12  A:   Your sigh?

[Her usual pattern after reassurance is to activate an underlying concern. I want to invite her to expand on this concern.]

89:1:13  P:   Why do I feel so bad?

89:1:14  A:   Can you do that over the weekend when I'm with, I mean, not with you?

[My intention is to continue to help her to make explicit her apprehension. In my slip, I suspect I am reassuring myself (and her) that she does and will after termination feel that I am with her. A latent problem in the sequence is whether to focus directly on my slip.]

89:1:15  P:   [*crying*] I don't want to leave you. I don't want to be well enough to. Oh, I'll take the well enough to, but not leave. To have you to talk to without having to shake you and say I want to talk to you like I'm an adult.... There are two things on my mind. One is a song about my best friend. [*singing*] You're my best friend.

89:1:16  A:   It surely is hard to part from a best friend.

89:1:17  P:   It sure is. It's increasingly clear to me how many good friends I have and how solid my relationship with my brother has become. There will be trouble, but I have faith now that we can weather it. With Judy, Sally, and Jim, it's more stable and I appreciate that a lot. Without you, I wouldn't have that. I had a dream over the weekend. I don't remember much. I was reenacting the situation as a little girl when I had a wooden dowel and I was masturbating my vagina. I was out of sight—attention getting. Another dream was about a bunch of women at the women's university where I did my undergraduate work. It was the same women—some married, some single—all dressed in white and lavender like wedding dresses, lacy chiffon. In the dream, I thought about being attracted to some of them because of their being happy, not because of their having big breasts or being angry and aloof. I was aware the angry and aloof women are not attractive. [*pause*]

89:1:18  A:   What was your situation in the first dream?

[The sequence has gone through rapid shifts. She ended her recitation of reassuring factors by noting her consolidated network of friends. She then brought up the kind of overtly sexual dream about masturbating that she would previously often have only alluded to. And finished with another dream about progress, about not being hooked on breasts to get maternal holding and cuddling or on angry aloof women—her mother and maternal aunts—but on women who are happy, her current aspiration. I had been puzzled by her references at the end of the first dream to being "out of sight" and "attention getting." I chose my puzzlement as the point for orienting my inquiry.]

89:1:19 P:  There wasn't much of a context. I was in a room upstairs. I had a smooth piece of wood. I'm looking at people and want them to notice me but they can't see me. It reminds me of a dream, I was crying and crying. Mother was saying I had to do something I didn't want to do. I was pleading, "Please don't make me." I had to marry a woman who was angry and hostile and made me feel terrible. I was saying to Mother, "It won't work, it will be bad." Mother was standing there [*mimicking*] implacable. When I first thought about the dreams in the beginning of the session, I thought I want to tell you something is wrong. I'm not ready to go.

89:1:20 A:  Do you want to tell me you are still caught up in masturbating and in a preoccupation with women's bodies?

89:1:21 P:  But I'm not. That's the funny thing. But that's what the dreams are saying.

89:1:22 A:  Um-hm.

89:1:23 P:  I don't want to go back to that in order to stay with you, but I don't want to leave you. If I just dream it, I cannot quite go back to it, but I can use it to bring it to you. To get you worried. To reassess the July time. It's hard to see how I'm going to be able to handle leaving you. I can't conceive it!

1/7/89

89:2:1  P:  I don't want to spend the whole next six months getting ready to leave. I have other things to do. I have to understand how I am with a man and how I can be. I'm thrown back into old ways, preoccupied with women and eating too much. We were talking about it on Tuesday, that it's the way I have to be in therapy to hang onto you. It brings up the possibility I could have a relationship with you not based on need. Not self-destructive. I do regressive.

89:2:2   A:   What do you mean?

89:2:3   P:   Not progressive, although objectively things look okay.

89:2:4   A:   It's for our alarm-triggering that it's so important to keep the regressive in the foreground.

[I am summarizing the understanding we have arrived at, painfully, after long periods of her remaining in or stirring up disturbed states. Then it was to activate or hold on to my attention through creating anxiety. Now it is to put the planned ending in question.]

89:2:5   P:   Yes. I guess. I'm astonished that when I sat down and planned my money and my dissertation, I am right on schedule. My dissertation is a little behind, but I will be done by the end of the year. I've been scrambling about money for a month. I overspent a little on presents for the meeting and I had my teeth cleaned. But I have a margin, so I'm okay I can do the dieting again. I have to work at it, but the margin is there too. Getting out of control a little doesn't kill me either. I don't have to get into a flap about any of these things— or get you into a flap. It should be comforting, but it's scary. Be careful what you wish for—I wished to be done here. [*pause*] [*sigh*]. I want to be ready to leave you, but I don't want to leave.

89:2:6   A:   To be ready adds a lot to your pride, to leave means a loss.

89:2:7   P:   Yeah. And I want the same from you. I want you to be ready for me to leave, but I don't want you to let me go. It's another part of the process—to attentively, carefully, be ready to let go of things that ought to be let go of. I ought to want to let go of you, you ought to want to let go of me. No. No. If you have someone you care about, you never let go. That's not sense, but it's hard to give up. Sometimes you can keep contact, but it can't be the same with you . . . I ran into Jim. He invited me to his house with the group. I couldn't come and I said, "No, I can't," but not very graciously. I think he's interested, but too shy to be direct. It's the way I am too. I thought I'd get a ticket for a play and ask him. I know he's not going with Alice now. It's awkward if I'm moving in July, but why not.

[She has expressed her concern about leaving in July on two grounds—whether she will be ready to accept leaving me and whether she will have dealt with her problems with "how I am with men and how I can be." She is now placing the second issue before us in her reference to Jim. Jim is the most recent in a series of men who demonstrate a characteristic ambiguousness with her. She gets caught up in the push-pull of such experiences, repeating her experiences primarily with her mother. I am pleased to have this issue before us.]

I didn't mention it to Judy and Joe. Judy closed up like a clam before. Phil said to do it, that Jim would like it and that Jim's 41—old enough. I know it sounds like I'm just looking for someone to take your place. I could stop, but I have enough perspective that with your help I won't get crazy and it'll be good to look at how I deal with men. [*pause*] I don't actually expect you to put down what I'm talking about. But I don't not expect it.

89:2:8    A:    Let's go into that. How would I put it down?

[She makes a direct attribution. I try to "wear it" to explore where she is placing me or I have wittingly or unwittingly placed myself.]

89:2:9    P:    What are you thinking? I'm leaving in July. "It's stupid to develop a relationship now." Or, "This guy hasn't asked you out and you're building another fantasy. You'll get hurt later—like with Karl." Or, "What do you need with a man? You should be independent." Or, "You don't need anybody else, you have me, at least for now. You're looking for someone to take my place—that's not very loyal." Other things too. "You're too old for him." Judy wants Jim to marry someone who can have kids with him. You could say that. [*pause*] I don't think you would say any of that, but I don't quite think you wouldn't.

89:2:10  A:    And what would be my motive if I did?

89:2:11  P:    You want me to be largely [*sigh*] *attentive* to you.

89:2:12  A:   I don't want to lose you—I want to be possessive. I want you to be loyal to me.

89:2:13  P:   If I think of you as my best friend, you want me to be your best friend. Not a friend to like me, respect me, or care about me. You just want me to be attentive to you. I feel that way about a lot of people I don't like—I want *them* to like *me*. It has to do with your ego.

89:2:14  A:   I want the flattery of your devotion, your full devotion?

89:2:15  P:   Yes. That's from my own way of thinking, but also Mom and Dad particularly. Mom was very jealous of my relationship with my aunt and Dad. She didn't want *me*, but she wanted me to be devoted to *her*. I have to admit, you haven't given me the slightest indication that you want me to be devoted to you, but my ego would want you to want me to be. It's a sad kind of importance. [*pause*] It is kind of sad, isn't it?

[I infer that she is feeling a need to be reassured that her plight is being understood.]

89:2:16  A:   It's sad in the sense you have to resort to that to feel good and to feel pride.

89:2:17  P:   Yes. It's sad in . . . I see a lot of people caught up in this way.

89:2:18  A:   How?

89:2:19  P:   Mother didn't want me around to bother with me, with my needs. But she didn't want me to go to Aunt Ada (paternal aunt) or Grandpa and see me have others doing for me. This person I want to love me but doesn't. I can get people to love me if they are jealous about me being interesting to someone else. What I need is someone to love me and not that and then give it up, but it's hard to do it. That brings me back to letting go of you and finding a relationship with someone where there is reciprocity.

89:2:20  A:   That means that I would have to let you go, and that means I'm not jealous, but that means I don't love you.

[I try to summarize the dilemma she has constructed for herself—and for me.]

89:2:21  P:   That doesn't have to be, but it comes out that way. It's a strange kind of love that won't give me what I need, desire, and deserve, but deny it to me from anyone else. Tortured, tortuous, and angry kind of love, Which reminds me of sex—tortured, tortuous, and angry.

1/8/89

89:3:1   P:   As I was driving over, I thought, I just have to tell you how depressed I am. So I tell you. I told you Monday, I'm using all my energy to take care of myself during the meeting and to manage my computer. I only want to be quiet. Not work on my dissertation, not at the lab or here. I just want to be quiet. I was thinking in the waiting room about what we talked about yesterday. It's the beginning of the year and my birthday is coming up. Yesterday it occurred to me that we might be getting to understand the relationship between sex and the way things get in the sexual realm. Mother didn't want to be around me, but she did want for me to be completely beholden to her.

89:3:2   A:   Beholden is worshipful.
[I chose "worshipful" as a descriptor (or metaphor) because as a little girl she had formed a strong idealization of her mother as beautiful and sophisticated—jewellike—and also because something of this early "worship" may have contributed to or been excited by her conversion to the Catholic church. Very occasionally that idealization entered in her vocal tone with me.]

89:3:3   P:   Yes it is! Total! Worshipful and [*pause*] I was going to say "dependent." Dependent in a certain way.

89:3:4   A:   Flattering?

89:3:5   P:   Yeah.

89:3:6   A:   Do you think that your depressions do that for me?
[Following her associations, the hesitant "dependent," I am led away from either admiration or religious metaphoric expression. Instead, I am brought back to her initial reference to depression. This is a reference not simply to an affect state but to telling me, meaning activating in me a response to need. I want to explore the relationship between evoking a response by idealization (flattery) and by protestations of depression.]

89:3:7  P:  They flatter you? I wouldn't have thought so. No, but perhaps I do. It seems opposite. Evidence of your failure—or mine.

89:3:8  A:  If I want you to grow up and manage well, it is my failure.

89:3:9  P:  Interesting. Yes, like push-pull—flattering you and slapping you in the face.

89:3:10  A:  Um-hm.

89:3:11  P:  My depression flattering? I need you—no one else can do what I need. I'd be a mess without you. On the other hand I say you're not as great as you're cracked up to be. I'm not sure why that phrase. Not as good as you would have me believe . . . I feel incredibly frustrated and angry! [*with feeling, as if she had been reluctantly following up an interpretation of mine and now was reacting to the constraint with resentment*] I want to thrash out and be free of you, of Mother, not be dependent on you.

89:3:12  A:  Just get rid of me!

89:3:13  P:  I'm not sure, get rid of being dependent and angry, but still have you to be related to in a more adult, mutual way. It feels like I have to fight with you to get independence, but I'm not sure it feels like from you, but from me. It's Mother I have to leave to be my own person. It might be good if I don't get a job this year, but finish in July and stay here, not have everything to deal with at once. Only leave town figuratively. I've been trying to decide on my own and report to you, not work it all out here. [*pause*] It's flattering for me to come and tell you all my troubles and how I appreciate what you do—which I do.

89:3:14  A:  But, then, do I have to keep you doing it to keep the flattery going? And do you have to keep it going to not be alone?

89:3:15  P:  I think you are more independent of the need for flattery than I am of the need to not be alone. If I found a man to be in love with, I could imagine we could have equal responsibility, but here no matter how independent I felt, I'm still the patient, the little girl, and you're the daddy—a comfort there won't be anywhere else. I have to learn everything kicking and screaming! [*pause*] It's not fair. I just get to where I trust you and believe you like me and I have to give it up. You're caught—there is no way you can do anything right. If you want to let me go and marry and grow up— you don't want me to be dependent. And if you did need me and kept me in analysis for the rest of my life, I'd hate you! [*chuckle*] I'd like your help in leaving, but I want it to be hard for you. It's hard for me, it should be hard for you too. Maybe it will be difficult in a variety of ways for you too. I haven't just learned to trust you, but you've learned to trust me, how to work with me, help me to see things.

89:3:16 A:   Having attained all that, I lose you.

[Often she works herself up to an angry outburst and then gives a self-conscious chuckle of mixed amusement and embarrassment. This is frequently followed, as now, by a useful period of insightful reflection that I want to follow up.]

89:3:17 P:   Um-hm. And having attained that, I'm not miserable all the time. That's got to be pleasant. [*pause*] I think I said at the beginning, this may help me see how things slide off into sexuality. Here things are clean and tidy. We can talk about different stuff. Feelings are not clean and tidy but ...

89:3:18 A:   Are you saying the messages I give you don't have the mix of stay–go, stand up–lean, a date–not a date, if he wants to okay–if not okay?

[From prior work, I am equating "slide off into sexuality" with being caught up in ambiguity. At this point, toward the end of the hour and week, I want to underline this as an area that needs exploration before ending.]

89:3:19 P:   It's not always good to clear up ambiguity. Sometimes it is, sometimes it isn't. That's your basic Thomistic answer.

89:3:20 A:   You did say my reference to ambiguous flattery was not what you were thinking.

[I take her response—the negation "not always good" and the teasing tone of "Thomistic"—as a gentle rebuke for feeling imposed on—a mild empathic failure. I acknowledge that I had heard her earlier negation.]

89:3:21 P:   It sort of was, but I'm thinking of something in a sexual way.

89:3:22 A:   Let's get to that.

89:3:23 P: Here I talk in a prescribed way about going out into the world and hoping to have intimate sexual relations with a man, John perhaps. I want over the next six months to look closely at that.

89:3:24 A: Um-hm.

89:3:25 P: Someone mentioned "Beauty and the Beast" as a story of a woman transforming the beast in her mind into something loving and lovely. I'm trying to make that same transformation. I grew up believing sex is an ugly thing.

89:3:26 A: Yes.

89:3:27 P: And I need to make a transformation to something loving and generous. I bring it in here. I don't think what I'm doing is cleaning it up. I get control of it by seeing what it has been. So what I see now that I've talked about it, is that in so far as there has been sex here, it's been verbal. You're encouraging me to talk about it, to think about it. I'm going back to a world where sex has old, destructive, ugly, angry facets to it. I realize that's not what has to happen.

89:3:28 A: Not a repeat of Michel.

89:3:29 P: Or Matt.

89:3:30 A: Yes.

89:3:31 P: [*sigh*]. Now I'll try to take that back to the issue of ambiguity—and I feel scared to do that. The problem with ambiguity is while I said I didn't like it, I tolerated it all too easily and didn't make a real effort to get things clear.

[I hear her as putting us on notice that before ending we must do more to resolve the debilitating effect on her self-regulation and self-confidence of years of enuresis. She "tolerated it all too easily"—it provided a way to keep her mother involved and concerned, as well as disgusted and frustrated, at a terrible cost to Nancy of humiliation and shame. That she "didn't make a real effort to get things clear" paralleled the lack of clarity about who was responsible for the sexual play with her brother (whom she knew she liked to be with and was important to). And because in his masturbating against her she was, to the best of her memory, totally anesthetic generally, the bed-wetting provided her with a nocturnal erotic life under her sole control but without clarity of responsibility.]

1/11/90

90:1:1  P:   When you came in I heard you fumbling with your
             keys. There was something erotic about it. It reminded
             me of a friend who graduated from the Ph.D. program.
             He was so excited, he came home after the party and
             managed to lean over the commode and drop his keys
             down. Keys are being independent, like graduating.
             And that can be much.

90:1:2  A:   Both exciting and frightening.

90:1:3  P:   Yeah. Being transported back to childhood. Flushing
             something of yourself down the toilet. It's amusing
             and frightening. At the lab, the supervisor wanted me
             to call immediately and ask about when I was going
             for my interview [for a teaching position]. I got rattled
             and called. I shouldn't have let her push me into it.
             Now I'm going February 10th and 11th. So I'll miss
             two days here at the worst time for me. But I have
             to live with it. I'll only have the 15th and the 17th
             and that's the end of my analysis. I have to live with
             it. Oy. I wish you could see me on the Wednesdays—
             the 9th and 16th. We'll live with whatever you can
             do. They do have another candidate who is coming
             the days I wanted to come. I had had the impression
             there was no one else, but the other person is from
             their school. I was foolish to think I was only
             competing with myself, that all I had to do was to
             keep myself together. Then I got home and found a
             message from Father Rocco. I knew it would be terrible
             and it was. [*In a droning voice*] "Your dissertation will
             require a lot of revision. There is a significant contra-
             diction." [*normal voice*] And I felt I wouldn't be able
             to do it. [*Plaintively*] I worry it will mess up the inter-
             view. [*Laughing*] I might as well kill myself now. No!
             Kill him! Then I got so angry at his message and
             thought, "I can't go on. I need things to go well.
             Don't just put obstacles in my way." I had a dream
             about being molested. At the lab. A young black guy.
             He was a technician in the dream. He was acting out
             anger against me because I'm a woman and white. He
             had the impression he can get away with it. He comes
             up behind me and starts rubbing his groin against my

leg. I say "Don't do that." He does it again. I say "Don't." He does it again. I put my leg against him with leverage. But I still can't get him away. So I scream for help, so the people in the next room will come. He reaches up and grabs my crotch and I really scream. I thought, "I'm glad I did that. I can nail him to the wall." Then I woke up. In the dream I said "nail him," like I have a penis—I have power. That is what I think about Father Rocco and the dissertation. He was acting out feelings about my being a woman, his hostility against me. I don't have to make excuses for him. He's an angry, vindictive man. A woman told me, "You are working with the most difficult man on the faculty." He treats everyone that way. He is an obstructionist and I have to be clear who *I am*. I'm going to be very positive—emphatic and direct—no more pussyfooting around. I'm not going to let this sidetrack me. That makes me feel independent [*all of this said with vigor*]. I need him, but I'm going to get him to do what I need. I think the problem lies in a section I had trouble with. I'll ask for help with it from him or someone. If I have to rewrite the whole thing, I will as expeditiously as I can. . . . You're being very quiet. It makes me think I'm missing something.

90:1:4   A:   I'm aware of your saying a lot, not of your missing anything.

[As I responded, I suddenly became aware that I had been so concentrated on listening and taking notes that I had not been responsive to Nancy in either nonverbal utterances or body movements.]

90:1:5   P:   I'm glad to hear you say that, but usually you say "um-hm."

90:1:6   A:   I haven't and you miss it.

90:1:7   P:   Maybe you're weaning me. I really like your hm-ing. [*pause*] Yesterday after the phone message [from Father Rocco], I felt undone. Then I reconstituted my sense of determination. I'm doing what I'm doing because it's me. I felt a real sense of independence, and that's good.

90:1:8   A:   Yes.

90:1:9   P:   I had a good day today.

90:1:10  A:   In your dream, what was helpful was the clarity with
              which you could see that the abuser was out of line.
              [I believed that both she and I had "reconstituted" our
              "determination," and that I could offer an intervention that
              indicated that I had listened empathically to her dream and
              was offering some direction to our exploration of it.]

90:1:11  P:   And the clarity of my response—I was clear and increas-
              ingly forceful. I woke and thought the next physical
              response was an elbow uppercut! I'm not letting myself
              get muddled in what is happening here. It would be
              so easy to say Father Rocco is right—I'm a lazy good-
              for-nothing. I did my best and he should too! I have
              to respond clearly and calmly and set the limits. My
              new slogan on the bathroom mirror from our discus-
              sion is *My happiness is my responsibility.* [*pause*] I think
              about leaving my analysis and I get scared and think
              I'm going to jump out of my skin. I'm anxious, but
              also excited and looking forward to the challenge. And
              also sexual. Everything today has a sexual flavor.

90:1:12  A:   From my playing with, fumbling with my keys, on?

90:1:13  P:   Yes. I am so much less guarded in my relations. That's
              good. I could meet someone. But what about sexu-
              ality? Have we done enough? I've never had a really
              successful sexual experience. I don't know when I feel
              I'm jumping out of my skin at leaving analysis. Being
              ejected. Not rejected.

90:1:14  A:   Launched?

90:1:15  P:   Yes. It's positive. I have to keep self-centered. Be quiet
              and calm.

90:1:16  A:   And you lost it a bit when the lab supervisor pushed
              at you.

90:1:17  P:   Right. I have to be aware that when people push at
              me, I have to look to see what's good for me. I can
              have both—launched and be calmly under control—
              but it's hard to maintain. Do you know the commercial
              on TV with the skier who hangs in the air? He is
              supported by an air flow, but he has to hold himself
              up too. He has to stay centered and keep his body
              under control.

90:1:18  A:   [I thought back to her statement that she has never
              had a really successful sexual experience.] Are you
              concerned that in intercourse you might have trouble

staying centered on your body, keeping your body under control while you experience the exhilaration of the whole experience?

90:1:19 P:  Yes [*crying*].

1/13/90

90:2:1  P:  I read what Father Rocco wrote. He's a Dr. Jekyll and Mr. Hyde. He only read a few pages. He complained about phrasing, and it was a quote. Then he asked for something that was there a few pages later. It made me furious. What should I do? Should I ask someone else to be the director? I'll still have to make changes. Will I gain? Steve thinks I will. His readers don't say his is junk, they suggest revisions. My analysis is—I'm not as attentive to details as I could have been while I am working on leaving here. He is a big jerk, but I could make it clearer. I can add a better flow rather easily. I must pay very particular attention to these details, not just the substance.

90:2:2  A:  Could you give me an example of a detail?
[Here I chose to request her to fill the narrative envelope so I could try to sense into it with her. I chose not to comment on the affect, which seemed to require no immediate affirmation or exploration.]

90:2:3  P:  Let's see. There are sentences with two clauses with an "and" in between. He said it's a grammatical error in that the two parts are not equal. He was so irritable in his comments. I shouldn't have given it to him right after he graded 100 papers. I'd made a direct quote, "cause leads to action," and he slashed it out. "No," he said, "cause leads to effect!" I used an analogy to a mirror. I didn't work it out as well as I could. He said the analogy has problems. He's right. All analogies do. But it is a good analogy. I need to make it more precise. I said, "as light deflects off of a rose." He said, "off the surface of the rose." I'm splitting my day, half for the paper for the job interview, and half for the dissertation. I went back and read the original book to see if I thought my best revision of that problem was accurate. Steve thought it was fine. Rocco said he can't comment because it wasn't clear enough. He said

revisions would have to be by the author, he can't do
anything with it. Brutal! My reason for saying I will
stick rather than bolt is if I don't get the position—
if I do, I don't need him—if I don't, a dissertation
with him as director is valuable. I still might switch
after the revisions he still wants. I'll have to think
about it. Claus would be the one, but he will want
me to include a lot of secondary sources and that isn't
what I want. I'm not sure it's a gain. Once a person
got a finished dissertation sent back by Father Rocco
because of the margins. She went to Claus and still
hasn't finished a year and half later. The dean might
be my second reader, but he's never directed a dissertation. He's nice and concerned. It's not clear going
somewhere else will be a gain. If I keep plugging along,
it might be best. Steve asked why do I want to stick
with him when he told me years ago I don't belong.
I did get through my M.A. thesis okay. Am I just
trying to prove to him I can do it? I don't think that
is very strong. I think I'm trying to get through.

90:2:4   A:   You're trying to get your work completed.
[She has been considering the nature of her position and
her choices in a very measured, contemplative manner, unlike
her hyper-emotional approach in the past. I offer a confirmation of her conclusion that she is not in the throes of
a rebellious, self-defeating effort like her I'll-show-you-Mother
bed-wetting.]

90:2:5   P:   Yes. I'm not sure it's better one way or the other. The
tiebreaker is his reputation is more impressive. I made
my choice and I'm acting on it, but I do feel as if I'm
beaten up, that I'm not taking care of myself. He said
he'd read it and we'd get together and talk. I see no
reason to talk and invite more unrelenting criticism. If
I come up with a precise question, it would be better
to talk with him about it. I don't want to hear his
general complaining. I think I'll use the technique I
used when Jane whined to me. I meant Nancy. [*In a
cheery voice*] "Oh thanks. I'll work on it and I'll get
back to you." I'd like to beat him with a two-by-four.
It makes me angry I have to do all this and worry
about his being in a bad mood. It's inappropriate. *But
my happiness is my responsibility*. If that's what I have

to do to get a job, it's what I have to do. [*pause*] I couldn't bear to go to Claus or someone else and have him say he agreed with Rocco. I almost couldn't let Steve read it because I was afraid he'd say Rocco is right, it's a piece of junk. After the revisions, I don't think I'll hesitate to get it to someone else. I couldn't without revising.

90:2:6   A:   If you agree, you might want to fix them in any case.

90:2:7   P:   Right. But why does going to another director require the same form? If I want to say he's a jerk—a lazy lout—it has to be the same. If I say he makes some right comments mixed with wrong ones and a lot of meanness, I can make the revisions. If I want another director, I can't try to prove he's a total jerk. I have to weigh that fact that I need help and he hasn't provided it on the substance of the problems.

90:2:8   A:   So vengeance, however good it might feel to you, isn't too practical?

90:2:9   P:   It won't work. The best vengeance is to get my dissertation done and make it good.

90:2:10  A:   Hm.

90:2:11  P:   It's interesting. Steve's questioning why I have stuck reminds me of Mother telling me you have this problem and that problem and you don't do this right or good enough. The other problem you and I talked about is why I have to fail to prove Mother wrong [to show her up as a bad mother]. The very best vengeance for [me with] Mother is [my] living a happy life and not proving her wrong. Being happy in spite. Vengeance doesn't have to be denied, does it?

90:2:12  A:   Denied?

90:2:13  P:   I was hearing that the vengeance I was trying to wreak was wrong! No. It's impractical, foolish.

90:2:14  A:   You may well feel like proving her wrong, but to do it now would be to demonstrate that it's her negative opinion that is wrong, that you can lead a happy, productive life.

90:2:15  P:   To do that requires I separate from her in a very important way.

90:2:16  A:   Hmm.

90:2:17  P:   I've not done it. I say, you owe me this. In a reasonable world Rocco would recognize that, but I have to

stop expecting it of him and being disappointed. I
have to just say he's wrong but not to stay tied up
with him or he with me. His being wrong is only tied
up with *him*. Does that make sense?

90:2:18  A:   Yes.

[Nancy is breaking very important new ground here.
Desperate clinging in the face of lack of support or absence
has always proven too strong as her anxiety would mount.
Her other aversive response would be to prove that the
failed parent was "bad" by being a failed child. She is definitively identifying an alternative path.]

90:2:19  P:   I've been shouting all day, been very worked up [*said
calmly, with self-acceptance*].


1/14/90


90:3:1  P:   Yesterday I said I didn't think I was taking very good
care of myself, although I think I am. I might be
coming down with a cold. I didn't run this morning.
It could be allergies. For some reason I am mad with
Jim. I realized it when I was talking to Jane. He is
arranging a party for me next week and he hasn't told
me yet. What does my anger at Jim have to do with
my taking care of myself? Jim takes care of himself.
What I'm angry about is that Steve said, let's do something for your birthday. I said I'd like that. We could
go to dinner someplace—Jim, Steve, and I. Good. Then
Jim said Jane will give a party. I think they conned
Jane into it to save money for Jim. Neither Jane nor
Jim has mentioned it to me. Jane apologized when we
were talking. She said it was largely her idea, and I
felt better. Perhaps I'm too hard on Jim. Oh, I finally
called Father Rocco. I didn't tell you yet. He was more
conciliatory. He told me George was giving a class I
should go to. I felt it was criticism, then I thought,
"It's not such a bad idea. I could learn from George."
I told Father Rocco thank you, that some of his comments
were helpful. I'm anxious to move along and have my
job interview. Rocco said he would be back in touch
soon. What I want is an honest, direct okay. What
does that have to do with Jim?

90:3:2  A:   Both are disappointers?

90:3:3   P:   That's interesting. I hadn't thought of that. How I'm
              disappointed by Jim. He remembered my birthday,
              engaged other people, but never communicated it to
              me. I don't feel disappointed, I feel *angry*. I was disap-
              pointed not to have a small, quiet dinner, but a noisy
              party. But why get so angry about being disappointed?

90:3:4   A:   "Jim takes care of himself."

90:3:5   P:   I don't really want him to take care of me, but as he
              is doing something for me, he ought to consult me.

90:3:6   A:   Not make an arrangement that suits his pocketbook
              and inconveniences Jane?

90:3:7   P:   It's not the way I want to celebrate my birthday. A
              patina of generosity, of caring, under which is lack of
              caring. Like Father Rocco—the way he softened on
              the call made me think he realized I thought he'd been
              a jerk. He said this was the difficult part, but when
              you get through it.... Sounding a positive note. It's
              his way of apologizing for being so critical. But he
              doesn't put forth any effort. I can say go to another
              person and maybe he'll help. But something more funda-
              mental is a way of being radically rule-directed as we
              talked about before—and angry. Father Rocco was angry.
              He was saying to me I'm a morally inferior person for
              handing him that stuff. That's what he was saying. It's
              hard for me to see what Jim did. The rule on birth-
              days is you must do something. Is he being manipulative?
              I'm circling around and not getting it—back to taking
              care of myself. A part of me says to take good care
              of myself is not to take this reasoned position with
              Father Rocco and the dissertation, but to vent my
              anger. Vengeance!

90:3:8   A:   Stamp your feet?

90:3:9   P:   I feel that way. By my stamping my feet, everyone can
              see my displeasure. But by not returning his call for
              several days, I was saying some comments were helpful
              and some were not. I want to say, "Don't be mistaken
              by my response that I'm buckling under!" That sounds
              like pride.

90:3:10  A:   Hm.

90:3:11  P:   It's a big problem. I'd rather have my pride, vent my
              pride, show my pride, than have my dissertation done?
              I don't feel I'm taking care of myself because I'm not

seeing that my pride is assuaged. It's a terrible conflict [*chuckling*], having to be so reasonable and logical and sensible.

90:3:12  A:  You say, chuckling.

90:3:13  P:  It feels so inadequate. I must show him how wrong he is. This is where I converge with the two of them. It's my desire to maintain moral superiority. They tell me I'm a sloth for not handing in my dissertation. I'll show you you're a sloth for not helping me. Back to Mother and you. I can see what's reasonable and the end looks appealing, but the cost to my pride is too high. We were saying all along the way I maintain my pride is through the position of being morally superior rather than getting my dissertation done and being reasonable. I hate your guilt.

90:3:14  A:  Does it make me morally superior?

90:3:15  P:  No, it reminds me of when I won't be here. I don't assume you disagree with me. Perhaps I should. I assume I'm saying what we've been saying.

90:3:16  A:  Yes.

90:3:17  P:  I don't need you to say mm-hm to know I'm correct [*crying*], but I sure like it.

90:3:18  A:  And you're saying you will miss it very much.

90:3:19  P:  That's what I'm saying. I just remembered a dream. I will miss you and that interaction—but you, too. I dreamt about Betty, who is pregnant. We were hanging out, talking. She looks beautiful, glowing. She delivers early, but everything is okay. She's up soon. She planned early enough that everything is okay. She's calm, self-assured. The way you are calm and self-assured. I wouldn't use the word "beautiful" for you. It seems funny for a man. Implicit is that I'm not calm and quiet, but in a sense I can be that too. Perhaps not with quite the serenity. I can get on the same road [*laughing*]. Another snatch of a dream. I'm masturbating, but not really—with my breasts by touching myself. It's kind of chaotic—"searching" is the word. With my hand I brush past my breast again and again.

90:3:20  A:  Something we've never talked about.

90:3:21  P:  It fits in with talking earlier in the week about sexuality and my being able to have sexual relations that would be fulfilling. I can't achieve it by myself. Coming to me, to my breast, and moving away. It connects with the notion of serenity and comfort. With self-fulfillment—what Betty and you embody. Knowing what you want and how to get there and fulfilling it. Babies come early. It happens. But you prepare for that. I know what that means in terms of self-satisfaction. Being able to take care of myself. Feeling comfortable and pleased by myself.

90:3:22  A:  Um-hm. Um-hm.

90:3:23  P:  Pleased with myself. It's still chaotic but I know what it is. I recognize it, how to achieve it, but I'm not in control of it [*sighing*]. One has to do with sexual satisfaction, the other, satisfaction with someone else. The other has to do with both. It's funny to think of my having this dream about this mother giving birth and relating it so clearly to you.

90:3:24  A:  After you think about how you'll miss me.

[I had a choice to refer—to the obvious symbolic reference to her "birth" as analogous with ending and with the *early* but prepared for. I chose instead to address the affect of missing, the sigh, the sadness.]

90:3:25  P:  That's interesting. After I think about missing you, it reminds me of how much I missed being taken care of by my mother. My birth mother. And how much I'm being taken care of by you. When I think of my mother, I think of loss in what she didn't give me. When I think of you, I think of the loss of the care and caring you did give me.


2/16/90 [This is the next to the last hour, midway through.]


90:4:1  P:  I dreamt I was climbing up a big hill to see the sunset across the lake. I'd seen it before and it was beautiful, but now the lake was almost dry—like a crater. The wind was blowing. The season has changed and it will return again, but now it's not so beautiful. I can accept that. There was a boy stomping around, collapsing the side of the bank. Since it was not full, he might destroy it. I thought I'd better scuttle for safer ground, away from the edge. [*pause*] The work with you is drying up. The winds of change. The boy was my brother. I have to be careful and not let him or anyone destroy the work we've done, to put it down. It's hard to see now how the lake can be filled again.

90:4:2  A:  Seasons change and rejuvenate—regenerate.

90:4:3  P:  Right. It was different when I went off to college. I was glad to be getting away, and my parents were glad to have me go so they could get on with the day's chores. Here I feel love and affection, and that in a way you are my best friend—and you are. Now it's time to transfer all of that to other relationships that aren't so circumscribed. I'm picturing leaving home on the bus with the door closing behind me.

90:4:4  A:  What are you finding?

90:4:5  P:  The hardest thing with you is to get clear and to stay clear, that you don't feel martyred to have me here or are anxious to have me go so you can do something else. That you do get pleasure from my accomplishments, and have empathy for my sadness, that you feel proud of my accomplishments.

90:4:6  A:  That I feel proud of your accomplishments as you have accomplished them.

90:4:7  P:  What do you mean [*slightly alarmed*]?

90:4:8  A:  Not more.

[I am emphasizing her justifiable pride in her actual accomplishments rather than her embellishments in fantasy by dazzling performances or saintliness and moral superiority.]

90:4:9  P:  [*nods*] What am I proud of? Proud that you don't want to kick me out so someone else can take my place. Proud that I am being considered for two fine jobs. Proud of my uniqueness that makes it possible.

# 4  Ten Principles of Technique

The topic of technique is tricky. Technique includes procedural rules, but procedural rules can become authoritarian restrictions. Technique includes conceptual principles, but conceptual principles can become arid pedantry. Technique can be taught didactically, but "didactic" can become lifeless and academic. The task for the clinician is to maintain one foot on solid, empirical ground and the other foot on the fertile soil of creativity, being careful that neither foot ends up in the clinician's mouth.

To the experienced clinician, technique is second nature, informed by experience and knowledge. Yet, discussions of technique are in danger of formalizing creativity and subverting the very spontaneity that is intrinsic to good treatment. Discussions of technique, rather than enlarging the clinician's perspective, can interfere with established, reasonably successful ways of working. The experienced clinician will recognize in our user-friendly, self-psychological technique both an attempt to codify what may already be familiar and congenial, and an attempt to legitimize what is often done, but not discussed openly in seminars on technique.

To the beginning clinician, technique is the sought-for answer to the questions what to do, and when and how to do it. Learning technique provides guidance and may decrease uncertainty. Nevertheless, technique as a formula can be misapplied and thus interfere with the inevitable uncertainty with which even the most experienced therapist must live (Moraitis, 1988; Franklin, 1990; Friedman, 1995).

In that case, technique can mechanize the therapeutic encounter and undermine the spontaneity we hope to promote.

A number of years ago, one of us (Lachmann) taught a continuous case seminar in which the sessions of an analysis he was conducting were presented to the class. The patient told a dream in which she was playing tennis. After a few comments about her tennis partners and opponents, the patient fell silent. The analyst waited awhile and said to her, "It's your serve." The patient then began to talk about her difficulty in taking the initiative. The class thought the intervention was clever. One of the students in the class was in supervision with the teacher-analyst. Lo and behold, when her patient fell silent during a session, she said to him, "It's your serve." Although the student's intervention did not quite fit because there had been no reference to tennis during the session, it was not far off. In fact, her patient did begin to speak. However, Lachmann's point had been to illustrate the use of imagery and metaphor as jointly constructed by analyst and patient. The material was not presented to teach a technique for enabling therapists to overcome silences. Although the student's misunderstanding did not damage her or her patient, neither did what she said promote creativity in technique. Taken out of a specific context, an "improvisation" can become a "ritual-ized script."

Therapeutic action is furthered by a mutually constructed creative communication in which an analyst "gets" a sharper insight into a patient's experience, and conveys this insight to the patient in a unique manner that enables the patient to feel "heard" or "under-stood." At their best, analyst and patient construct an experience that could not have occurred between this analyst and any other patient. No matter how familiar an interaction may look to the analyst, how "right out of the textbook" it may feel, only the unique-ness of analyst and patient's mutually created, shared experience can lead to heightened, affective moments (Pine, 1981; Beebe and Lachmann, 1994) that become transformative.

It is easier to formulate analytic technique than it is to teach analytic creativity, spontaneity, or intuition. With these caveats in mind, we list and illustrate "principles" in the art of psychotherapy and psychoanalysis. We will use clinical material from the treatment of Nancy to illustrate these principles.

We have originated some of the principles that follow; others we have borrowed and modified. The specificity with which we have been able to describe the ten techniques derives from our applica-tion of them in our own therapeutic endeavors—and especially in teaching and supervising others. They have come to the foreground of our thinking against the background of our theories of self psychology, infant studies, motivational systems, and of self and mutual regula-tions.

## THE TEN PRINCIPLES

### 1. Arrangements that Establish a Frame of Friendliness and Reliability and an Ambience of Safety

Psychotherapy and psychoanalysis are best conducted in an ambi-ence of safety for both patient and therapist. In the analyst's manner,

and in the formal arrangement of the treatment, a frame of friendliness, consistency, and reliability is established. Our accent on these
"human" aspects of the therapeutic encounter can be contrasted with
those techniques that accent the role of frustration in analysis. However,
we do not suggest that an analyst gratify a patient's requests, wishes,
or idiosyncratic expectations without question. Rather, we suggest
that the analyst respond affirmatively to whatever will help to establish a frame or set of boundaries within which both analyst and
patient can participate effectively. We do not propose that an analyst
set out to provide a patient with a specific beneficial experience that
may have been missed in the course of development. We do believe,
however, that *understanding* what the patient needs and wishes to
have provided constitutes a therapeutically necessary and legitimate
form of provision and gratification. We agree with Blatt and Behrends
(1987) that the "use (or misuse to be more precise) of the relationship to create compensatory experiences must be distinguished from
a process in which the analyst allows the analysand to construct the
relationship in ways which *temporarily* meet infantile needs in order
to be able to interpret the constructions to the patient" (p. 282).

We illustrate the establishment of an ambience of safety by describing
two crises from the beginning of Nancy's treatment, which occurred
prior to the first week of the sessions reported in Chapter 3. The
arrangements for the analysis had been consolidated. Hours had been
scheduled that took into account Nancy's school and work commit-
ments. She used the couch without discomfort.

The first crisis was prompted by the analyst's practice of ending
sessions by saying, "Our time is up, now." On one occasion, Nancy
was having a difficult hour, crying bitterly as the end of the session
neared. The analyst stated his ending phrase in a sympathetic tone
with a prolonged "now." Nancy said, "Don't give me that patronizing 'now'!" The startled analyst said "Okay" and Nancy left. During
the following session she described her resentment at being patron-
ized "when being thrown out." She believed the tone of sympathy
was not for her benefit but to ease the analyst's conscience, a belief
the analyst accepted. He resolved not to end the session in his usual
manner. But he was unsure of an alternative that would retain a
frame of friendliness and safety. He asked Nancy how she would like
him to announce the ending. She answered that he should just convey
the message directly and flatly, and say "the time is up," because
that is what he meant. The analyst did so without incident but also
became sensitive to any inclination to shift his tone from appropriate concern to placating condescension or patronization. In addition

he was ready to bring these issues to the forefront of the work whenever they appeared.

The second crisis concerned the analyst's fee. Nancy was paying a somewhat reduced fee and talked a great deal about her money worries. She hated the arrangements in the laboratory in which she worked. Increasingly, she found the conditions dangerous, as errors in testing and reporting were common. She announced that she had to leave her job for her self-respect and safety. She pleaded for a further reduction in her fee, as well as for the option to delay payment of her bill until some undetermined later date, as she had arranged with her previous therapist. Otherwise, she stated with increasingly hysterical emphasis, she would have to stop her analysis.

After a brief reflection, the analyst refused her demand. Although he was uncertain of all the facts, he doubted the practical necessity for the reduction that she claimed she needed. Additionally, he recognized the serious possibility that she might bolt because of his refusal. His main reason for refusing was that he did not want to offer his professional services at a further reduced fee or under the arrangements she proposed. He recognized that the frame of the treatment might not now feel friendly or reliable, or contain the ambience that *he* required, and he believed, that *they both* required, for therapeutic success. Within a relatively short time, Nancy arranged for more satisfactory and better paying work, and she began to regard her problem in regulating her finances as an integral part of the analysis.

Establishing an ambience of friendliness, consistency, reliability, and safety is not confined to the opening phase of treatment. We analysts must pay constant attention to issues of our manner of approach throughout the analysis. The ambience of friendliness and reliability is often placed in jeopardy by the manner in which the analyst handles a patient's need or desire for information. Despite Stone's (1961) objections, in discussions of analytic technique, responding to a patient's questions continues to be equated with providing gratifications that may interfere with the motivation to analyze.

In our view, responding to a patient's questions can promote the analytic exploration of the very issue raised by the patient. For example, when Nancy asked (83:1:3), "How can you do this all day, listen to this?" the analyst did not silently abstain, but responded (83:1:4–6) "[*Pause*] does it put me at risk for getting out of control? [*pause*] That I get stirred up as a result of what you're talking about." In his response, the analyst did not counter with "What makes you wonder about my ability to listen to you?" or "What makes you wonder how I can do this all day?" or "How do you imagine I can

do this all day?" We recognize that parrying a question with a para-
phrased restatement is a perfectly reasonable intervention designed to
elicit unconscious fantasies. However, we have found that such standard analytic responses often disrupt the openness of the interaction
rather than carry the exploration forward. They heavy-handedly throw
the spotlight on the patient, gratuitously reminding him or her that
he or she is the patient in analysis; that the analyst makes rules about
a one-way informational flow and the patient must comply. They imply
that what the patient attributes to the analyst is all based on the
patient's fantasy, his or her curiosity as a source of shame, and that
it is up to the patient to account for raising such a question.

None of these standard restatements conveys the extent of the
analyst's continuous immersion in the patient's subjective experience.
Specifically, at this point in Nancy's analysis, restatements by the
analyst would not have conveyed his awareness of the sexual material that had just been offered. Thus, the analyst articulated his
understanding of the relevance of Nancy's sexual references ("getting
out of control") by connecting them to Nancy's question. By retaining
the continuity of the content and of the transference attributions, he
reinforced Nancy's ability to articulate her sexual fantasies. In addition, the standard restatement interventions carry the danger of increasing
the patient's self-consciousness rather than increasing her sense of
safety. To address this danger, we offer the second principle.

### 2. Systematic Application of the Empathic Mode of Perception

Our method of conducting treatment is based on the systematic
application of the empathic mode of perception, whereby the analyst
gains information to orient himself or herself by listening from within
the perspective, the state of mind, of the patient. For example (85:1:7),
the analyst's listening is guided by his sensing that Nancy's state of
mind indicated she was delicately balanced between remaining in an
affect-rich contact that would promote joint exploration and developing an aversive affect state that would disrupt cognition and preclude
joint exploration. He deviated from a free-floating attentiveness to
keep Nancy from plunging into an aversive affect state. That is, he
risked an approach that she might experience either as positive and
helpful or as humiliating and patronizing. The analyst also became
somewhat puzzled over Nancy's reference to their "nonhysterical"
talk as "decadent." He was guided by a conviction that particular
designators may serve as metaphors with ties to significant unconscious beliefs. Alternatively, to concentrate on his own "puzzlement"

could only have interfered with sensing himself more closely into Nancy's state of mind. As it worked out, his phrase "old-fashioned virtue" led to an unexpected confluence and a momentary attunement.

In a later hour (85:2:14), a different path was shaped. Here Nancy's affects were relatively clear and consistent. The analyst could follow or lead and remain close to her state of mind as she energetically pursued the exploratory work, linking present and past. The analyst entered into a playful enactment with her, at her invitation. However, he chose content that reflected, as best he could infer, Nancy's immediate wishes and the limit of what could be said without interfering with the ambience of their jointly expanding awareness.

Later in Nancy's analysis, another example of the analyst's empathic immersion in Nancy's state was noted when she spoke about her mother not wanting to be around her. She added, "but she did want for me to be completely beholden to her" (89:3:1). The analyst responded, "Beholden is worshipful" (89:3:2). At that moment, the analyst imagined Nancy as a little girl looking admiringly at her mother, whom she regarded as beautiful and perfect. Sensing the nuance of the little girl's feeling, the analyst chose the concept of "worshipful" over the more manifest meaning of "beholden" as indebted to. Nancy's choice of the archaic-sounding word, "beholden," rather than a more modern term, probably also contributed to the analyst's association. Because he had been able to sense himself into Nancy's experience, he enlarged "beholden" in a way that was accessible to her, but was not immediately available. She could then further pursue the experience of being in a "worshipful" state (89:3:3), "Yes it is! Total!"

The empathic mode of perception is an all-important way for therapists to gather data about the subjective life of patients. To feel the analyst's continuous attempts to grasp empathically the nature of their experience can be an enormously gratifying experience for patients. To assess the success or failure of the analyst's attempts at empathic understanding requires monitoring of the sequence of exchanges as we will describe in our tenth principle. The empathic mode of perception serves as an overarching principle, one that takes precedence over the others we will be citing.

### 3. We Discern a Patient's Specific Affect to Appreciate His or Her Experience; We Discern the Affect Experience Being Sought to Appreciate the Patient's Motivation

We listen empathically to appreciate and resonate with the experience of patients and to infer when we can, the patient's motivation as he or she would recognize it. Recognizing a patient's discrete affects, moods, and affect states (see Chapter 5) is crucial to discerning, from the patient's own perspective, the experience the patient is describing and currently having. Recognizing affects is not a cognitive activity, although cognition is involved, but is primarily the result of attuned resonance, of feeling along vicariously. To know that an event triggered affection, or indifference, or fear, or anger, or shame, or pride, or awe, or calm is a prerequisite for the analyst to appreciate the experiential meaning, the salience of the event for the patient. For the analyst to understand the patient's motivation requires another step: to discern what the patient's associations and actions reveal to be the affective goal (the selfobject experience) the patient seeks. We investigate whether the patient seeks a specific experience—such as the relief of a physical dysregulation, the pleasure of intimacy, a sense of efficacy and competence, sensual enjoyment or sexual excitement, or the lessening or removal of an aversive state. At a more general level, we explore whether the patient seeks an experience of vitalization in response to feelings of depletion or a soothing experience in response to feelings of being overwhelmed with an intense emotional state.

Frequently the patient's motivation can be inferred relatively easily. Nancy's desire for the attention of the priest and the analyst on the weekend (83:1:1) was for the experience of a sense of closeness and the affirmation of her importance to people she admires (an attachment motivation). In contrast (87:1), the motivation behind the feeling of paralysis with which she had ended the session prior to this hour was inexplicable at the time. Then, when the analyst brought it back into focus (87:1:9), she indicated her motivation in saying, "the paralysis was to avoid drawing the conclusion it's not a friend who does this stuff" and thus preserving the illusion of a positive attachment experience to her aunt and to Jane. On other occasions, the analyst may incorrectly infer a motive, such as the analyst's presumption (83:1:8–9) that Nancy's desire to know how he dealt with his sexual arousal served to enable her to use him as a mentor or model and achieve preservation of her sense of self-cohesion in that way.

Our third principle of technique takes into account the relative difficulty for analyst and analysand of exploring the analysand's experience and motivation, and offers the analyst a guide for sequencing his goals in comprehension. Often the analyst must glean the affect as a first step. Only slowly then can knowledge of an event or exchange being talked about be built up.

For example, at the beginning of session 87:1 Nancy spoke about her chronic constipation, depression, and sense of moral failure. She referred to her aunt and to her friend Jane, and stated that there is "nobody in the world that I'm special to" (87:1:1). In his response, the analyst attempted to bring her affect and her motivations together, "Would that feeling pressure you to want to try again with Jane and your aunt?" Evidently Nancy felt that what she had been conveying, so far, had been understood. She could now go to the heart of the matter, "Perhaps, I do feel a devastating sense of aloneness" (87:1:3).

In his response, the analyst had articulated what he grasped as Nancy's feeling of pressure, a competition between attachment motivations and an aversive reaction, her dread of reexperiencing a disappointment or rebuff. Having felt understood, Nancy could then articulate her sense of aloneness directly. In so doing, she anticipated continued understanding from her analyst and could therefore risk bringing into their relationship her struggle between seeking the intimacy of attachment and the aversiveness of withdrawal. From the vantage point of our technical recommendations, conveying understanding gratified Nancy's need to feel attached to her analyst, and enabled her to build on that attachment. When analysts succeed in grasping both the affect and the selfobject experience being sought, they can recognize which motivational systems have been activated and which have receded into the background. We will discuss this sequence in greater detail in Section 9 of this chapter, when we consider interventions made from the patient's point of view.

### 4. The Message Contains the Message

Two specific aspects of the patient's communications that require a primarily cognitive focus by the analyst are recognizing the message and filling the narrative envelope. The empathic mode of perception, as we have stated, defines our overall perspective and provides a background ambience that enables other activities between analyst and patient to move into the foreground when required.

Traditional psychoanalytic training is replete with technical recommendations, such as when the patient talks about the present it is a resistance against revealing important memories from the past, and when the patient talks about the past it is a resistance against revealing important transference feelings in the present. From this perspective, it is believed that the "true" message of the patient is always concealed. The sought-for meaning is either the opposite of what is manifest or is buried beneath the analysand's communications.

Instead, we propose that "the message contains the message." By "message" we mean the communicative flow of the patient, that is, any particular statement and the context of what preceded it and what follows it. As delivered by the patient, the message is a complex amalgam of shadings and nuances; gestural, vocal, and facial displays; transitions into and out of topics; emphases as to what is deemed foreground and what provides background, and "hints" that subtly illuminate the communication. All of these manifest aspects of the "message" can be surmised, inferred, and evaluated only from the delivered message. If fully appreciated, they can be as revealing as a baby's face when compared to poor Yorick's skull.

The proposal, "the message contains the message," is often misinterpreted as downgrading the role of unconscious motivation. In line with our description of unconscious mentation (*Self and Motivational Systems*, Chapters 5 and 6), we discuss factors that lead to the barring or opening of awareness. We conceptualize an ever-shifting surface on which previously inaccessible material becomes consciously accessible. The rate of shifting depends on how open to change an issue is or how entrenched an aversive pattern may be. By providing an ambience of safety through the systematic application of the empathic mode of perception, and by attending to the patient's affect and to the selfobject experiences being sought, optimal circumstances are provided for the patient to explore, ever more deeply, his or her unconscious world. In addition, when the analyst's presence remains minimally intrusive, a minimum of iatrogenically rooted opposition is stirred up. In this way, interactively organized resistances are kept to a minimum. The delivered message can contain all the message required for the exploration of the moment in an ongoing treatment because, as analysis progresses, the patient feels less need to maintain a protective privacy and a defensive withdrawal. As the surface constantly shifts, the message will contain ever more personal, meaningful material.

The previously described illustration (87:1:3) of the analyst's empathic grasp enabling Nancy to access a "devastating sense of aloneness" also illustrates the shifting surface of Nancy's experience. Her communication, "I am painfully alone," was heard as the message. At that point, the analyst did not assume or interpret that Nancy was warding off any other feelings toward him by walling herself off, that is, through a defensive withdrawal into aloneness.

### 5. Filling the Narrative Envelope

Filling the narrative envelope (Stern, 1985) refers to activities whereby the analyst asks orienting questions: who, what, where, when, and how. Such information may be necessary at a particular moment so that the analyst can better grasp the patient's narrative.

The narrative envelope contains the themes and variations of lived experience from the late toddler period on. The elements of who, what, where, when, and how are organized into a temporal structure having a beginning, middle, and end. The relative sophistication of these elements depends on the development of cognitive capacities. But by the age of two or three the central features of this organization can be recognized in speech and dreams. The richness and variation of the narrative increases from simple early schemas, to the somewhat stereotypic scripts of three- to six-year-olds, eventuating in complex, imaginative stories.

The finding that lived experience is remembered in the form of narratives or event schemas (Nelson, 1986) has direct significance for analytic technique. Caregivers and infants comprise a system of mutual influence. In early life the experiences on which narratives are based are mutually constructed. Caregivers immerse the infant in a world of communicative looks, sounds, expectations, and procedural predilections. Each partner is also impacted by the temperament of the other.

The shadow of the other also falls onto the agency of the self—even when experiences and the memories abstracted from them are organized primarily as though the individual is alone. Thus mutual influence, each partner's motivational systems being impacted by the other's, is built into human experience (Mitchell, 1988; Stolorow et al., 1987). This fundamental relatedness of self to others, organized and communicated in narrative form, provides the basis for treatment. Prior experience of an aversive nature is similarly organized, but the tendency toward omission and disjointedness in the narrative is increased. The expectation of mismatched responses is also built in. The path to awareness and communication is then burdened with suspicion, deception, and resistance. Frustrated by failures to decipher a disjointed or fragmented narrative, analysts may rely on a theory of resistance to "explain" the problem. We propose that the analyst help the patient develop the narrative by inquiry. Because episodic memory formation is similar for analyst and patient, an analyst's introspection and empathy will help in the construction of narratives dominated by obfuscation.

A further influence on technique lies in the clinical finding that coherence of narrative presentation has a beneficial effect on treatment. In the analysis of children, mutual understanding is facilitated when a child can present or construct a coherent event in symbolic play. The same applies to adult analyses. The cues we use to unravel repressed or disavowed motives, fantasies, and beliefs often remain meaningless fragments unless incorporated in a relatively coherent narrative of an event or in a dream. No matter how symbolically rich a patient's slip, specific association, or isolated dream element may be, we cannot enter the state of mind of the patient without an episodic schema or representation into which to place the symbol. In fact, we have tended to regard a patient's ability to relate experiences in coherent affect-rich narratives as an important facet of psychological mindedness and a major contribution to successful therapist–patient matching.

The timing and technique of helping patients to relate their past, current, and immediate experience in organized renderings of who, what, where, when, and how requires tact. Analytic participation can range from merely indicating empathic sensing to encouraging the treatment process by asking for examples or further elucidation of an unfolding story. By remaining open to emendations of our organization of the analytic experience, we can encourage an equal openness on the part of the patient. At times, the questions who, what, where, when, and how may be experienced by an analysand as insensitive, demanding, or intrusive. Generally, a disruption resulting from questions about narratives may be easily navigated and require minimum exploratory efforts for repair. Occasionally they may be massively disruptive. In the latter case, both the analysand's propensity to become disorganized as a result of any initiative of the analyst and the possibility that the analyst "fled" from a particular intimate moment into an "information gathering" mode need to be considered.

The analyst successfully helped Nancy to fill the narrative envelope when Nancy stated that she looked at her analyst from the couch to be reassured (83:1:16). Uncertain what she meant and needing her lead to orient him, he asked, "Reassured in what way?" Once oriented, he could address Nancy's need for attachment and explore this need through further inquiry. The analyst did not assume that her need for reassurance necessarily indicated infantile dependence, or masked hostile, voyeuristic, or seductive feelings toward him. Similarly, in the third hour of that sequence (83:3:19), the analyst inquired "In the imperfections you experience me as having, is the one about my going away the most problematic at this time?" He implied that the narrative of her complaints had come across to him as discursive and that identifying the central complaint was necessary for him to be able to understand her main meaning.

### 6. Wearing the Attributions

Given our overriding interest in maintaining an ambience of safety, we must consider the extent to which a patient's negative or positive fantasies about the analyst can disrupt the analytic dialogue. These attributions by the patient may be contrary to the analyst's view of himself or herself or of "reality." Both the analyst's countertransference and a theory that places a premium on "defining boundaries and supporting reality" may prompt the analyst to confront these attributions in order to promote realistic perceptions. In contrast, we encourage the analyst to "wear the attributions."

When a patient indicates that the analyst looks more tired than usual, appears angry or pleased, is looking forward to a vacation, or losing interest in the work, the analyst must try to see himself or herself as experienced by the patient. The clues that the patient picks up about the analyst's feelings and character often point to expectations and areas of interest from the patient's prior lived experience and provide associative pathways to experiences within the clinical exchange. The analyst, with attention wandering over the patient's attribution, can often acquire unexpected information about how his or her therapeutic approach is regarded by the patient. The analyst's self-awareness can be expanded through intuitive responsivity in wearing attributions or engaging in an enactment. These are times when analysis facilitates an exploration of both partners and what experiences and motivations each triggers in the other.

In recommending that the analyst wear the attributions, we advocate neither verifying the patient's fantasies nor asking the patient to collude with the analyst in an overt "pretense." Rather, we advocate the widest possible openness to a consideration of the attribution as having an immediate source in the clinical exchanges. Once analyst and patient regard the attribution in this way the implications of the attributions for the patient can be explored. Several beneficial consequences follow when analysts open themselves to a full consideration of patients' attributions. First and foremost, the analyst's openness and interest promote an exploration of intersubjective aspects of the transference that is less likely to occur if an assumption of distortion and projection on the patient's part introduces a critical, dampening voice into the proceedings. Second, a sense of continuity is maintained within the session. Whatever material the patient introduces, including qualities attributed to the analyst, is open to exploration—irrespective of its manifest or "interpersonal" effect. The exploratory ambience and its safety are maintained for the patient.

Third, it provides an opportunity for "play" within the analytic session. The fact that the analyst is "wearing" the clothes supplied by the patient cements a special bond between them. Such "playfulness" can promote intimacy or become a source of danger. In either case the analytic dialogue is furthered as the effect is then explored.

For example, in the first session presented (83:1:3), Nancy challengingly portrayed the analyst as perversely exposing her and himself to sexually stimulating talk. The analyst took on the issue (83:1:4), "What you asked before, does it put me at risk for getting out of control?" Nancy responded (83:1:5), "That's a possibility. I see others. You have these feelings—pleasure, excitement." The analyst then wore her attribution (83:1:6), "That I get stirred up as a result of what you're talking about." However, in this instance the analyst could not sustain being the recipient of the patient's fantasy that he perversely enjoyed the prospect of pushing her toward the limits of her ability to control herself. Instead, he moved away from the "heated" issue of his presumed sexual arousal and focused on depicting himself as a "mentor."

### 7. The Joint Construction of Model Scenes

Analyst and patient construct model scenes to organize the narratives and associations of the patient, to capture important transference configurations and role enactments, and to focus further explorations of the patient's experience and motivations. Model scenes can be derived from a variety of sources, such as a theme from literature; a dream image; a fantasy; or a longstanding conflict, fear, or expectation of the patient. In the analysis of Nancy, three model scenes were derived from traumatic childhood events from different developmental epochs. These scenes came to be understood by her and her analyst as occupying pivotal positions in her motivations. They were:

• a memory from Nancy's fifth year, sitting on her father's lap and then suddenly being banished. This memory was gradually elaborated to include a construction that Nancy felt her father's erection, believed herself to be bad, the cause of his discomfort, and therefore was banished from his lap. This model scene thus contains the conviction that girls are seductive unless they go to great lengths to prevent it. Furthermore, Nancy and her analyst inferred that boys and men were seen as helpless reactors to a girl's revealed bodies and charms. Thus, if a man becomes aroused, it is the fault of the seductive woman and he bears no responsibility for it.

• a construction or reconstruction of Nancy tugging at her mother's leg and sensing the stiffening of her mother's body as she resisted Nancy's importuning. This scene was gradually elaborated to include Nancy's memory of her mother lifting Nancy's brother onto the kitchen table, and asking him to sing to her. When Nancy climbed up as well, her mother told her that she couldn't sing. These model scenes contained the theme that Nancy was with a caretaker who was capable of reaching for, lifting up, affirming, and praising another child, a boy, but not her.

• memories of Nancy's brother using her body to masturbate against and insisting that she cooperate in the masturbation. This scene provided a further enhancement of Nancy's memories of sitting on her father's lap and revealed an additional reason for her intensified sense of shame, guilt, and worthlessness.

These three model scenes will be elaborated with clinical detail in Chapter 7 where their relevance to sexual abuse and the eroticized transference will be discussed. The three scenes, taken together, illustrate a family collusion that placed Nancy in conflicted, no-win circumstances. The over-all analytic process can be looked upon as the working through of the model scenes derived from her experiences of overt sexual molestation by her brother, covert sexual involvement by her father, and longings for nurturance derived from experiences with her mother.

### 8. Aversive Motives (Resistance, Reluctance, Defensiveness) Are a Communicative Expression to Be Explored Like Any Other Message

Resistance analysis has held a major place in the development of analytic technique. In fact, it provided one definition of what makes a treatment "psychoanalytic." We do not place a premium on resistance analysis or defense analysis, or on analyzing a patient's reluctance to reveal material. So, what is the place of resistance in the user-friendly technique?

We understand "resistance" from the perspective of the five motivational systems. Resistance, defensiveness, and reluctance all illustrate degrees and aspects of aversive motivations. When resistance is viewed as an aversive motive that dominates the patient's goals at a particular time, then the patient's "resistiveness" is understood as a need to react with a form of antagonism or withdrawal. The aversive motivation is then regarded as on a par with other needs that are being explored. Some aversive motivations are themselves goals of analysis. We are pleased when a patient such as Nancy can consolidate a response of exerting power to oppose abuse and can be effective in engaging in controversy. We are pleased when Nancy can recognize the disadvantage to her of trying to overcome obstacles by rash attempts to dazzle and instead applies self-restraint. The aversive motivations that are traditionally conceptualized as "resistance" in analysis are reactions or responses to experiences that trigger negative affects and threats to the cohesion and vitality of the sense of self. The aversive experiences may be expectations of recurrences of past traumatic interactions or actualizations in the clinical exchange. To view the occurrence of resistance during the clinical exchange—the patient's or the analyst's—as reactive, is of particular importance in maintaining the analytic ambience. Then the trigger for the aversive motivation in the session, as well as the patient's (or analyst's) tendency to react aversively under certain circumstances, is open for exploration. Patients are not made to feel that they are at fault for responding in a manner that interferes with the analyst's attempt to help them. The goal shifts from an attempt to set resistance aside and get to the "real" material that lies sequestered or to make conscious unconscious mechanisms of defense. The goal is also not to make resistance disappear, which is impossible in any case, but to explore any experience of aversion that can be brought to the foreground of the analytic work. Thus, in our view, defense interpretation is not a special or central aspect of analytic work. Each motivational system is explored when it is dominant.

When we discern from a patient's associations that he or she desires companionship or to be mirrored or to find a sexual partner or to be better able to complete a work task, we try to help him or her discover the context in which the desire arises and its present and past meanings. We approach a patient's tendency to express antagonism and withdrawal in a similar way—we ask what the context is in which the aversion arose and what is the present and past meaning of the particular form of its expression. To achieve optimal appreciation by the patient, a desire for companionship or mirroring or a sexual partner or to achieve competence must be interpreted in a manner the patient can recognize and experience from his or her point of view. Similarly, to be comprehended effectively, manifestations of antagonism and withdrawal must be interpreted in a manner the patient can recognize and experience from his or her point of view. A significant difference is that the motivations of the physiological, attachment, exploratory-assertive, and sensual-sexual systems

are most often experienced as going toward a desired goal, whereas
the motivations of the aversive system are most often experienced
as dealing with or getting away from an undesired state. Clinically
we find patients giving signals of distress and appeal that are easily
recognizable as indications of aversiveness and a call for a response
comparable to a child's signal to a parent for remedy and relief.
Nancy often indicated directly or by a loss of concentration, a
diminished affect, falling into silence, or bodily rigidity that something the analyst had said or something she was recognizing was
triggering anger, fear, shame, or sadness. Frequent examples of
this occurred during discussions that centered on her disappointment, anger, and criticism of her mother, brother, and aunt. In
these situations, the analyst's task is relatively straightforward. The
analyst can observe from the more traditional position of the outside
observer and then, placing himself or herself in the patient's perspective, offer a question or a suggestion about the nature of the
aversive response and its triggering source. For example, the analyst
often would ask Nancy: Do you have the sense from your silence
now that we got into the troubling area of your hurt feelings
about your brother and then your desire to not put your devotion to him in jeopardy? Very often the aversiveness will take on
a more complex form, one embedded in a repetitive, resistive pattern.
This pattern of resistance derives from a habitual triggering of an
expectation of something aversive occurring whenever a particular
need or desire arises. Conscious awareness is rarely complete. Either
the need or desire, the expectation of the aversive response, the
antecedents of the expectation, or the existence of the entire pattern
may be inaccessible to awareness. Although repetitive, these
patterns, especially those that seem adaptive, may be difficult for
patient or analyst, or both, to recognize, or, if recognized, to
discern the full meaning of. Because they are difficult to identify,
they tend to become habitual in the treatment and appear as roles
in which analyst and patient play out their parts with limited
awareness. Nancy often returned from a weekend or holiday break
in a state of upset or depression. She would describe an event at
the lab or at school that had upset her. The analyst would take
up the event as the trigger for her distress and a useful exploration would follow. The repetitiveness of this pattern was not
recognized for some time, with the partners playing out their expected
roles of troubled patient with complaints, helpful analyst ready to
take up the problems. Once the analyst did recognize the pattern,
however, Nancy reacted to his inquiry with obvious reluctance and

fear. The fear alerted the analyst to her concern that something bad would happen. Both Nancy and the analyst were familiar with her fear of being shamed for complaining, but this pattern indicated something more. The analyst got his cue from the role he had taken, as he began to be less willing to attend the upsetting event of the weekend and Nancy became more upset as a result of his subtle shift. They then pieced together that Nancy had the fixed expectation that the analyst had spent his weekend delighted to be free of the burden of her care and that on his return he would continue his indifference to her as long as he could. She needed to ensure his reengagement with her by arousing his anxiety over her distress. Without it he would treat her as her parents did, relying on her ability to take care of herself and then out of sight out of mind. The understanding Nancy and her analyst achieved resulted not in the elimination of the pattern, but in its being more readily acknowledged and worked with. The 85:3 hour began with Nancy's acknowledgment of progress, but her usual weekend depression. She recognized that if everything was in order, she would have no excuse to avoid the sexual problems that she had been considering. She became limp, still, and silent. The analyst, rather than pursuing the obvious purpose of the resistance, tried to encourage Nancy to explore her experience. Nancy: "Fog. I feel I'm in a fog, when I try to think about my sexual problems." The analyst, taking this as a full recognition of her aversiveness, invited her cooperation to explore it and asked "Can you penetrate the fog to sense any of the factors?" This led to a flow of useful associations.

In stating the technical principle that aversive motivations are explored like all other motivations, we move away from the traditional importance given to repression, isolation, projection, identification, and negation to get to a latent conflict. We believe that as the sources of aversive experiences, especially those occurring during the treatment, are explored, the patient's increased sense of safety will guarantee the relative openness of the path to awareness. Alternatively, we place great significance on the problems that arise during role enactments. Many of these arise from repetitive patterns of aversive responses embedded in relational schemas, such as Nancy's need to bind the analyst to her through guilt and anxiety over her suffering and failures. Any of a long list of comparable responses to aversive experiences and expectations may pull the analyst into affective verbal and nonverbal enactments. The initial problem often is recognizing that what is happening in the clinical exchange is the result of deception by denial and disavowal of the patient to himself or herself and/or the analyst or the analyst to himself or herself and/or the patient.[1] Or it may be that a quality of irritability is mounting by virtue of the subtle use of provocation by either partner or threats of harm to the self by the patient. Emptiness in the exchanges may be due to submissiveness, dissociation, suggestibility, or overidealization. A subtle form of arousal may result from seductiveness under a variety of guises. States of difficult-to-explain confusion in the exchanges may result from pseudostupidity, rapid shifting of positions, and frequent contradictory stances. The analyst may feel crowded out by being talked at (not with), or may feel encroached on by shadowing or by the patient's sticky preoccupation with him or her. This partial list conveys the often subtle forms of resistance that require analysts to be drawn in enough to get clues from their experience, and then to identify the particular trigger to the intersubjective context that has developed. The next step, often the most difficult, is to help the patient to recognize the experience from the patient's point of view. Then and only then do we believe effective, nonblaming, nonshaming interpretation can take place. The interpretation is focused on the intersubjective context and the mutuality of triggering in the interplay of enactments.

The possible triggers for the patient's aversive reaction are derived from the contributions of both analyst and patient. We take into account the *analyst's* transferences, empathic ruptures, narcissistic vulnerabilities, misattunements, and blind spots, as well as the *patient's* propensity to react aversively, under circumstances when other motivational systems could be, or might have been, activated. The patient's aversive responses often are triggered by breaches in his or her expectations. Such breaches occur when expectations of having a selfobject experience are ruptured—whether these expectations are in the foreground or the background of the analyst–patient interaction. Investigating fluctuations in selfobject experiences simultaneously repairs their breach and addresses the aversive motivations.

---

[1] Slavin and Kriegman (1992, 1994) correctly state that inevitably there are times when the interests of therapist and patient diverge and clash. "We tend to talk as if the therapist's discipline, role, and understanding can enable therapist and patient to transcend the self-interested efforts at influence which are part and parcel of all human relating. . . . *Both* patient and therapist must confront the elaborate system of protective self deceptions that maintain their own subjective bias. This confrontation forms a crucial—yet greatly underemphasized—dimension of the treatment process"(1994, p. 2).

### 9. Three Ways in Which Analysts Intervene to Further the Therapeutic Process

Based on empathic listening, the analyst's most frequent interventions are presented from within the patient's point of view. We do not propose that the analyst simply echo the words of the patient. Rather, the analyst selects and focuses, highlights and questions, articulates subtle or "hinted at" affects and states, and spells out transference implications of the patient's associations. Often the intervention will follow the form of "Is this what you are telling me?" or "Can you say more about that?" or "Do you mean?" These interventions are designed to continue the flow of associations, promote the paths to awareness, and enlarge the areas of material available for investigation. The dialogue between analyst and patient increases the terrain available for exploration—terrain that had previously been unavailable or inaccessible.

For example, in session 87:1, Nancy elaborated on her sense of "moral failure." This sequence also illustrates the analyst speaking from within the patient's experience. Having discerned the patient's experience, the analyst is then prepared to convey what has been discerned. Nancy spoke of her "trouble with Jane" and her feeling of depression that she is "not special in an intimate way with anybody." She continued, "It's ironic that in the middle of the [church] service, I'd be so aware of feeling alone. I reminded myself I have lots of friends who love me. I was overcome with hopelessness nevertheless—a fear I'd never be close, always on the fringe." In her lengthy opening monologue, Nancy alluded to feelings of jealousy about Jane's special relationship with the minister, Charles. In addition, she complained about her "aloneness" in spite of having lots of friends who love her. Neither of these issues were inaccessible to her. Given a receptive ambience, Nancy can be expected to explore these problems in her own time. The analyst could therefore articulate what he had discerned about Nancy's affect, motivations, and reparative strivings. Thus, having sensed himself into Nancy's affect state and motivations, her needs for attachments and affiliation, he could speak to her from within her point of view. He said (87:1:2), "Would that feeling pressure you to want to try again with Jane and your aunt?" Nancy's response justified how and where the analyst positioned himself vis-à-vis her. She continued (87:1:3), "Perhaps. I do feel a devastating aloneness and I feel it as a consequence of my own actions."

Another illustration of addressing the patient's experience from within the patient's point of view is found in session 89:1. With

termination only about a year away, Nancy spoke about her reluctance to leave the analyst. For a moment she even considered not
being well enough to leave so that she could hold on to him. The
analyst might have picked up the residuals of Nancy's dependency.
She had considered a "flight into illness" to retain a dependent attachment. When she said (89:1:15), "You're my best friend." He commented
(89:1:16), "It surely is hard to part from a best friend," thus artic-
ulating Nancy's dominant affect state, affectionate yearnings. Nancy's
ability to struggle with her conflict over her dependent attachment,
and her anticipation of loss, was respected. But, more important,
speaking to Nancy from within her experience avoided the danger
of ushering the patient out of analysis by tilting toward independence over dependence and suggesting that psychological health required
renunciation of archaic ties. Understood as a selfobject experience
rather than as "dependency," Nancy's tie to her analyst can remain
and gradually become abstracted and depersonified. As Nancy elaborated later (89:3:11), "I want to be free of you, of Mother. Not
be dependent on you." The analyst said (89:3:12), "Just get rid of
me." Nancy continued (89:3:13), "I'm not sure, get rid of being
dependent and angry, but still have you to be related to in a more
adult, mutual way."

The dialogue that follows from interventions reflecting the analyst's
empathic listening perspective is, however, never continuous, smooth,
or unimpeded. And, no matter how artfully the analyst conveys
comprehension, and no matter how attentive the analyst is to the
patient's affects and selfobject needs, speaking *only* from this perspective does not an analysis make.

*Another kind of intervention required of the analyst includes illumi-
nating a recognizable pattern, or communicating feelings, appraisals, or
impressions from the analyst's own perspective.* In these instances, the
analyst has shifted from an empathic, interpretive listening mode to
an empathic, interpretive observing stance vis-à-vis the analysand's
experience (Lachmann, 1990). This stance is not a departure from
the empathic vantage point, but it does stretch it toward a potentially more confrontational interaction. Under these circumstances,
a degree of tension may characterize the analytic ambience. The
patient may be receptive to these appraisals and be just about ready
to grasp a new perspective, or he or she may be aversive to the
intrusions of the analyst's impressions. In the course of their dialogue,
analyst and patient pay particularly close attention to those interventions that have had some disruptive effect.

In session (85:2:5), Nancy spoke at length about her sexual history, her sex play at age 10 with a girl friend, and being sexually molested by her brother. [*Pause*] "My brother would rub against me. Against my leg, my stomach, until he had ejaculations. I felt very dirty." The analyst restated her account (85:2:6), "You didn't have a sense of being appreciated for yourself but for the purpose you served?" Nancy began to speak in generalities (85:2:7), "I'm angry at men for taking women as receptacles. I'm angry at women for being vulnerable enough to let it be carried out, and worse, to invite it." The analyst now spoke from his perspective, in that he applied Nancy's general comments to herself (85:2:5), "And that makes you feel bad about yourself that you were inviting it, the alternative of being unnoticed was such a painful choice."

In the next session, (85:3:1) Nancy said, "When I left Tuesday your last statement made me feel bad." She then worked herself into a momentary outrage. As her anger abated, she reminded herself that the analyst said that the alternative of being unnoticed was so painful. We regard this sequence over the two hours as an example of the analyst speaking from the vantage point of an observer who was aware of and sympathetic to a conflict Nancy faced between two aversive choices. Her subsequent associations indicated that Nancy was ready to work with this perspective.

*A third group of interventions in analysis, which we call "disciplined spontaneous engagements" between analyst and patient, are difficult to classify.* They lie within the overall therapeutic frame, but outside the usual pattern of association and reflective response. "Disciplined" refers to a full appreciation of and dedication to the maintenance of the analyst's ethics and fostering the analyst's generative intent. "Spontaneous" refers to the therapist's often unexpected comments, gestures, facial expressions, and actions that occur as a result of an unsuppressed emotional upsurge.

Disciplined spontaneous engagements may be prompted by some untoward event, breach, or miscommunication that requires a human response. Disciplined spontaneous engagements of a dramatic sort were rare in the treatment of Nancy. One was precipitated by Nancy's demand that the analyst change his way of ending the sessions. The analyst's authenticity required that he accept that he had unwittingly engaged in a role response to her distressed state. His tone was an attempt at soothing that was indeed patronizing as it played out between them. Implicit in Nancy's response was the attribution, "You don't want to face that you are throwing me out by the clock and want to sugarcoat it. Don't play the saint (mother) with me!" The analyst, accepting his need to change, then had to deal with his second problem—his uncertainty as to how to proceed. His spontaneous response was to ask Nancy directly how she would prefer he end the session. Her suggestion, "Just tell me the time is up" and his acceptance (with relief) placed them on a footing of relative equality.

A second disciplined spontaneous engagement occurred when Nancy, again in a great state of distress, announced she would have to have a change in the fee arrangement. In this instance, the analyst responded to the challenge of Nancy's emotional appeal, and the threat to the continuity of the analysis, by engaging directly in a confrontative refusal. He regarded his own need as the decisive factor in the engagement, buttressed by his intuitive guess that Nancy was exaggerating the seriousness of her economic need.

We recognize and applaud the analyst's capacity and readiness to intervene when intersubjective authenticity is at stake—to offer creative, innovative, ad hoc, unplanned, and unexpected interventions. Such interventions seem to spill from the analyst's mouth, often to the surprise of both analyst and patient. These moments are best viewed as uniquely constructed between a particular analyst and a particular patient at a crucial juncture in analysis. They are better left as "tailor-made" moments than converted to "mass-produced" technical interventions or generalized principles.

However, these spontaneous comments do not have to await some special moment. The analyst's empathic stance, and ability to "play" with the material presented by the patient, provides the soil from which these creative gestures can spring at any moment in an analysis. For example, session 83:1 began with Nancy's expression of reluctance to engage in the session. She then spoke about her disappointment in the priest who did her conversion. Later, she said to her analyst (83:1:9), "I think of you as my dad. [*pause*] You represent a verboten character." The analyst responded (83:1:10), "Your father?" The analyst's comment was packed with more meanings than the analyst had been aware of when he made it. Nancy quickly picked up the broader implications of the analyst's comment, she said "you, Dad, and Christ" (83:1:11). Such interventions illustrate the analyst's access to his own pathway of increased creativity and spontaneity without loss of control over the issues that are salient for the patient. Such inadvertent double or triple "entendres" are familiar aspects of social discourse, but are generally not given sufficient credit in widening the levels of communication between analyst and patient. They illustrate the relationship between preconscious mentation and wit (Freud,

1905). In a similar vein, the term, "old-fashioned virtue" (85:1:16) slipped out of the analyst's mouth. Such odd comments are typical of the vast array of subjectively organized phrasings and idiosyncratic imagery that make every analysis unique. These interactions, like "It's your serve," defy categorization and range from "jarring" disruptions of the analytic relationship to "golden moments" or "turning points" (Wallerstein, 1986) in analysis. Spontaneity, wit, double entendres, and play pave the "royal road" to consciousness.

### 10. We Follow the Sequence of Our Interventions and the Patient's Responses to Them to Evaluate Their Effect

In our discussion of the user-friendly principles, we have emphasized the analyst's role in the therapeutic dyad. In so doing, we have understated the complex interactive process that accounts for therapeutic action. The analyst's spoken words, as well as silences, facial and vocal displays, and other forms of nonverbal communication are part of the sequence of interventions that affect the patient and contribute to the organization of the transference. In our view, interpretations are best not offered in "chunks" toward the end of a session as is customary in some analyses. Rather, complete interpretations (Glover, 1955) that cover wish and defense, past and present, transference and resistance are best coconstructed by analyst and patient and conveyed piecemeal, throughout the session. In digestible bits, the analyst tracks the patient's affect and association, responds with another construction/intervention, and then further tracks the patient's response. When a disruption occurs, attention to its effects takes precedence. At such points, the analyst makes inferences to understand the nature of the rupture and his or her role in its occurrence.

We consider a unit of time (a session or a week of sessions) to provide the continuity necessary to encompass an interpretive sequence (Lichtenberg, 1992). We include a wide range of interventions: investigative, confirming, affirming, reflecting understanding, explaining the process, and developing and repairing ruptures (Lichtenberg, Lachmann, and Fosshage, 1992).

We have retained the term "interpretation" because of its historical roots in psychoanalysis. But, more important, we recognize and include the multitude of facilitative interventions that are usually not credited with contributing to therapeutic action. Recognition of the wide range of interventions that contribute to therapeutic outcome (for example, see Wallerstein, 1986) broadens the concept of interpretation, more accurately represents psychoanalytic technique as it is practiced, and recognizes the interactive process that constitutes therapeutic action. Through the sequence of interventions, the analyst conveys a coherent sense of purpose and the interventions thereby attain a cumulative effect. The back-and-forth of the analytic dialogue deepens the interpretive sequence, transforming both participants in the analytic process.

Interpretive sequences in Nancy's treatment can be tracked in sessions 85:1 and 85:2, where the work of prior sessions comes to fruition. Nancy's sense of "badness" and decadence slowly gave way. Her sense of her analyst and herself began to shift. Sometimes a line of interventions leads to "dead ends." For example, in the first session (83:1), the analyst followed Nancy's associations in response to his interpretation that she wanted to use him as a model for regulating sexual arousal (83:1:8). After a compliant "could be," she left this theme. Her subsequent associations were not about using the analyst as a model, but to the analyst as a "verboten character" (83:1:9). The analyst sensed that his intervention was essentially inconsequential. In such circumstances the analyst may lie low and then reorient to discern the patient's concerns.

Perhaps the intervention about "regulating her sexual arousal" was derived from a then current concern of the analyst, rather than based on insight into Nancy's motivation. She did not react affectively to it, neither aversively nor enthusiastically. Although Nancy sensed that her analyst was "off," she did not respond as though she experienced an empathic failure. Even if she had such an experience, it was apparently not a serious enough "failure" to require time for self-righting or mutual exploration. Both analyst and patient let the intervention pass without further notice as they attended to other associations.

In the next hour (83:2), the interpretive sequence covered Nancy's dream. As the analyst followed Nancy's associations during the hour, he recognized that Nancy had related her dream at the beginning of the hour. She then spontaneously came back to it later. He concluded that both the dream and her associations contained a common motivational thread—aversiveness to a man whom she experiences as a sexual provocateur, but who denied his responsibility for the sexuality of the encounter. In relating the theme and her associations, the analyst discovered that he and Nancy had enacted the very issue he was addressing. He was the "provocateur" in "relating" with Nancy. She had remained more passive and she and her analyst thereby fell into an enactment whereby Nancy could plausibly perceive him as a provocateur.

In this interpretive sequence, the analyst tracked Nancy's affect, associations and reactions, and potential ruptures in their dialogue.

He also tracked his own affect and associations, and considered how his experience may further, obstruct, or enact the issues he and Nancy were addressing. Our attention to the interpretive sequence aims at keeping the subjectivity of both analyst and patient, as well as their "intersubjective conjunctions and dysfunctions" (Atwood and Stolorow, 1987), in the forefront of the analyst's attention.

We chose a somewhat arbitrary starting point for the interpretive sequence described, Nancy's sense of "badness." The sequence led toward Nancy feeling blamed, "bad" and "responsible," when men felt sexually aroused by her. She expected them to hold her responsible for having provoked them. In the course of the exploration of this theme, the analyst made interventions that were off the mark, but which, when recognized, permitted the analysis to continue. For example, in the enactment of "blameless" provocateur-analyst and responsible seductress-patient Nancy felt increasingly "trapped" (83:2:21). For the moment, the transference became "real" to Nancy. The analyst attempted to extricate both himself and Nancy by an "empathic" comment, "Your sense of being trapped in a situation that *seems* manifestly unfair." However, he implied that her sense of unfairness was entirely her construction. Nancy, understandably, responded with anger (83:2:24–25), "What do you mean *seems?*"

In the following session, Nancy was still angry. She likened the analyst to her sadistic brother who pulled the wings off a fly and watched with pleasure as it squirmed. He was a "scientist" and sadist, a clever deceptor. The safety of the analytic relationship enabled her to simultaneously experience her analyst as a sadist who enjoys taunting her and as the benign, caring figure who has demonstrated that he can accept her experience. He has done so by having articulated her experience from allusions, hints, and scattered associations, and has done so from within her perspective.

Nancy cried when she said to her analyst, "Before this when I got really angry with you I could tie myself down by reminding myself you seem to be a decent man. You look benign" (83:3:1). The analyst responded, "If my very presence and my benign appearance invite your interest and curiosity, that becomes part of the problem" (83:3:4). The interpretive sequence continued throughout the session with the analyst "wearing" Nancy's attribution of him as a sadist, tempter, and cheater ("If my very presence . . ." [83:3:22]). Throughout this interpretive sequence, Nancy's experience with her father, mother, and brother, and her current experience with her analyst (her ability to articulate her fantasies and fears about her analyst), have become gradually consolidated.

Our ten principles of technique are formulated to achieve the traditionally recognized analytic goals of expanding the patient's awareness and self-reflection, forging links between the patient's past and present that provide an emotionally rich context for current experience, and decreasing impediments within the patient to past, emotion-laden experiences. We propose that these principles further these goals by increasing the likelihood that patient and analyst can navigate their interactive process with a minimum of interference from theoretical rigidity and a maximum of therapeutic creativity.

Commenting on *Psychoanalysis and Motivation*, Lawrence Friedman (1995) states

> If analysts perceive through Lichtenberg's prism, patients may see the analyst as more *specifically* empathic, more readily at the service of the patient's momentary state. [The analyst's] non-authoritarian flexibility will make him seem less professional, more "into" his patient, less distant . . . and less judgmental . . . because "bite-size" motivations [even when supplemented by model scenes] are just like facts of neutral nature [pp. 444-445].

Our principles of technique can lessen the "suspiciousness" that often characterizes psychoanalysis. When psychoanalytic treatment is viewed through the prism of the motivational systems, the often interpreted concealing, defensive, and resistive efforts of the patient can be seen as expressive. This theoretical feature can impact treatment enormously. When the analyst follows a theoretical model that does not place a premium on suspiciousness toward the resistive, avoidant patient, the analyst is more likely to become aware of his or her feelings of affection, anxiety, and anger toward the patient.

Our principles of technique are designed to be friendly toward both the patient and the analyst. As analyst and patient engage in an exploration of the patient's states, affects, moods, and the intrapsychic and intersubjective dimensions of their interaction, these principles also place the analyst in an optimal position to access his or her own subjectivity.

# 5　Affective Experience

## The Golden Thread in the Clinical Exchange

*Every intervention made by the analyst has attached to it the implied question to the patient: "Is this what you are trying to say that you feel?"* (Boesky, 1990, p. 577).

*Affects amplify experience. They either make good things better or bad things worse* (Tomkins, 1962, 1964).

*Object love strengthens the self, just as any other intense experience, even that provided by vigorous physical exercise, strengthens the self. Furthermore . . . a strong self enables us to experience love and desire more intensely* (Kohut, 1984, p. 53).

These three references approach affective experiences as they emerge in psychoanalytic treatment from different angles. They provide a scaffold for the discussion that follows. Boesky (1990) proposes that every analytic intervention addresses feeling as conveyed by the patient and as received, understood, and communicated by the analyst. We develop Boesky's comment by proposing that learning what the patient "feels" involves exploring a continuum ranging from transient categorical affects, through moods, to all-engrossing states of intense affective experience.

Each affective experience involves a feeling, a physiognomic expression, and, often in addition, an autonomic nervous system reaction. By "categorical affects" we refer to the experiences of enjoyment, happiness, pleasure, anger, fear, sadness, shame, humiliation, embarrassment, guilt, distress, contempt, and disdain. These affective experiences are relatively easily recognized and labeled by both experiencer and observer. They are commonly triggered by an identifiable source. Thus, when Nancy was angry at her dissertation advisor's failure to respond in a timely fashion, the analyst and she could recognize the source and the easily understood form of the emotional response. The term moods, in our usage, refers to affect experiences that last longer and are often more pervasive. For example, Nancy's anger when triggered by Father Rocco's failure to respond to a phone call would at one point dissipate into relief when he called back a day later. But after repeated failures, chiding, and discouragements, her mood became one of prolonged low-keyed resentment and disillusion. Linkages to past comparable experiences and transference associations made her moods more complex and longer lasting. By affective *states*, we refer to more intense all-engrossing affective experiences, those that are so all-engrossing that cognitive capacities are constricted and compromised, like those of a child during a temper tantrum. Only the immediate sensing of the affect has cognitive significance. Affect states may be short-lived or as enduring as malignant hatred and grudge carrying after a perceived narcissistic injury. Nancy's description of states of bone-crushing depression during weekends are examples of an incapacitating experience. She would be unable to work, finding it difficult to follow her exercise plan, write letters, or talk with friends.

Analysts find that their interventions are or are not consonant with the particular kinds of responses that help to further explore patients' communications—each position on the continuum calling for differing facilitative responses. We further assume that interventions, through their impact on the affective experience of both participants, contain a transference–countertransference dimension in which emotion is central to the exploration of the motivations underlying the clinical exchange.

Every clinical exchange constitutes a lived experience for both analyst and analysand. Consistent with Tomkins's (1962) perspective, when an analyst affirms a patient's positive affect, the good experience is enhanced; and when an analyst is drawn into an affective state of rage, shame, or hopelessness, the clouds become even darker. The significance of this amplification process will be apparent when we detail the continuum of positive to negative affects, moods, and affect states. By an appreciation of the significance of affective experience, we are in a better position to consider the therapeutic implications of the analyst's encouragement, recognition, positive and negative enhancement and containment of the emotional aspect of all clinical exchanges.

Kohut (1984) proposes a reciprocal relationship between the experience of emotion and the experience of one's self. The sense of self is strengthened through invigorating, intense, heightened, positive affective experiences. A strengthened sense of self, in turn, allows one to experience affects more intensely. The strengthened self may then respond to and communicate affects more clearly. In so doing, one's own affective experiences may be more clearly appreciated reflexively and thus be more available for sharing and conceptual understanding in the clinical exchange.

## A CONTINUUM OF AFFECTIVE EXPERIENCE BASED ON
## DIRECT CLINICAL OBSERVATION

The significance of emotions in psychoanalysis has seesawed from its initial centrality in abreaction as strangulated affect caused by traumatic events. The salience assigned to affects diminished greatly during the period when the emphasis was on drives. Affects then were considered as derivatives or by-products of the drives. Greater significance was then assigned to anxiety in the structural hypothesis. As a signal of potential danger to the ego, anxiety became the basis for the automatic institution of defensive measures. Within this core hypothesis of ego psychology, theorists wrestled with the place of emotions (Rapaport, 1953; Spitz, 1957). The modern era of affect theory began with Tomkins (1962, 1964). With many valuable contributions in between (Stern, 1985; Emde, 1988a, b) the modern concept has led to comprehensive reviews and reformulations of great merit (Schore, 1994; Jones, 1995). We place our own essential view in common with this contemporary trend based on infant research, neurophysiology, and clinical observation. Here, however, we choose to follow a different course. We will take a "naive" approach based on common experience in order to make a particular point that is important to our approach to the clinical exchange. We will develop our thesis that discrete or categorical affects, moods, and affective states each have different impacts on both patient and therapist. This assumption is necessary to substantiate our belief that any clinical experience requires the consideration of not only the traditional intrapsychic and intersubjective perspectives but also a third perspective—an assessment of the affective-cognitive state.

Although we recognize that affective experience changes in complexity from those that are innate and directly triggered in infantile life to subtle couplings of feelings and symbolic cognition and appraisal, we have chosen to base our designations of affective experience on ordinary verbal usage by adults. That is, we use terms that patients would use to describe their inner experience and that we would use to call attention to their affective experiences and our own. We have chosen not to follow any of the available attempts to distinguish between affect, feeling, and emotion (Basch, 1976), innate affects, affect auxiliaries, and affect coassemblies (Tomkins, 1962, 1964), primitive affects and derived emotions and feelings (Kernberg, 1992) or affects in schematized forms such as signal anxiety and unconscious guilt (Freud, 1926), an affective core (Emde, 1983), organismic distress (Mahler, 1968) or basic anxiety (Sullivan, 1953).

We acknowledge the validity of the linear empirical effort that under-
lies each of these efforts at a scientific classification. The approach
we take is guided by our belief that in adults affective experiences
and their designators are individualistic. For example, what seems
like guilt to one person may seem more like shame to another. Thus
the pairings and diagrams we will offer are, of necessity, arbitrary
in their specifics. Other choices could easily be made for the pairs
and groups we will present as exemplars of our main goal—to call
attention to the distinctions among discrete affects, moods, and affective-cognitive states.

Affective experiences tend to suggest pairings of positive and negative, or hedonic and anhedonic as shown below.

| | |
|---|---|
| Affection | — anger |
| Contentment | — envy |
| Pride | — shame |
| Happy | — sad |
| Courage | — fear |
| Moral goodness | — guilt |
| Energetic | — tired |
| Self-assured | — insecure |
| Competent | — ineffective |

When a patient states that he or she is sad, this feeling is apt to
be paired by patient and analyst with happy—which, of course, sad
implies the patient is not.

An imaginary line representing affect neutrality can be drawn between
the principal pairs (Figure 1). The positive affects that ordinarily we
observe people seeking opportunities to experience are above the
line and those that people ordinarily are aversive to are below the
line.

| Affection-trust | Benevolence Contentment | Pride-respect | Courage | Optimism-hope |
|---|---|---|---|---|
| Anger-distrust | Envy Jealousy | Shame-humiliation-embarrassment | Fear | Sadness |

| Moral goodness | Energetic-active | Self-assurance | Effectance-competence |
|---|---|---|---|
| Guilt | Tired-passive | Insecurity | Ineffectiveness-uncertainty |

Figure 1

Another imaginary line can be drawn above and below the line that represents affect neutrality to indicate a range comprising experiences of discrete affects and moods (Figure 2). The lines above

Affect to
mood line _____
                    More intense, longer lasting, more situational resistant

                              Positive affects

Neutral        Less intense, evanescent, immediately situational sensitive
line           _____
               Less intense, evanescent, immediately situational sensitive

                              Negative affects

Affect to    More intense, longer lasting, more situational resistant
mood line    _____

## Figure 2

and below lines are boundaries that delimit affects that are experienced sometimes as less intense, evanescent, and responsive to situational change (those nearer the neutral line) and sometimes as more intense, longer lasting, and more resistant to moment-to-moment situational change (those away from the neutral line). The affective experiences or moods away from the neutral line are often influenced by temperament (for example, shyness and shame-proneness) and are often considered an identifying aspect of character or personality.

During the clinical exchange, feelings within the discrete affect to mood lines of both analyst and analysand are in or relatively accessible to awareness. When one affect is barred from awareness because of aversiveness—for example, anger is suppressed or lightly repressed because of shame, recognition of the shame and its purpose will allow both shame and anger to become consciously experienced. Emotions between the discrete affect to mood lines are relatively easily available to free association, reflective awareness and expanding insight. Those affective experiences that lie outside these lines, those that constitute *state* changes, present greater challenges for analytic work (Figure 3).

### WHAT RESPONSES BY THE ANALYST ARE EVOKED BY DISCRETE AFFECTS, MOODS, AND AFFECT STATES?

Those affective experiences above the neutral line—affection, contentment, pride, courage, optimism, goodness, energy, assurance,

| | Rapture-idealization | Imperturbable self-satisfaction Compulsive benevolence | Self-perfection-idealization |
|---|---|---|---|
| State | | | |
| Affect-mood | Love Trust Affection | Contentment Generosity | Pride-respect |
| Neutral | | | |
| Affect-mood | Anger Distrust | Envy Jealousy | Shame-humiliation Embarrassment |
| State | Rage-suspicion Hatred Vengeful | Malicious spite Irreconcilable dissatisfaction | Shame state-avoidance Secretive |
| Reckless abandon | Elation | | Righteous hauteur Moral superiority |
| Confidence | | | |
| Courage | Optimism-hope | | Moral goodness |
| Fear Worry | Sadness | | Guilt |
| Terror Panic | Pessimistic Depressed Self-pitying | | Abjectness |
| Frenetic-agitated | Arrogance-grandiosity | | Omniscience-omnipotence |
| Energetic-active | Self-assurance | | Effectance-competence |
| Tired-passive | Insecurity | | Ineffective-uncertain |
| Deenergized Apathetic | Demoralization Helplessness Victimization | | Ineptitude-inadequacy |

Figure 3

effectiveness—generally convey to the patient a sense of safety for telling the analyst his or her thoughts. Alternatively, distrust, envy, shame, fear, sadness, guilt, passivity, insecurity, and ineptitude generally lead to guardedness in self-revelation. Because discrete affects and moods are relatively sensitive to context and open to self-reflection, their appropriateness to current conditions is often easy to assess.

A simple confirmatory response will tend to provide patients with an affirmation of a positive affect or mood. Negative affects and moods can be confirmed (or disconfirmed) as an appropriate response to their trigger by the analyst's interest and inquiry (Figure 4).

| Positive affect and mood | _____ | Safety | Verifiable in keeping with context |
| Negative affect and mood | _____ | Guardedness | |

Figure 4

The type of expectation that may lead to either a discrete positive or negative affect or mood can then relatively easily be brought into awareness, revealing transferential configurations of varying intensity and historical longevity.

Affectively intense states likewise carry experientially a sense of safety or guardedness. Rapture, imperturbable self-satisfaction, self-perfection, reckless abandon, elation, hauteur, frenzy, grandiosity, and omnipotence all carry the patient along on thoughts and behaviors that seek neither counsel nor question. Safety is experienced as dependent on the preservation of the state. Interventions aimed at deflating the aggrandizing or dangerous aspects of the state expose the analyst to being regarded as the danger, rather than the state itself. Prolonged and/or intense suspicion, hatred, irreconcilable dissatisfaction, mortifying shame, terror, depression, self-pity, abjectness, apathy, victimization, and inadequacy all tend toward guardedness as a general orientation. Challenging its validity or even inquiring as to its source will often place the analyst at risk for being implicated in the aversiveness, whatever its origin.

The affective states conveying a sense of safety and those conveying a sense of guardedness are paradoxically similar in that both are a source of resistance to investigation and change. The patient who is experiencing a state of rapture, hyperidealization, and various forms of self-aggrandizement will be exceedingly reluctant to reflect on, examine, or lose the temporary sense of security he feels. Much has been made of whether these states, often lumped together as "grandiosity," are defensive or the result of deficits. We feel that the clinically significant fact about them is that their origins usually lie in a combination of prior difficult or traumatic experiences, that conflicts invariably play a part in their development, and that each instance requires investigation as to its meaning. Reluctance to change is inherent; thus an analyst's failure to recognize the patient's insistent effort to preserve the sense of safety is apt to be experienced as an empathic failure. The perceived empathic failure in turn leads to increased defensiveness—now iatrogenic in origin—and often to a change to an aversive state. To complete the paradox, an aversive state of rage, mortification, phobia, enervation, helpless dependency, self-pity, and ineptitude may be clung to with the desperation of a person clinging to his last hold on security. These states are indeed dystonic and aversive, but the patient may regard them as familiar, as an aspect of identity, and as a powerful safeguard against a new experience of hope, disappointment, and failure. The analyst may help by understanding the motivation to cling to the state and, by way of reassurance, remaining with the patient during the state (affect containment). Questioning the "reality" of the aversiveness and depreciating the seriousness of the current context by an interpretation of the past "real" source often is experienced as an empathic failure and confirms the patient's need for guardedness.

## LINEAR AND NONLINEAR ASPECTS OF AFFECTIVE EXPERIENCE DURING THE CLINICAL EXCHANGE

Thus far we have described discrete affects, moods, and states as following a linear mode of action leading to reaction: The analyst fails to remember something the patient has said. The patient feels hurt and angry. The analyst acknowledges the failing and the reaction it triggered. The patient's affectionate-trusting feeling is restored. Or the patient brings up an event of which he or she is ashamed. The analyst, ostensibly to encourage the patient's recognition of a pattern of such events, notes several instances, including those in the clinical exchange. The patient experiences this as being immersed in shame and feels mortified. He or she can hear nothing of the analyst's intent and derives, for the moment, no understanding— only misery from which the patient wishes to escape. The analyst's recognition of the disruption and acknowledgment of his or her part in it may limit the intensity of the shame-state response. Nonetheless the patient may become avoidant and secretive for days, during which the analyst's consistent presence helps the mortification to abate. These linear descriptions of disruption–restoration sequences provide excellent guides for analysts to understand common treatment experiences. They fail to do justice either to *qualities* of affective experience or to the subtle moment-to-moment *dyadic* affective *communication* (Beebe, Jaffe, and Lachmann, 1992) that takes place between partners who have an established familiarity (analyst–analysand, caregiver–child, wife–husband). "Mother and infant jointly construct the rules of negotiating social relatedness. These rules guide the management of attention, turn taking, participating in discourse and affect sharing" (p. 73). As the later dyad of married couples and analyst–analysand become established, each partner begins to anticipate and predict the other's feelings, thoughts, and conversational gambits. This leads to the familiar sense of "finishing" each other's sentences almost as soon as they begin.

Thus far we have spoken of affective experiences as discrete entities to which each culture gives a linguistic descriptor. Each affective experience involves a feeling, a physiognomic expression, and often an autonomic nervous system reaction. Affective experiences do not simply turn on and off like a lightbulb, they have qualities that Stern (1985) has described as crescendo and decrescendo, surge and fade, bursting and fleeting, explosive and drawn out. These qualities add to the vitalization of overall self-experience that is coincident with emotion, that is, the rise and fall of emotions creates a sense of liveliness when needed or soothing and calming when needed. The result is a sense of aliveness and cohesion of the self.

Stern made another finding that provides an important corollary to the clinical situation. When caretakers were attuned to the activity of babies, the babies, while seemingly unaware, responded by an augmentation of their emotion. In psychoanalysis, when patients experience the analyst's empathic perceptiveness and often his or her attunement as well, the sense of liveliness, both personal, and in the shared exploratory goal, is enhanced. The recreation of this experience of vitalization and cohesion—what we have referred to as a selfobject experience (Lichtenberg, Lachmann, and Fosshage, 1992)—then becomes itself a goal for both patient and analyst. For example, during a period in the middle phase of her analysis, Nancy had been reluctant, because of shame, to experience and express her affection for the analyst. As she struggled with her feelings, that is, with a fuller recognition of both the shame and the affection, the hours had a subdued, draggy quality with Nancy reachieving a degree of vitality by shifting the topic to areas of work and her studies. Then in a series of hours she and the analyst were able to interpret a dream and construct a model scene involving present and earlier expectations that she would be regarded as a foolish girl having a crush on a man who was too aloof or deadened even to notice her growing fondness. As she experienced and expressed her humiliation at the anticipated rejection, her voice became animated, her suffering palpable, and the analyst's responses took on a quickening responsiveness to acknowledge and confirm the intensity (the surging nature) of her feelings. Defiantly she exclaimed she would once again risk feeling her love and appreciation for the analyst, adding her rage at him for his unavailability. In this series of hours, the openness to her feelings, the shift from burst to fade, from explosive defiance to a more drawn-out expression of affection, gave to both Nancy and the analyst a sense of individual and shared vitality.

Patients who can experience more fully their affects and moods, both positive and negative, gain a sense of self-authenticity, of being in touch with their needs, wishes, and desires and thereby gain an enhanced cohesion. Analysts who are empathically perceiving their patient's affective fullness, their crescendos and decrescendos, gain a sense of intersubjective involvement and participation in a vitalized and vitalizing experience and thereby an enhanced cohesion. The analyst's task in successfully helping patients to expand their awareness and expression of positive and negative emotions within the discrete affect and mood range involves sensitive listening and a level of involvement relatively easy to enter into and draw away from, a moment of attunement and a moment of more conceptual awareness.

One person's attunement to another's affect is never exact. Mothers can capture babies' rhythmical affect responses, slightly speeding up or slowing down the pace and flow in keeping with an intuitive perception of their mutual needs. Careful observation of analyst responses during successful moments of empathic perceptiveness may reveal that the analyst's verbal tone and physical activity approximate the patient's surge and fade. Careful observation also may reveal the analyst's using a slightly calming tone for an excited patient or a slightly more animated tone as intuitive encouragement to a subdued patient.

### THE ANALYST'S WALKING AN AFFECTIVE-COGNITIVE TIGHTROPE: AFFECTIVE EXPERIENCES AS TRIGGERS FOR ROLE ENACTMENTS

In addition to providing an opportunity for attunement, each discrete affect and mood exerts an evocative power on the analyst to engage the patient more directly—for example, to respond to anger with anger, or to react to haughtiness or envy with criticism, or to sadness with sympathy. The possible responses by anyone to the emotions of another are many. As the patient consciously and unconsciously pulls one way, the analyst by his own immediate or characterological proclivities may go along with the patient's thrust or pull in one of many other possible directions. In comparison to the relative ease with which analysts can remain empathic attuned listeners to their patients' emerging discrete affects and moods, intense affect *states* press the analyst toward greater involvement. Often the involvement may take the form of a specific affective and role response that the patient expects the analyst to enact. The enraptured patient does not want the analyst to intervene to help him modulate his or her affection or recognize the illusions he or she has built up; rather the patient in a state of enrapture demands the analyst's participation in the experience, either as the loved one—the object of the rapturous attachment—or as promotor, encourager, co-believer in the goal, if the beloved is another. The pull on the analyst is for involvement, not for listening and interpreting: be it, do it, react, confess, admit, oppose; in short, to up the intensity and join the state somehow, some way. The patient's view of how to obtain or preserve a sense of vitality or cohesion—however maladaptive or unstable—is to have the analyst respond in a role concordant or complementary to his affective state. In the face of the pressure of the patient's expectation, the analyst is required to perform a difficult emotional balancing act, to walk an affective-cognitive tightrope. The analyst must be sufficiently emotionally involved to experience whatever concordant or complementary response the enactment pressure evokes—anger, indignation, sympathy, jealousy, boredom, sexual arousal, sleepiness, and so on (Racker, 1968).

On occasion the analyst may react with an immediacy that surprises both participants. A patient who had been emotionally abused as a child reported picking his son up and shaking him in a terrifying manner whenever his son's provocations got to him. For a long time the analyst had struggled with his impatience and frustration as the patient's intense shame and guilt triggered the patient's immediate plunges into first pseudo-deafness and then sleep, which made it impossible to even discuss the episodes. Then, after much understanding of his aversion to considering his abusiveness, he began to acknowledge and work with the issues—going back and forth between his own childhood abuse at the hands of his parents and his current rage outbursts. For him, shaking his son was like shaking the slats on his crib in desperation to get his sleeping depressed mother to

come. As the last hour of the week was nearing an end, the analyst
was ruminating to himself that although he found the patient to be
an essentially caring and well-meaning person he had difficulty feeling
friendly toward him at times. The patient, in a rarely expressed state
of desperation, said to the analyst, addressing him directly by his
name, "But what am I to do?" The analyst, without any reflective
thought, responded, with a mixture of annoyance, authoritive direct-
ness, and pleading: "Be his friend." The hour ended with the somewhat
stunned patient standing and looking at the equally stunned analyst
and saying, "Oh, that's what I should do. Be his friend." This phrase
became the motif for associations for months.

In this instance, the analyst was both emotionally involved with
the patient's frustration-rage and with the patient as an "abused child."
The abused child was both the patient and the patient's son. Two
model scenes organized the configurations of the transference–countertransference enactments that were taking place in the sessions. One
drew on the experience of the abused child in the crib desperately
trying to get his mother's attention. The other was of the organically
hard-of-hearing father's turning a deaf ear to his son's plight. The
transference repeated the original mother–son and father–son interactions, but the analyst was in the position of being frustrated, discouraged,
and/or rageful when the patient first "went deaf" and then fell asleep.
That is, the analyst was pulled toward the emotional state of a desperate
child who failed to get the attention of a deaf father and a sleeping
mother. The shift in the treatment occurred when, after considerable
analytic work, the patient could tolerate oscillating between two shame-
guilt states, that of being an intolerant abuser and a helpless, abandoned,
abused child. A shift in the patient's state from being "deaf" and
asleep (like his parents) to frustrated and abused (as he felt as a child)
enabled the analyst to connect with the patient as an abused child.
The shift occurred because the patient could now tolerate the recollections of being frustrated, rageful, and despondent both as victim
and victimizer. Previously, on those occasions when the patient had
fled into deafness and sleep, the analyst had been left to cope with
painful experiences of frustration and disappointment in his effort to
move the analysis forward through exploration or even reflective consideration of what was happening. The only goal possible for both was
established by the patient's motivation being limited to his desire to
be soothed back into an awake state of contact.

By asking the question, "What am I to do?" the patient indicated
not only a restoration of contact but a shift from helpless despon-
dency to a belief something *could* be done. The analyst's response,

"Be his friend," reflected the analyst's recognition that, based on his own positive connection to the patient, the patient was a person capable of friendly attachment, rather than being limited to victim–victimizer exchanges.

In asking the question, the patient had transcended his pessimistic conviction that he was doomed to experience one side or the other of the aversive relationship with his unavailable, unreflective parents and could acknowledge and tolerate his shame, abuse, and frustration. The analyst's spontaneous response reflected what the abused child-patient needed from his parents, what the patient's son needed from his father, but most important, the friendliness the "struggling" analyst felt was possible for the patient and himself (as well as the patient's son) after the success they were now having following many discouraging disrupted clinical exchanges.

In other instances, the analyst's response to a patient's intense affective state may be intense but contained. A very distressed young woman in the early months of treatment was crying hysterically about an incident that, while minor, was obviously very distressing to her. The analyst, to his consternation, found himself suppressing a sadistic giggle. Associating to his affect, the analyst remembered that the patient had mentioned often being provoked and teased by her family. The analyst also recalled participating with others in the cruel teasing of a female classmate and his regret on hearing later that the young woman had had an emotional illness. The analyst regained his composure and made comments appropriately sensitive to the patient's distress, to which the patient showed little response. As the hour drew to a close, the patient expressed doubts about the treatment at the same time that the analyst was wondering when this slowly developing treatment might get some momentum. The analyst acknowledged the patient's doubts, said he too wondered about possible sources of problems between them, and wondered if she had any feel for what might be interfering. After a moment's hesitation, she stated she thought the problem was her fear of ridicule. The analyst felt how energized their emotional responsiveness had been in the form of an enacted complementary dyadic communication of sadistic ridiculer and provocative victim. The analyst consequently experienced a sense of optimism about their ability to respond to and with each other and bring about a successful treatment. The next series of hours were spent exploring her fear of ridicule in both her current and past experiences, with a resulting increase in openness of emotional expression during the sessions.

Both examples demonstrate the analyst's openness to spontaneous role responsiveness and affective expression. Each response by the analyst helped move the treatment forward, each in a different way. The inward sadistic giggle provided information to the analyst of a complementary affective response, helping him to identify a bit of prior lived experience of the patient and himself that was being recreated at that moment. The analyst confined his response to his internal dialogue. In his judgment, the working alliance and sharing of information was not yet ready.

The situation with the male patient was quite different. Patient and analyst had worked together for a long time and had shared extensive information. Despite the breakdown of openness to one another that characterized the moments of blockage to the patient's self-reflection, the ground for a successful intervention was prepared by many experiences of jointly expanding awareness. In one sense this background made the analyst's spontaneity possible and "safe"; in another sense the background of frustration and concern for the patient, his son, and the analyst's own sense of efficacy made the affect state of distress and impasse unbearable. A sense of necessity gave impetus to a disciplined spontaneous engagement, but the successful outcome was prepared for by the solidity of the intersubjective affective connection in which the exchanges occurred.

Affective states that propel patient and analyst toward action rather than exploration are apt to occur under some predictable circumstances. In Chapter 6 we present an example from Nancy's analysis in which the analyst's outrage at Nancy's passivity and rationalizations in response to insulting treatment by her aunt pulled the analyst into an enactment. The analyst stated the patient's claim for better treatment rather than analyzing her failure. In this instance, the effect was to confirm her right to expect more from her family members. It was not experienced as abuse or an encouragement to dependency on the analyst, but we must recognize that when we sway into an interaction the outcome is not predictable. But whatever the reaction is, it can furnish material for further exploration.

Some affective states may develop insidiously, building up when themes, motives, and feelings are either unrecognized or their significance unappreciated. At other times, an affective state may be triggered by a crisis in the life of either patient or analyst, such as a divorce, an illness (Schwartz and Silver, 1990), the loss of a job or expected promotion, death, or loss of a pregnancy (Lazar, 1990; Gerson, 1994). One group of patients often diagnosed as borderline, especially those who have suffered profound trauma at any time in life, may be unable to tolerate an illusory space without loss of a sense of authenticity in the clinical exchanges. These patients may demand that the analyst react more directly to their unbearable, extremely absorbing affective states. A central feature of affective states is that whatever their origin (analysts' failure to recognize patients' affective needs or their own, crisis-driven altered self-states, or the requirement of a severe pathologic transference expectation), the impact will be experienced in the intersubjective realm as a pressure for more intensified direct reactions. The ordinary stances of analyst to patient and patient to analyst will be more difficult to maintain, and increased self-revelation on both their parts is more apt to occur. In a treatment that has been well established and in which exploratory-assertive motives have been dominant at moments, interactions and revelations of self often may prove beneficial.

In walking the tightrope, we can expect the analyst to sway in the direction of varying degrees of direct emotional involvement without falling off. We know at times this sway takes the analyst beyond feeling to such actions as forgetting appointments, scheduling two patients, making errors on bills, and the like. While action responses of this sort inevitably cloud the intersubjective realm of the treatment, the origin of the particular action may or may not be specific to the analyst's attitudes and feelings about the specific patient involved. It may be in response to the analyst's feelings about his practice as a whole, his financial state, or some other temporary distracting aversion. In any case, to recover his balance the analyst needs to wonder what affect state he has failed to recognize and experience more directly. When it bears directly on the clinical exchange with the patient, the analyst needs to discern through the empathic mode of perception (extro- and introspection) signs of an unrecognized triggering pull for a response such as sympathy, sexual arousal, attack, or tuning out and exclusion. Falling off the tightrope occurs in an obvious form when actions the analyst resorts to lie outside professionally acceptable behavior, and in less obvious forms when the analyst cannot restore an empathic mode of perception first with himself and then with the patient. Another danger lies in the analyst's making an unexamined assumption that whatever he feels or does reflects solely a direct involvement in a role or trap the patient has consciously or unconsciously set for him.

The sway to the other side of the tightrope has the analyst restricting his own affective involvement to remain as close to the neutral line as possible. He becomes the silent, distant, cold, "ungratifying" analyst so often caricatured as the "classical" analyst of the 50s and 60s that

Stone (1961) decried. Though the arguments often centered on correct
or incorrect interpretations of what was intended by neutrality and
abstinence, the main result of the failures of the period lay in the
crimped affective engagement that could be created between patient
and analyst. Arguments about whether patients required optimal frustration to be motivated or optimal attunement to fill deficits missed
the point that an exploratory-assertive motivational system is always
potentially available to explore intersubjective experiences—but an
analyst's stiffness and rigidity may preclude the needed affective engagement from developing. The sway on the tightrope to an affectively
impoverished clinical exchange may be so subtle that only after the
fall—an interruption or a bland, meaningless termination—can it be
recognized.

## AFFECTIVE EXPERIENCES CHARACTERISTIC OF THE
## FIVE MOTIVATIONAL SYSTEMS

Thus far we have taken a phenomenological approach to discrete
affects, moods, and affect states, and to how we work with ours and
the patient's during treatment. We have used nine sets of opposites
as examples. Obviously, the list could be many times larger. What
are the limitations of the model we have used of affective experiences above and below a neutral line? To make this inquiry we return
to the five motivational systems.

The principal affective experience in the attachment system is the
sense of intimacy. This feeling arises in both the dyadic relationship
with mother and father (and any other frequently available person
or pet) and, in more complex forms, in triadic relationships where
shifting desires and rivalry enliven the intimacy. Thus, affection, trust,
love, contentment, generosity, pride, respect, courage, optimism, and
moral goodness would all be affective experiences that arise in the
course of positive attachment experiences. Likewise, to the sugar of
these feelings, the spice of moments of anger, doubt, envy, jealousy,
fear, shame, and guilt intensify an attachment experience. Feelings
of efficacy and competence are central to the exploratory-assertive
motivational system. The whole group of negative affects, moods,
and states are experiences that reflect dominance of the aversive motivational system in either separate or combined forms of antagonism
and withdrawal. Being energetic and self-assured is more reflective
of the state of the self than of any of the systems.

The affective experiences associated with the systems based on the
need for the regulation of physiological requirements and the need

for sensual enjoyment and sexual excitement differ in some ways from the patterns (Figures 1, 2, and 3) we have presented. The affective experiences in these two systems involve to a much greater degree bodily derived sensations in patterns that bear the stamp of the rhythms of bodily needs and hormonal tensions.

We have described (Lichtenberg, 1989) physiological requirements that come under psychic regulation throughout life: nutrient intake, elimination, breathing, tactile and proprioceptive stimulation, thermal control, equilibrium, sleep, and general physical health. We distinguish these physiological requirements and the psychic regulation they require from those silent bodily occurrences such as the function of the spleen, liver, and so on, which are not open to awareness. We have suggested a basic innate schema for feeding is: a need for nutrient intake → the sensation of hunger building to an affect of distress (crying) → sucking and intake experience (variably rapid diminished distress = relief) → a sense of enjoyment and a sensation of satiety (with a state change to another motivational need). The success of the psychic regulation of this pattern is measured by the infant's achieving a recognition of the existence of hunger and satiety as self-identifiable sensation-affects. Self-recognition of hunger and satiety is only achieved as an outgrowth of sensitive dyadic communication between caregiver and infant with the caregiver picking up the signals of the infant's rhythms. In clinical work with many adults we neither can nor need to pick up the subtlety of these formative dyadic exchanges. The pattern of hunger–eating–relief and satiety, when well established, needs little exploration. But in the increasingly frequent encounter with eating disorders, eating or not eating, satiety and overeating and vomiting raise a specter of affect disturbances that may or may not harken back to the basic schema having been ill formed (see Lichtenberg et al., 1992, pp. 138–145).

Breathing offers another example of the affect patterns involved in regulation of a physiological requirement. During the clinical encounter, breathing as sensation could be considered as remaining mostly outside the awareness of both partners—in a neutral zone. A possible exception may lie in the breathing qualities that influence the affective-evocative potential of speech. In certain particular situations that occur during treatment, breathing itself comes into direct or indirect awareness. In states of excitement, either pleasurable arousal or fear and anger, breathing accelerates noticeably. In states of diminished arousal, avoidance and suppression of affect, or drowsiness, breathing slows. In situations in which breathing is interfered with during colds, sinus infections, and asthmatic attacks, the threat of air-passage blockage evokes discomfort with the potential for rapid rise to the panic instantly evoked by a sensation of suffocation. When traumatic experiences involving suffocation have occurred, such as a patient's almost drowning or as in the case of Nancy when Matt would hold his hand over her nose and mouth, memories can recreate the sensation with accompanying panic. Our hypothesis is that during analysis, even when breathing appears to go unnoticed, breathing rates and depth, along with postural changes and stomach gurgles, all enter into the subtle nonreflective dyadic communication. Subliminally attended, these less direct affect-sensation indicators provide a background source of information that adds to the vitalization of the foreground verbal-affective flow, or gives an indication of a flat-devitalized state not obvious from the verbal flow, words without music.

In our view the affect goals of "sexuality" are far more varied than that conceptualized by libido theory. In that theory the model is that of orgasmic discharge—a slowly rising (foreplay) and then more rapidly mounting excitement state (coitus) with orgastic discharge (pleasure) and a steep decrescendo of sensation with relaxation (satisfaction). Observation of the "sexual" life of infants and adults indicates that two paths are open from approximately nine months on: (1) A need for sensual enjoyment arising as general distress and irritability or a specific sensation in a sensual target zone → soothing, stroking, rhythmic rubbing by self or other → *either* relief of distress and irritability and specific sensations of pleasure with reduced general tension or (2) Relief of distress and irritability and specific sensations of pleasure with heightened focal and general sensations of sexual excitement. One path involves sensual sensations that can either rise or fall in intensity with enjoyment. One path involves sexual excitement that rises in intensity toward a climax. The path involved in sensual enjoyment may utilize sensations widely distributed across the body—the mouth, skin, anus, as well as the genitals and across sensory modes—sight, sound, taste, and touch. The path involved in sexual excitement may utilize all the other sources of stimulation, but the focus is concentrated on the penis or vulvo-clitoral-perineal area. Sensual enjoyment tends to incorporate feelings of tenderness toward the self or others, whereas sexual excitement tends to incorporate feelings of thrust and power as doer and/or recipient and often a heightening intensification that comes from a sensation of pain. The sensations and affect comprising the total experiences of both sensuality and sexuality may be "autoerotic" as pattern but not in origin or psychic content. The lived experience of sensuality and sexuality arises from within the intersubjective exchanges of caregivers and infant. Thus, the pre- and postsymbolic representations of these experiences bear the stamp of their dyadic and triadic sources in imagic forms that easily reverse the roles of doer and done-to. The sensual and sexual experiences often include a dreamlike quality of fuzziness and reverie that enhances the interchangeability of subject-object representations. The fluidity of active-passive, masculine-feminine gives these experiences a heightened potential for tapping into multiple domains of dyadic and triadic experience. However, for patients whose self-cohesion is vulnerable, the fluidity of representations is often a source of fear, guardedness against loss of boundaries, and, consequently, intimacy-limiting avoidance (Mitchell, 1993).

The affective patterns that characterize the experiences associated with the psychic regulation of physiological requirements and the sensual-sexual motivational systems are particularly rich sources of metaphoric expression. We conjecture that the crossover from the sensation-rich lived experience of the presymbolic child and later symbolic use of verbal coding affords a particular poignancy to sensation-derived metaphors such as: I could eat you up. Don't be such a tight-ass. You take my breath away. What a nauseating thing to say. You're trying to climb to dizzying heights. Cool down. A red-hot mama. What a poker he's got.

The significance for the clinical exchange of this prevalence of "sensation" language in the metaphors of each motivational system lies in two directions. First, the metaphors orient us to the affectively rich potential of what is being spoken about. Second, the metaphors often enable the patient to make discursive distancing references that may need to be brought nearer to the actual lived experience. A patient may say she was "touched" by what the analyst said, but without expanding the meaning of touched in the specific affective form—she felt affection or felt affirmed or helped to experience the sadness she was suppressing, and so on.

Now that we have completed our survey of affects, affect-sensations, moods, and affect states of each of the motivational systems, we will consider the relationship of affects to each other. In our diagrams, we presented pairs of positive and negative discrete affects, moods, and states as extensions of related emotional experiences. Anger, when not responded to, often will spiral into rage, but an angry person who has been ineffectual in overcoming a frustrating situation can respond by entering a shame state or becoming depressed.

Likewise, an ineffectually angry person can seek calming from overeating and/or sensual seeking. Similarly, an attempt to establish shared affection when not responded to can spiral to a rapturous preoccupation, a state of grandiose indifference to others or rage, depression, abjectness, extreme self-pity, anorexia, or obsessive sexual excitement seeking. What can we conclude from this statement of complexity, from the implication that in some circumstance the arrows in the diagram might go from any affect or mood to any positive or negative affect state? Each person has from his or her lived experience proclivities for intensification or spiraling to an affect state when any flexible affect is perceived as not having been responded to in a needed or desired manner. We must follow each patient's communications to track the vicissitudes of all emotions, the sense the patient has of the therapist's success or failure in understanding and responding, and the potential and pathways for affects to spiral to states. We believe, along with Friedman (1995), that "if an analyst learns to sort affects along several, separate motivational axes, he will very likely develop extra sensitivity to nuances of meaning and feeling" (p. 444).

**TECHNIQUES THAT CONTRIBUTE TO
FEELINGS OF SAFETY**

What technical approaches enable analysands to feel safe enough both to recreate affect states that represent important lived experiences that are necessary to explore, and also to prevent the states from becoming entrenched barriers to reflective awareness? The empathic mode of perception is key. As the analyst succeeds in recognizing the analysand's affects and moods and in understanding the motivations involved, affects tend to remain flexible, expanding awareness develops, and a sense of safety is established. In Friedman's (1995) words, "love or the illusion of love is shown when someone supports a person's subjectively felt thrust" (p. 446). When the analyst inevitably fails in recognizing an affect or mood, and/or the motivation present from the patient's point of view, an affect state triggered by the failure often will follow. A characteristic of many such failures is patients' perception of themselves as being treated as an "object," their subjectivity ignored or overlooked (objectification, Broucek, 1991). As patient and analyst live with (contain) the affect state and begin to explore its triggering by the empathic failure, the patient will have opportunities to correct the analyst's perception of the source of the disruptive state change. By his or her openness to the analysand's perceptions, the analyst affirms the analysand's capacity to make reflective observations and to *exert influence*. This self-assertion helps to lessen the asymmetry of patient and "expert" and itself triggers affects of efficacy and competence, a counterbalance to the disruptive state. Often an additional factor may be present. The patient may identify the analyst's role in the disruption as the patient perceives (Hoffman, 1983) him or her to be and often this attribution is made in affect-state terms: "You get silent and nurse your hurt feelings when I don't accept an hour you offer me." Or "You talk like you know everything and I know nothing." Or, "You're too confident that you are attractive to understand how I feel." These attributions of hurt withdrawal, omniscience, and self-perfection provide opportunities to explore the impact of one person's state on another if the analyst allows herself to "wear" the attribution. By being open to the premise and allowing oneself to sense into the state, sometimes recognizing a dimly perceived aspect of the self that has been influential in the intersubjective realm, the analyst can model a willingness to explore the impact of an affect state as it inevitably influences a dyadic relationship.

# 6 Transferences

## How We Understand and
## Work with Them

To begin our discussion of transference, let us turn to the first reported session of Nancy's analysis, then in its second year (83:1). Nancy addresses her hurt and disappointment concerning the unavailability of her priest and, in a similar vein, her depression related to the weekend unavailability of her analyst. She mentions the stress of her exams, followed by her sexual "fantasies of being close and making love." She then reflects about the analyst to whom she is relating these matters. She hopes for a trusting relationship, "I trust I can confide in you and talk about it and feel better." Yet, a different, frightening percept of the analyst also emerges, creating conflict: "On the news I heard about a psychiatrist who raped his patient. Here I am bringing all this explicit sex stuff in. What kind of person are you to want to hear about it, help me with it? Isn't there something perverse about it? What in all these cases gets out of control? The potential is there." The analyst wears the attributions of the "rapist" to further the elaboration of in the here and now and inquires: "What you asked before, does it put me at risk for getting out of control? . . . That I get stirred up as a result of what you're talking about." Nancy reflectively replies that this is a possibility and that he (the analyst) has to do something with his pleasure and excitement. Reiterating her hope and fear, she declares, "If I entrust myself to you, I want to know you are able to deal with the stuff I bring up. I'm selfish—you could get out of control, or get deadened, unable to empathize." She then relates this frightening percept of the analyst to her experience of her father: "My relationship with you—I think of you as my dad. I was very close to him. I had to deal with feelings that would creep up. I have to deal with my own feelings about you—regardless of anything else. I'm aware of strongly

---

Several portions of this chapter appeared in Fosshage (1994) and Lichtenberg (1990).

135

stifling my curiosity about your life, desk, car—far removed from you personally . . . You represent a verboten character."

Nancy then delineates themes derived from problematic thematic familial experiences, which are currently active in the relationship with the analyst, concerning, Who was the seducer? Who was the seduced? Who was responsible? She says, "I'm not allowed to go around not fully dressed. Not being fully clothed all the way is attempting to seduce. . . . So I got mad—the same stuff as Dad—I have to wear clothes to not disturb him. Nobody cares how it disturbs me! It's not fair. Why do I want to look and turn away? There's another class of verboten interests. . . . I feel in all these cases I'm in the wrong and that's not right." Nancy presents a condensed but clear statement of the conflict that has been organized in relation to the analyst. She seeks to express sexual curiosity with its associated feelings and fantasies. Nancy's need for sexual excitement was consistently thwarted in her development, leading to years of genital anaesthesia. As her sexual longings became manifest during the analysis, she was filled with shame and guilt. She feared that in expressing even curiosity someone, either the man (father, brother, analyst) or herself, would get out of control and that, regardless of who would lose control, she would ultimately be responsible for the seduction (what Ornstein, 1974, has described as the dread of the repetition of the past). This leads into our discussion of the nature of transference and its two central aspects.

Patients enter an exploratory psychotherapy with two broad groups of conscious and unconscious expectations. With dread, they expect to find in the treatment situation experiences that conform to prior problematic relationships. This expectation corresponds to the familiar model of transference as derived from conflict and trauma. Patients also expect their current analytic endeavor to provide growth-enhancing possibilities. These divergent expectations in dialectic interplay influence the construction of the analytic relationship from the patient's perspective. This model of transference is similar in broad outline to Freud's unobjectionable positive transference and corresponds to Kohut's selfobject transferences when these are understood in a figure–ground relationship to the pathologic repetitive dimension (Stolorow, Brandchaft, and Atwood, 1987) or representational configuration (Lachmann and Beebe, 1992). We regard it necessary to explore both the transference constructions based on expectations of past problematic relationships and the expectations of new beginnings (Balint, 1968; Ornstein, 1974). We delineate the contents, affects, and conflicts associated with each, their sources in the present and past, and, of greatest importance, their interplay.

For Nancy, three abiding transference constructions stand out. In one configuration, the analyst becomes the sexually threatening male and abandoning female separately or in combination. In another view, the analyst and analytic situation become a vehicle for soothing and calming, for attention focused on self-regulation, and for a thoughtful self-reflective approach to problems. Nancy created a third configuration by her distrust of the second view. A stance of the analyst that at one moment she experienced as steady and thoughtful became diffident and indecisive, and a welcomed willingness of the analyst to engage with her in a consideration of sensual-sexual problems was then experienced as threatening and seductive without consummation or commitment.

## ORGANIZATION MODEL

In a significant departure from a drive-displacement model (see Fosshage, 1994), we, in concert with others (Gill, 1982; Stolorow et al., 1987; Lachmann and Beebe, 1992), view transference experience as occurring within an interactive field and as variably codetermined by patient and analyst. The model we use assumes that all experience is organized: (1) in conjunction with the context that is impacting perceptually, (2) in response to whatever motivational system is dominant, and (3) in accordance with expectations based on prior experience that have been generalized and presently activated. Transference refers to those particular experiences of analysands that focus on the analytic relationship.

Organization models of transference have emerged over the past decade and reflect a transition from positivistic to relativistic science (see Wachtel, 1980; Gill, 1982, 1983, 1994; Hoffman, 1983, 1991, 1992; Hoffman and Gill, 1988; Stolorow and Lachmann, 1984/1985; Lichtenberg, 1989; Lachmann and Beebe, 1992; and Fosshage, 1994). While corresponding with what Hoffman and Gill refer to as the social-constructivist view, we designate it as an organization model (Fosshage, 1994) to reflect the significance of the developing sense of self for the organization of experience. In its focus on the ongoing perceptual-affective-cognitive organization of experience, the model is anchored in recent developments in cognitive psychology (Bucci, 1985), infant research, (Stern, 1985), and psychoanalytic developmental psychology (Lichtenberg, 1983).

From our vantage point, the view that Nancy displaces and projects drive-organized distorted infantile object representations onto the analyst does not provide the encompassing view of the interaction

between analyst and patient that we hold as definitive of the transference. Of course, thematic patterns established in her past exert a
dynamic influence but they are organized in the present in accord
with an immediately perceived context. We do not view her disappointment in the priest as a displacement from her disappointment
in the analyst, or from her parents, but as organized by the *same
thematic emotional experience* that was triggered in her perception of
each situation. Nancy's message is her disappointment in the absence
of the other. In contrast to assuming Nancy's disappointment to be
a displacement and shifting the focus to prior experience, we follow
changes in Nancy's cognitive-affective state, occurrences in the analytic
relationship, and thematic patterns that shape her perception of particular contexts. For example, Nancy's weekend separation from her analyst
may have increased her vulnerability to the priest's lack of attentiveness, and increased her susceptibility to disappointment. To view her
emotional response as a displacement would depreciate the authenticity of her disappointment with the priest as an event with its own
meanings, motives, and nuances to be explored. Furthermore, Nancy's
desire to discuss her sexual feelings and fantasies triggers an image of
the analyst that contrasts with her disappointment in the priest. She
conceives of the analyst as a hoped-for and trustworthy man who is
able to manage her and his own sexual feelings. She also conceives
of him as frightening. He could become sexually aroused and lose
control, or has protected himself from sexual arousal by deadening
his feelings, as she had for most of her life. To view perceptions of
the analyst as ongoing patterns that emerge, organize, and construct
the analytic relationship compels the analyst to be alert to his and the
patient's variable contributions to the triggering of these perceptions.
Consequently, the analyst is drawn to live more fully in the here and
now of the shared transference experience. Nancy's analyst, for example,
engaged and explored the here and now of Nancy's transferential experience by inquiring, "What you asked before, does it put me at risk
for getting out of control?" (83:1:4). We propose that the exploration
of the patient's experiential themes facilitates psychological reorganization through new relational experiences that increase the patient's
perspective. Nancy became increasingly aware of her expectations of
encountering a seductive, out-of-control male and the origins of these
expectations in her relationships with her father and brother. Her
expanded awareness enabled her gradually to gain freedom from this
restrictive perspective and enabled her to create sufficient personal
space to lay claim to her own now reevaluated sexual desires.

## ORGANIZING ACTIVITY: SELF AND
## MOTIVATIONAL SYSTEMS

We begin life with innate patterns of needs and responses that coordinate the satisfaction of those needs with the responsivity of caregivers. As a consequence, a sense of self develops that becomes a center for initiating, organizing, and integrating motivation and experience (see Lichtenberg, 1989, and Lichtenberg, Lachmann, and Fosshage, 1992). Affects amplify and create personal meaning in lived experience and their abstracted memories. By the third year, lived experiences in the form of events and event memories are organized as narratives. Each new perception is influenced and categorized through two simultaneous modes of processing—the logical, linguistically anchored, secondary process (generally left cerebral hemispheric functioning) and the sensory-metaphoric, imagistic, primary process (corresponding with right cerebral hemispheric processing) (Holt, 1967; McLaughlin, 1978; McKinnon, 1979; Noy, 1979; Fosshage, 1983; Lichtenberg, 1983; Bucci, 1985, Dorpat, 1990). Each lived experience is affected by the motivational system dominant at the moment and by the state of self-cohesion. Simultaneously with these intrapsychic factors, each lived experience is shaped by the pulls of an intersubjective context.

The organizing activity we speak of does not produce replicas of prior experiences, but creates new lived experiences modeled on significant features of prior experiences. Let us consider one sequence of Nancy's lived experience in this light. We assume from the clinical evidence that Nancy's mother, on her return to their home, did not create for Nancy a rich, warm sense of intimacy and attachment. This experience of being cared for by a (depressed? apathetic? withdrawn?) mother doing her moral duty was abstracted from innumerable interactions and generalized to an expectation that Nancy could not count on a warm reception, especially from a maternal figure. By the age of three, these abstracted lived experiences coalesced in the narrative of Nancy pulling on her mother's skirt only to feel her mother stiffen in an attitude of refusal and rejection. When we turn to the clinical exchanges, we find that the lived experiences and the narrative "memory" shape the new creations. Nancy became aware, for example, that out of her anticipation of rejection by men, she would, protectively, partially withdraw and communicate unavailability.

## TWO BROAD GROUPS OF SELF-EXPERIENCE

Experiences that contribute to vitality—for example, the experience of the caretaker's responsive attunement to the child's need for affirmation—occurrences we refer to as selfobject experiences (Kohut, 1977, 1984; Lichtenberg, 1991; Lichtenberg, Lachmann, and Fosshage, 1992), are particularly influential organizers of new creations. Selfobject experiences facilitate the psychological development of the child and motivate the adult to recreate comparable experiences of positive affect-laden attachments between self and other. In her early years, Nancy's company was welcomed by her grandfather, who would chase her brother away when he tormented her. In the analysis, Nancy sought to recreate a similar feeling of welcome and protection from the analyst.

In contrast, those experiences that involve thematic misattunements will tend to organize expectations that lead to the dominance of one motivational system, often aversiveness, at the expense of other motivations, such as attachments. For example, Nancy felt that her mother never developed a warm attachment to her, as she had with her brother, and, instead, resented her as a burden added to her already hard life. Nancy's experience illustrates that an absent or denigrating parent, by disrupting the child's unique developmental process, contributes to the formation of expectations of misattunement and organizations of self and self-with-other based on aversiveness: shame, guilt, fear, and anger. Nancy viewed herself as a person with "wrong" wishes and desires and as the responsible seducer who, therefore, had to constrict herself. A conflicted, debilitating identity such as Nancy's persists as an organizer because it produces a temporary sense of cohesion derived from strong affects and a sense of stability derived from a familiar sense of self. Nancy's feeling that she was in the "wrong" persisted, despite her desire to feel more positively about herself. The variety of self schemas, together with shifting motivations and interactions with others, contribute to the moment-to-moment self-states and to the more pervasive and continuous sense of self.

## TRANSFERENCE–COUNTERTRANSFERENCE: EXPERIENCES OF THE OTHER CONSTRUCTED BY PATIENT AND ANALYST

Although analysis requires placement of the patient's immediate experience in the foreground, both patient and analyst enter the psychoanalytic arena with their respective prior lived experiences and shifting motivational priorities and self states, and thus create a unique experience with one another. Based on past experience, the patient constructs repetitive self-enhancing and self-debilitating expectations and assimilates them into the analytic relationship. Self-enhancing patterns contain and convey the patient's expectations that needs will be met and self-cohesion furthered (Kohut, 1977, 1984; Stolorow and Lachmann, 1984–1985). When entering psychoanalytic treatment, the patient's hope for a different and growth-producing experience is an attempt to self-right. Nancy described at the beginning of treatment that she tended to drift along and hoped that someone would light a fire under her. Self psychology's contribution has been to monitor closely the success and failure of the patient's search for selfobject experiences and vicissitudes in the development and maintenance of a resilient, vitalized sense of self.

Analytic exploration of self-debilitating patterns and their origins generates a new perspective and, by contrast to the positive, often new, relational experience occurring in the analytic relationship, gradually leads to symbolic reorganization (Chapter 9). Sexual feelings for Nancy, whether her own or others', consistently triggered feelings of her being wrong and the responsible seducer. As she gradually became aware of this pattern and its origins, she was able to slowly gain freedom from its dominance and to establish new, more enhancing views of herself that enabled her to become orgasmic. In other words, analysis focuses on exploring and gradually transforming the pathological configurations, while forming and bolstering the vitalizing configurations.

Both the analysand's strivings for developmentally required selfobject (vitalizing) experiences and the recreation of problematic expectations oscillate from foreground to background (Stolorow and Lachmann, 1984–1985). When Nancy's background experience of the analyst was of a trustworthy, interested, involved coexplorer, she was enabled to relate with affective liveliness a problem she was having with either a roommate's exploitation or the analyst's vacation "abandonment." On occasion, Nancy would verbalize her recognition and appreciation of the analyst's helpfulness and consistency in the face of her aversive emotions. Alternatively, when Nancy experienced the analyst as failing to understand, as being misattuned, or experienced her stress increasing after she failed an important examination, the background experience of affirmation and support was ruptured, bringing those needs to the foreground. Understanding the triggers for repetitious aversive patterns tended to repair the ruptures and to reestablish the background selfobject experiences.

In contrast to viewing countertransference responses as limited to the analyst's personal pathology, we view the analyst's countertransference to embrace the full spectrum of the analyst's experience of the patient (Fosshage, 1995b). The analyst's experience of the patient is constructed by his or her perceptions of the patient and of the dual aspects of the patient's transference as well as by his or her prior lived experiences, motivational priorities, self states, selfobject needs (Bacal and Thomson, in press), and psychoanalytic models. Pulled by both the patient's problematic relational constructions and hoped-for, vitalizing wishes, the analyst's experience of the patient serves as a central guide for exploring the patient's experience. Throughout Nancy's analysis, the analyst had to struggle with a variety of responses to her reactions to threatening or abusive situations. On one occasion, Nancy's wealthy aunt promised her a gift of a modest sum that would help Nancy not to feel pressed to overwork, and the analyst shared Nancy's relief at this prospect. He also felt pleased when after a long interval of silence Nancy said that, although very reluctant, she would ask her aunt about the promised gift. Nancy then reported her aunt told her she had decided not to send her the money because Nancy would only waste it on her analysis. Terribly upset, Nancy called her brother in the hope of receiving solace, only to be told that he thought Nancy was a fool to do anything to risk her eventual inheritance from their aunt. Believing he was feeling along with Nancy, the analyst suggested she was disappointed, hurt, and angry at both responses. Nancy responded that at first she was angry, but she quickly "realized" that her aunt had a right to do what she felt best with her money and was only trying to protect her, and her brother was doing the same. At this point, the analyst experienced fury that quickly moved from aunt to brother to Nancy—with a generous helping of impotence thrown in. Nancy went on to ask why her aunt should give or leave her anything anyway. What claim did she have on her aunt for either money, help, or concern? At this, the analyst's sense of outrage powered his entering the role enactment taking place between them with his own value judgment: "You are her sister's daughter, she is your aunt." The analyst's reaction can be seen as an identification with Nancy's suppressed rage and as a direct attack on her—for her passivity in response to being teased with unkept promises, for turning to her brother (despite the knowledge that he would usually take any opportunity to humiliate her further), and for the slur on the worth of analysis that constituted the family attitudes (a personal reason of the analyst to remind Nancy of family values). We don't believe the outcome of this "countertransference" experience of the patient is predictable a priori as either destructive or helpful. The sequence that followed indicated that Nancy experienced it as an empathic confirmation of her having a place in her family that called for responses of sensitivity and concern.

## SELFOBJECT EXPERIENCES WITHIN
## THE ANALYTIC RELATIONSHIP

The analysand's hopes and expectations of evoking selfobject experiences from the analyst are fundamental motivations for the analysand's engagement in the analytic endeavor. Self psychology has emphasized mirroring, alterego, and idealizing selfobject transferences, all of which are cornerstones of the attachment motivational system. We believe that the application of the motivational systems theory enlarges the types of selfobject experiences that emerge within the analytic relationship.

### Regulation of Physiological Requirements

Self psychologists have demonstrated that disturbed regulation of physiological requirements in patients can result from primary disturbances or deficiencies in mirroring, alterego, or idealizing experiences. This conception was based on the observation that when a sense of empathic connection was restored after a disruption, the physiological disturbance would end. Nancy frequently would report periods of constipation over weekends that would abate when a mirroring, twinship, or idealizing transference experience was restored. In contrast, many disturbances of eating, eliminating, sleep, breathing, and equilibrium appear to be primary defects in lived experience. Some primary disturbances are the result of innate dysregulation such as coeliac syndromes, infantile asthma, eczema, tactile sensitivity, sensory hyperreactivity, and so on. More commonly, developmental disturbances are the result of failures in coordination between caregivers and child. Once specific failures in physiological regulation occur they frequently become the source of disturbances in attachment experiences. At times, the interweaving of a primary dysregulation and attachment deficits are difficult to disentangle. Nancy's infantile eczema is probably a primary skin disturbance, but it was associatively linked to her sense of failure to be held and fondled sensually by her mother. Whenever her eczema recurred during the analysis, she experienced discomfort, embarrassment, and an intense craving for being held physically by the analyst. The analyst could not discern if the craving that had been unresponded to triggered the eczema or the eczema triggered the craving. When there is a long-standing dysregulation that is current—for example, a dysregulation of hunger and satiety or sleep disruption—the affect states related to these disruptions, and the current motives related to them, require specific empathic focus to understand the particular failure of selfobject experiences suffered by the patient. This understanding will increase perspective and aid the patient in achieving physiological regulation in the affected areas. When patterns of eating, sleeping, or exercising are being considered, the transference experience for patient and therapist is apt to be a shared interest and concern. Alternatively, when these same issues of regulation trigger recreations of prior empathic failures, the transference experience will involve aversive feelings.

### Attachment and Affiliation

In addition to affirming, twinship and idealizing, attachment selfobject experiences can include a variety of features that can be more specifically referred to as guide, advocate, mentor, sponsor, lover, and rival. Nancy, for example, looked to her analyst as a mentor to help her to regulate herself in a variety of ways, including her relationships to men, her graduate work, and her finances. Affiliative selfobject experiences can involve the family, team, country, religion, and professional group—all with specific allegiances to values and ideologies. Religious affiliation was important to Nancy as a positive source of intimacy. Rather than her nuclear and extended family, where she felt criticized and rejected, she looked to religious groups for inclusion and acceptance. This led to her search within the intersubjective atmosphere of the analysis for her reading of the analyst's position. Was he opposed to her conversion to Catholism, as was her family? Was he opposed to religion as a "neurosis," as she knew some psychoanalysts were? She knew that he did not work on Rosh Hashanah and Yom Kippur, and so inferred that he would be supportive. She concluded from the way that he responded to the issues she brought up that he wished to help her achieve a positive sense of affiliation.

### Exploration and Assertion

Exploratory and assertively motivated behavior can create a plea-sure of efficacy and competence, an inherent self-enhancing aim. Successful exploration and assertion, exercising talents and skills, creates a selfobject experience. Past experiences accruing to this motivational system will trigger attitudes that will affect the patient's willingness to articulate and explore his or her internal process in the analysis. When Nancy entered treatment, she had begun doctoral studies and was well aware of the vitalizing experience of using her talents. She spent many sessions discussing problems involving learning, teaching, writing, and test taking. Based on her early strong exploratory interest and the encouragement she received from her father to inquire, she easily established an investigative approach with the analyst. She enjoyed the sense of efficacy that she gained from understanding meanings and solving problems in and out of the analysis. As with her father and brother, her faith in her ability to do exploratory work was easily lost if a professor or the analyst failed to offer her affirmation or if she discovered or inferred a prejudice against women (then she might resort to the use of her intelligence she had employed in adolescence—to set the man up to make opinionated statements she could ridicule). With the analyst, she both admired his carefully thought out interventions and gently derided his slowness as diffidence. Alternatively, if she felt he was ahead of her in drawing a conclusion, she often experienced a strong sense of shame, of being exposed as not quick like her brother. As she became less plagued by negative self-feelings, partic-ularly feeling "in the wrong," and by her desire to rush and dazzle, she was better able to pursue her work with clearer focus and to navigate relationships concerning her dissertation with more effec-tive assertiveness.

### Aversive Antagonism or Withdrawal

To be able to become angry and to avert a perceived threat or hurt can both protect the individual's self-cohesion and enhance feelings of power. In augmenting exploration and assertiveness in overcoming obstacles, aggression can increase our sense of efficacy. The child needs an empathic parent to be both ally and adversary (Wolf, 1980; Lachmann, 1986). As allies, parents confirm that through their chil-dren's refusals—their vigorous statements of opposition and preference—children strengthen their developing sense of self. As adversaries, parents provide children with a firm, indestructible opponent against whom to mobilize forces of anger, reasoning, and persuasion. The combination of ally and adversary gives children the opportunity to learn the sense of power that derives from augmenting assertion with anger, and thus to be effective in controversy. Similar experiences within the analysis can vitalize the patient's sense of self.

Nancy frequently would return home from a long exhausting weekend at the laboratory and begin to experience panic that she had made an error in a test that would be fatal to a patient. She would have to call the lab and be reassured. From the aversive transference position with the analyst that he asked too much of her while his help was inadequate, Nancy and he drew the inference that she also felt this way at work. Detailed inquiry into her relationships at the job in the laboratory that she had first described as superior, indicated she had allowed coworkers and supervisors to overload her with the more difficult procedures. Her great sense of responsibility for the patients and her high standards of efficiency made her vulnerable to the flattery of the supervisor's importunings. Behind that lay her resentment that she had had to take care of her mother during migraine episodes that often were triggered by her mother's critical reactions to her. Added to this dually aversive experience in her early life with Mother was her sense of guilt at not looking after her mother in her final illness. As these multiple threads of aversiveness were being explored, she began to protest directly to her coworkers and supervisors and to institute a policy of recognizing and caring for her own needs. The controversies that followed sometimes distressed her, but her panics disappeared.

### Sensual Enjoyment and Sexual Excitement

Motivations can center on seeking sensual enjoyment and/or sexual excitement. Sensual enjoyment can diminish the intensity of overstimulation or aversiveness by soothing, calming, preparing for sleep; or it can increase receptiveness to erotically arousing stimuli, leading to genital arousal and sexual excitement. A patient might seek sensual enjoyment in the analytic relationship and become especially attuned to gently rhythmic vocal tones, the restful ambience, the aesthetically pleasing decor, and symbolically feeling "touched" and "comforted." In her search for the sensual that was so absent in her relationship to her mother, Nancy, for example, would either look at or fantasize about the round, warm breasts and bottoms of women. Gradually her sensuality could also lead to sexual arousal.

Traditional psychoanalytic theory has taken sexual excitement and orgastic discharge as the central, even sole, aim of the sensual-sexual motivational system. However, we have noted that when a person feels endangered, sexual excitement may be sought, not as a primary goal, but as a means to obtain vitalization to repair a depleted state. Although this often might be the case, sexual excitement as it emerges within the analytic relationship can clearly offer self-enhancing pleasure. Nancy gradually and tentatively allowed herself to experience sensual longings and sexual arousal toward the analyst in dreams and away from and during the sessions. These experiences carried their own weight in the treatment as the working out of problems in the sensual-sexual motivational system, rather than as solely or primarily displaced attempts to desperately repair attachments. The repair occurred directly in the recovery of sensation in Nancy's genitals after years of anaesthesia. Following this important gain in sensuality, she had her first experience with orgastic excitement. The overall result was that for the first time she felt like a "complete woman."

Using the five motivational systems as guides to recognizing transference experiences works best when the major themes of the patient's associations and the feelings that go with them are clearly distinguishable. Affection and the search for intimacy easily can be distinguished from anger and the pursuit of vengeance or interest in play or work and the goal of competence. Commonly, complex symptoms and personality traits are amalgams of multiple motivations. Nancy's enuresis and demand for quickness, dazzle, and risk-taking are examples.

As a result of Nancy's inclination to let her money, her plans, and her resolutions about studying, her weight, and smoking slip away, the analyst felt somewhat in the position of observing a recurrent relapse into bed-wetting. Thus the generalized tendency of gaining and losing control occurred in each motivational system, the enuresis itself being a condensation or compromise formation from many sources that can only be pieced together from bits of analytic exploration throughout the treatment. The earliest source was Nancy's sleeping in her parent's bedroom until the age of three. The resulting exposure to their sexuality and nocturnal arguments made the night a time of overstimulation rather than rest. Further, her being "expelled" from the bedroom was seen by her as the result of her making a nuisance of herself. The resentment she felt was greatly augmented by the feeling that as soon as she was toilet trained, at age three, she was required to carry her potty up the stairs herself and put herself to bed. Thus began her lifelong feeling that as soon as she made a developmental advance, her mother took advantage of it to free herself of the burden Nancy represented to her. This gave a negative affective tinge to all advances in the analysis and became a specific problem in ending Nancy's analysis. Enuresis served as a means to deal both with the excitement states that continued with her brother and with her resentment toward her mother. On occasion during her analysis, when the excitement or resentment was triggered, she was afraid to and occasionally desired to wet the couch. Mainly the enuresis provided her with a means to keep her mother in a persistent involvement with her—getting her up, cleaning sheets, and berating her. Finally it ended when Nancy had stopped the sexual activity with her brother, thus reducing the sexual excitement, and after her mother had offered her money. Nancy felt that her mother had at least responded to her with a gift of something she really wanted.

During childhood, Nancy had looked to her older brother, Matt, for guidance on how to live. Through Matt, she had learned to rush full speed ahead without paying sufficient attention to the cues she needed to better regulate herself and her activities. She wanted to dazzle, to rush, and succeed like her "brilliant" brother and, consequently, often felt out of control and unsuccessful in her efforts. Gradually, through the analyst's calm and methodical attitude as expressed in his manner of exploration, he began to stand for the more relaxed, contained approach to life. In a moment when she was developing this new attitude, Nancy said, "I told myself I have to relax, to take things as they come, to look at them with you, and everything will by okay" (85:1:1). She "loved him for it," for it helped her gradually to gain control over a number of areas in her life. Yet, she also "hated him for it," for self-regulation required change and stole away from her her feeling of exhilaration and power. Nancy's striving for independence and power had been developed in part to counter her long-standing feelings of devaluation. Consequently, Nancy's trusting attachment to her analyst undermined the source of power she derived through her identification with her brother. At times, Nancy felt that the analyst, like her brother, would encourage her to take risks by entering into frightening situations and then reject her, berating her for her presumed cowardice. Several hours (not presented in this volume) were spent in Nancy's reliving a climbing excursion on a mountain, during which Matt kept his outstretched hand just out of the reach of his terrified sister. With any motivation, Nancy might feel the analyst was either restraining her excitement and leading her to be a boring mediocrity or encouraging her into scary situations and then not giving her his hand to help.

## EXPLORING THE TRANSFERENCE EXPERIENCE WITHIN AN INTERSUBJECTIVE CONTEXT

We have stated earlier that the patient and analyst variably code-termine the creation of a transference experience, and that the range of contribution for each varies from minimal to considerable. We now address two possible errors that can be alleviated by the analyst's awareness of the variable range of contributions of both partici-pants. We may err in the one direction when we ascribe the patient's current experience as exclusively the product of the patient when the analyst has contributed significantly. In the other direction we may err when we insistently seek for significant origins of the patient's experience in the analyst's responses or attitudes when the analyst has contributed minimally. When Nancy's analyst stumbled into a role enactment and pressured her to address additional mean-ings of a dream, interactionally creating seducer-seduced roles, he initially reported ingenuously denying his responsibility for the pres-sure. Nancy perceived (but did not project) his ingenuousness and became angry at him for having denied his responsibility (83:2:16–27). If he viewed her percept as a projection, he would again deny responsibility, thus continuing to replicate a pathogenic scenario. The analyst's recognition of his contribution to the interaction advan-tageously positioned him to validate her perception. Through his subsequent acceptance of Nancy's anger, and his understanding and acknowledgment of his contribution to it, he was able to facilitate the repair of the rupture. Alternatively, when patients are preoc-cupied with troubling expectations that they regard as contrary to what their experiences with the analyst's responses have been, the "old" conflict-laden and the emergent affirmative views are main-tained simultaneously. Nancy struggled between percepts of her analyst as either a trustworthy or an "awful" human being (83:3:17). Although the analyst's responses, over time, reinforced her hoped-for experience and emergent percept of the analyst as trustworthy, the patient's "older" expectation at this moment was not contributed to by the analyst, but was primarily generated intrapsychically. An analyst's assumption and insistence on his or her participation would, in this instance, obfuscate the patient's intrapsychic struggle with these two percepts.

The process of psychological reorganization breeds cognitive dissonance (Festinger, 1964). The struggle with cognitive dissonance is amply demonstrated in Nancy's questioning: "I'm not at all certain you're not just an awful human being. Who are you? Am I doing the right thing by coming? Can I trust you? Yet, I find myself not wanting to be separated from you" (83:3:17). Interpretations that are too dissonant with the patient's percepts will meet with aversiveness and disrupt analytic exploration. Remaining close to a patient's experience and gradually introducing a new frame (interpretation) will enable a patient to remain open to and gradually assimilate a new perspective (understanding).

The complex manner in which a patient organizes his or her experience of the analyst within the analytic relationship usually can be illuminated only after repeated efforts of recognition, conceptualization, and revision. Through empathic inquiry patient and analyst over time identify a repetitive experience occurring within the analytic relationship. The patient's description of the same experience in other relationships further validates that it is thematic. Often, we can begin to explore the history of the experience and, on occasion, a patient easily leads us to seminal experiences (model scenes) of the past. In other instances, the patient's experience of the analyst is so intense that the experience can only be "lived in" by analyst and patient (what we refer to as "wearing the attributions"). To "wear the attributions" means to explore and to fill in as if the attributions are true (to the patient they are true). Any exploration that moves away from the ongoing intense experience in the analytic relationship, whether it is identifying a theme or historical antecedents, can be experienced as invalidating the patient's current perceptions. If a patient feels a loss of the validity of his or her experience, the patient will tend to avert further exploration. In contrast, an analyst's nondefensive willingness to wear the attributions, as well as timely acknowledgment of his or her contribution, enables the analysand to feel heard, and in turn, to become more reflective. With the analysand's perceptions validated (that is, identified as his or hers and having a "reality"), and with increased reflective space, empathic inquiry toward identifying the experience as repetitive and exploration of the analysand's contribution to their experience can gradually proceed.

Expectations derived from past traumatic experiences may be triggered in the analytic relationship when the analyst's repeated interactions confirm those feared expectations. The consistency of intense aversive experiences may jeopardize the conditions necessary for the analysis of an unfolding pattern. The sense of a background selfobject experience may be disrupted and the intensity of the affective state may render cognitive processing and reflection impossible. The analyst's recognition that a background selfobject experience has been disrupted can alert the analyst to modify his or her behavior in order to decrease his or her contribution to the transference. For example, a patient's proneness to feel intruded upon and obliterated, eliciting intense aversive reactions of withdrawal, will require the analyst to become less verbally active so that the work can proceed and the patient's readiness to feel intruded upon can be explored. Kohut (1977) noted that for certain patients the "understanding" phase of the analysis needed to be extended before the "explanatory" phase in order to create the requisite developmental experiences and, we add, to offset pathogenic experiences. We believe that for all successful analysand–analyst pairs, some modifications in the analyst's behavior occur, often unconsciously, as part of their ongoing mutual regulation (Jacobs, 1991; Lachmann and Beebe, 1994, 1995; Fosshage, 1995a). In working with patients where a seriously injurious experience is being recreated in the treatment, understanding the patient's plight may be conveyed through actions, where words alone will not suffice (Balint, 1968; Bacal, 1985; Jacobs, 1991; Malin, 1992; Lichtenberg et al., 1992; Lindon, 1994; Fosshage, 1995a).

## TRANSFERENCE AND "EXTRATRANSFERENCE"

Some analysts posit that all communications, including extratransference discussions, contain transferential referents that need to be continuously examined. In so doing, an analyst places the analytic relationship consistently into the forefront of the analysis, a procedure that we, in concurrence with others (see Wallerstein, 1984), believe potentiates disruptions in the analytic flow and makes some interpretations of transference contrived. Moreover, an analyst's persistent focus on and reference to the analytic relationship, when, for example, a patient is speaking about other relationships, can subtly invalidate what the patient assesses to be important and undermine the patient's direction.

To deem the analysand's discussion of a relationship outside the analytic relationship as "extratransference" unfortunately assumes that the analysand is latently speaking about the analytic relationship.

The triggering of a particular thematic experience in an outside relationship does not necessarily indicate that it is simultaneously operative
in the analytic relationship. Forcing a patient's discussion of others
into transference inadvertently may make the analyst as a presence
in the patient's life more ambiguous than it is. The patient may
experience the analyst as telling the patient that the analyst does or
should matter more than is confirmed by the patient's authentic
experience. In our view, all of the patient's communications within
the analytic setting have transferential meaning; however, the meaning
may not be related to the content but to the process of communicating (Fosshage, 1994). For example, a patient describing to the
analyst a painful abusive experience with another person, either current
or of long ago, is most likely not "latently" experiencing the analyst
as abusive (that is, interpreting the content as applicable to the transference), but is experiencing the analyst as sufficiently safe and protective
to be able to communicate the painful experience (that is, interpreting the communicative process as having transferential meaning).
For the purpose of expanding awareness jointly, the exploration of
the experience and especially the feelings involved may be carried
out optimally in focusing on the particular setting in which the
patient brings it up.

In conclusion, transference, as we define it, refers to the analysand's
experiences of the analytic relationship and the organizing patterns
through which they are constructed and assimilated. Although analysis
requires placement of the patient's immediate experience in the foreground, both patient and analyst enter the psychoanalytic arena with
their respective prior lived experiences and shifting motivational priorities and self states, and thus create a unique experience with one
another. The patient variably constructs and assimilates the analytic
relationship into repetitive self-enhancing and self-debilitating expectations that were established through past experience. The analysand's
hopes of evoking the selfobject experiences necessary for ensuring
cohesion and vitality of the sense of self serves as the fundamental
motivation underlying the analytic endeavor. Applying motivational
systems theory to enlarge and specify the types of selfobject experiences sought within the analytic relationship, we believe, positions
analysts advantageously to understand the shifting motivational priorities of their analysands.

# 7 Dreams

*The Special Opportunity to Explore*
*Provided by Sleep Mentation*

Let us begin our discussion of dreams and their use in the clinical situation by focusing on Nancy's second dream in the reported sessions (85:4) and the subsequent interplay between Nancy and her analyst.

Nancy reported having dinner with Karl, a date, which called up a lot of "stuff." She was concerned that Jim, her housemate, would be jealous—that was the way it had been in her family. She described her brother, Matt, and her fear of his jealousy with regard to other men. "When I was in high school and college, everyone let me know my place was to be with my dad and my brother. Any boy I brought home was not good enough because he was a threat" (85:4:5). Once, she was speaking on the phone with a man whom she was dating. He was asking her to return to his place, for he was feeling lonely. "My brother heard me talk and said you know where your place is" (85:4:5). She then remembers a dream:

> In a dream I had last night I was on the floor picking up something. Jim came over. I put my arm around his leg. Only it wasn't his leg, it was his crotch. When I realized it, I tried to back off, but he wouldn't let me. I was trying to give him an affectionate gesture, let him know I had not gone and then it got misplaced—literally [Nancy continued to fill out the dream narrative as well as to associate to it]. I was thinking about the feelings I was having with Karl—they didn't come up in context with him, but displaced to Jim. Maybe it's not surprising. Starting with Karl—but where does it come from? You suggesting it's from my living with my family, my memories. In the dream one thing was apparent about making mistakes. My first was misconstruing where I placed my cheek. Then his in not letting it go. That is like my brother. I was not trying to get my face near his genitals. I was trying to share affection. That's what I was trying to do in the dream as well (85:4:5).

The analyst responds: "In the dream, what were you doing to begin with?" He explains: "Throughout the hour Nancy has been carrying forward her associations with little need for encouragement or focus. I wanted her to remain in touch with the dream imagery and I was curious about the beginning image which had not been clear to me" (85:4:6).

The analyst first clarifies the patient's dream experience to understand the meaning of the dream—our first technical guideline for working with dreams. With the same question, the analyst additionally facilitates the patient's reconnection to her affective experience in the dream, which will enable patient and analyst to explore and use the dream more meaningfully—our second technical guideline.

Nancy answers:

> I don't know. I was down on my knees picking up something. A note card maybe. He comes in. I want to make a gesture of affection, put my arm out and lean my face against—it would be his knee or upper calf. Then the size perspective changed, from child to adult. It's important because that's what gets played out here—feeling childish ... I just had a question: Do I understand the importance of what I'm saying? [*sigh*]. The answer is "No." Like when I say something, and you say it back to me, and then I see it [85:4:7].

Nancy elaborates her dream experience. She sees herself as first wanting "to make a gesture of affection." Then the size perspective shifts from child to adult, she relates this shift to the analytic relationship, and confusion ensues. In the subsequent exchange, Nancy is able to accept her affectionate needs and expression. She inquires if there is something more "scary" and, with the aid of her analyst, begins to lay claim to her sexual curiosity. Yet, sexual curiosity was tainted: "My parents feared an interest in my body and others would lead to depravity" (85:4:21). Following Nancy's description of further conflict-inducing messages in her family, her analyst summarizes: "And seems to retain the flavor of either 'it's your fault' or 'it's not your fault, it's the fault of someone who won't take responsibility'" (85:4:24). Nancy responds: "That's what it had. What am I supposed to do with that? [*argumentative*] That's the way the messages came across to me" (85:4:25). Nancy apparently had taken her analyst's comment as somewhat critical, which gave rise to her aversiveness. Feeling that it was possible to reengage her in a reflective process, her analyst returns to the dream, "In your dream you do parcel it out in a clear fashion" (85:4:26). He uses the dream to shed light on the issue of responsibility with regard to affectionate and sexual desires and behavior. Soon Nancy says, "I started thinking, 'It takes two to tango.' Then I lose it, and I'm back to 'It's all my problem.' Then I think, 'Kids need adults to learn.' It's a real problem for that not to be available" (85:4:31). She then follows: "I can take responsibility for wanting to know about everything. I was a very curious little girl. But curious isn't perverted. If it becomes perverted, it's because something is wrong" (85:4:33). Reevaluating old attitudes, Nancy arrives at a new position of acceptance of her sexual curiosity.

The dream's imagery reveals and offers an opportunity to explore conflictual issues involving the meaning of and responsibility for the expression of affection, sexual desire, and sexual curiosity. In the dream, Nancy makes clear that she was trying to express affection. There were, however, "two mistakes" in the dream: The first "was misconstruing where I placed my cheek," and "then his in not letting go." She declares: "That is like my brother. I was not trying to get my face near his genitals. I was trying to share affection" (85:4:5). Although the conflict over who is responsible for sexuality is apparent in the dream, Nancy's reference to the two mistakes "parcels out," as her analyst notes, what was her responsibility and what was her brother's. In working with the dream, her analyst used her dream mentation in conjunction with her waking mentation to explore and clarify further these troublesome, conflict-ridden issues. In so doing, he remained close to the thematic structure evident in the dream scenario, illustrating our principle, "the message contains the message." He did not translate dream images in an attempt either to understand the dream or to bring it into the transference, but stayed with the dreamer's imagery and immediate associations to conflicts involving affection, sexuality, and responsibility—conflicts that had arisen in part out of her relationship with her brother and were currently being triggered by her recent dinner date and relationship to her male housemate.

As is evident from this example, we approach a dream as a narrative. As we listen to a dream narrative, as with any narrative, we pick up and reflect to the patient the main affects, themes, and gist of the story to clarify and amplify the dreamer's experience within the dream. In referring to a dream as a narrative and to the gist of the story, we follow Sloane (1979), who believed it was central to dream interpretation that the analyst identify the sense of the dream, "its plain or essential meaning," its "quality or general tenor" (p. 39). Sloane, as do we, regarded the explicit affect expressed in the dream along with the general feeling tone as essential to understand the dream's meaning. Accordingly, we might reflect to a patient "So you were frightened in your dream when you thought your child was in danger" or "You were calm in the dream despite all the moving about." We inquire about unclear events of the dream and the dreamer's experience of them in order to understand them. As we focus on an affect, we try to connect it to its source in the dream. We do not recommend general questions, like, "What do you associate to the dream?" or "What does the dream mean to you?" because they tend to be too open ended, often fostering an affectless, intellectualized approach to the dream. To facilitate the patient's reentering, and the analyst's entering, the dream experience, our inquiry tends to take the form of questions like, "What were you experiencing when that happened in the dream?" and "What were you feeling when this occurred?" After clarifying the dream experience, we then attempt to connect it to the patient's experience in waking life.

This illustration brings us to our theory of dream formation and a more detailed account of technique in working with dreams.

## THEORY OF DREAM FORMATION[2]

We view dreaming as a complex mentational process that takes place in a sleep state. Its central function, as with waking mentation, is to process information. It utilizes variably the dual modes of cognition—the imagistic, sensory-dominated, primary process mode and the linguistically anchored, secondary process mode (Holt, 1967; McLaughlin, 1978; Noy, 1969, 1979; McKinnon, 1979; Fosshage, 1983, 1987; Lichtenberg, 1983; Bucci, 1985, 1992; Dorpat, 1990). These modes appear in the dream in the form of sensory images and spoken and unspoken words, respectively. Just as the words are placed in a logical, coherent fashion to shape meaning and cognitive focus, so too are the images placed in a sequential order to express meaning and further affective-cognitive processing (Fosshage, 1983). Sensory images tend to evoke more affect (see Epstein, 1994, for a review), which clarifies why dreaming (especially REM dreams, which are more imagistically dominated) can be so powerful. The sequential ordering of images, like a movie, dramatically depicts the dreamer's concerns and attempts to resolve problems of daily life. We believe that these images are chosen not to conceal, but to further the mentational efforts of the dreamer (Fosshage, 1987). Accordingly, dreams provide an invaluable resource for understanding a person's struggles, conflicts, and strivings.

The dream model we use assumes that all dreaming experience is organized: (1) in conjunction with the context that has impacted

---

[2] Several portions of this section have appeared in J. Fosshage's "Dreaming as a Royal Expression of Unconscious Mentation: A Current Perspective," presented at a Conference of the Toronto Institute for Contemporary Psychoanalysis, September 24, 1994, Toronto, Canada.

perceptually (although perceptual cues may occur at night—for example, a distant train whistle or a cold room—the perceptual context usually involves what has occurred in the previous day or days), (2) in response to whatever motivational systems are dominant and/or are in conflict, and (3) in accordance with organizing patterns, based on prior lived experience, that have been activated.

Dream mentation, like waking mentation, serves to develop, maintain, and restore psychological organization (Fosshage, 1983). We refer to our model as the "organization model of dreams," for the core process and function of dreaming is to organize data. In a similar vein, Atwood and Stolorow (1984) have referred to the dream as "the guardian of psychological organization" (p. 103). On the basis of REM and dream content research, Greenberg (1987, 1993) perceives dream function as "integrating information from current experience with past memories in order to produce schemas which are organizers of complicated behavioral tasks" (p. 3). From a neurophysiological perspective, Winson (1985), studying the evolutionary development of brain structures, posits similarly that the dream's function is integration, that is, a systematic processing of information (p. 295). And based on REM and dream research, Fiss (1986, 1989), in concurrence with us (Fosshage, 1983), has suggested that dreaming facilitates the development, maintenance, and restoration of the self.

### Development

Dream mentation, as waking mentation, can contribute to the development of psychological organization through creating or consolidating a new solution or synthesis (Jung, 1916). In contributing to development, new perceptual angles are achieved and new ways of behaving are imagistically portrayed. Proponents of information-processing models (for example, Breger, 1977) have suggested similarly that new perceptions and experiences are matched with permanent memories and solutions in a continual "reordering and enriching of the associative structure of the permanent memory" (Palombo, 1978, p. 468). In a review of the research, Levin (1990) concludes

> In general, the experimental evidence has demonstrated that REM sleep, and dreaming in particular, has functional utility in the consolidation, integration, and processing of affect-laden information, usually of a conflictual or negative quality. [Moreover,] [i]ncreased REM and dreaming appears to be associated with the ability to use fantasy effectively and to engage in divergent [creative] thinking and holistic problem solving [p. 37].

In one session, Nancy was reflecting on how many good friends she has, a new state of affairs. This triggered a recollection of the previous night's dream involving "a bunch of women at the women's university where I did my undergraduate work. It was the same women—some married, some single—all dressed in white and lavender like wedding dresses, lacy chiffon. In the dream, I thought about being attracted to some of them because of their being happy, not because of their having big breasts or being angry and aloof. I was aware that angry and aloof women were not attractive" (89:1:17). In her dream she turns away from women who are angry and aloof—women who are similar to her mother—and has less need of women with "big breasts"—seeking nurturance. She is feeling, in contrast, attracted to "happy" women. In her dreaming she is imaging and furthering her developmental effort to seek a more vitalizing attachment with women.

Another example of dream mentation furthering developmental movement is a dream reported by Ms. D. Ms. D is a physically attractive, pleasant young woman with a good sense of humor who entered treatment because of insomnia, hair loss, depression, and anxiety. She was painfully responsive to criticism in the law firm where she was a middle grade associate. Her confidence was at a low ebb and she attempted to compensate by working long hours and being compliant to the demands of her male partners. Exploration of her suppressed assertiveness and disavowed antagonism revealed a strong connection to her childhood fear of displeasing her mother, who had twice been hospitalized for depression. In time, she evidenced considerable improvement and was asked to join a group of three male partners who left the larger firm to form a specialty firm of their own. She was flattered to be asked, but extremely hesitant. Her father had squelched his ambitions and consistently advised her against the risk of leaving a "secure" job. She became anxious that her old partners would be offended and her new firm would fail. Nonetheless, she negotiated effectively with the three men and joined them. In a session just before her analyst was to be away for a week, she described her mixed feelings about insisting with her new partners on certain necessary arrangements or slipping back into her old inclination to be compliant—a good girl, "secretary" posture. Her analyst was unusually active in taking the role of mentor suggesting that these early days with the new firm might be critical in her establishing the kind of presence she wished to project—full-fledged lawyer or a submissive "secretary."

On her analyst's return, Ms. D reported that on the night of the previous session she had a dream that she thought was unusual and hopeful. She was in a room standing at one end of an operating table. Her analyst was at the other end. On the table was a baby. The unusual thing was that the baby was going to have a baby. Her analyst turned the baby—from being directed to him to being directed at her. Out of the baby came a full-grown woman.

Ms. D thought the full-grown woman represented her as she was taking her place in the new firm. Her analyst asked her about turning the baby around. She said that this was his way of saying to her that it is she, not he, who would bring this about, a turn around of her previous expectation that by her compliant good little girl supplications to him, he would make things right. She knew her passivity and avoidance was babylike and that the dream was telling her she could get herself to become a grown-up. The dream helped to provide her with a new vision of her ability to consolidate her sense of herself as a "full grown woman."

### Maintenance and Restoration

Dreaming, like waking mentation, can serve to maintain and restore psychological organization and self-cohesion. Kohut's (1977) description of the "self-state dream" (Ornstein, 1987) is an example in which dreaming efforts are aimed, in the face of a threat of self-fragmentation or dissolution, to restore a positive, cohesive sense of self. Regulation of affect in these dreams is central. When we have, for example, insufficiently expressed our anger and aversiveness in reaction to a perceived threat during the day, we may attempt to set the situation right in our dreaming—an effort to regulate affect and restore self-equilibrium.

Nancy, for example, described her reaction to Father Rocco's critical phone message about her dissertation. Initially feeling defeated, and then angry, she recalled a dream (90:1:3). She was being molested by a black man. Her first attempts to ward him off failed. Then, as she screams for help to the people next door, she feels empowered and realizes that she can "nail him to the wall." The dream's images graphically portray how she experienced Father Rocco's call as tantamount to molestation, her initial failures to ward him off, and then her empowering scream. She found a way in her dream to express her feelings and restore her sense of power and agency. Her connecting to the dream in telling it enabled her to become internally more definitive, assertive, and invigorated vis-à-vis Father Rocco. Relating and affectively connecting to a dream in a waking state facilitates the integration of the psychological movement that occurred in the dream state.

Restoration of psychological organization, however, does not always involve movement toward "health." One can reestablish and fortify a familiar but more problematic "mental set" (organizing pattern) in dreaming as well as in waking mentation. For example, a person's success may be experienced, based on the past, as threatening to the other and, therefore, to the selfobject tie. A dream may serve to reassert the more familiar, less anxiety-producing negative view of self as inadequate, restoring the selfobject tie and a modicum of psychological equilibrium. We can discern this occurrence only through understanding the dreamer's characteristic self-view, combined with a close tracking of the day's events that led up to the dream event.

As we dream, we use and reveal our primary patterns of organizing our world. Dreaming, like waking mentation, can serve to maintain or transform these patterns. Images of self, other, and self-with-other are intricately portrayed imagistically. Object-relational struggles and conflicts emerge and are resolved or not. Affects, motivations, conflict, selfobject experience—all aspects of one's experience are engaged and revealed in the dreaming process. Nancy's dream (90:1:3) of her struggle with the molester, for example, tells us an elaborate story. The story dramatically involves a relational struggle with the other as attempting to sexually dominate her out of his anger toward her, a repetitive theme in her familial life. Her initial attempts to assert herself fail. And then, in a moment of self-resilience, she finds the fortitude and strength to scream loudly for help to the people next door—a view that there are others who will come to her aid and a changed view of herself as empowered and capable of defending herself.

### Dream Content

Freud's manifest-latent content distinction, central to his model of dreams, was based on drive theory, in which the latent drive impulses or infantile wishes had to be disguised and transformed into the manifest dream in order to preserve sleep. His postulation that all dreams involve a defensive (disguising) transformation of the underlying latent content is unique to the classical model and differentiates it from all other dream models. Once drive and energy theory are eschewed, it is no longer theoretically necessary to posit the ubiquity of defenses in dream formation.

We believe that dreams—through affects, metaphors, and themes—directly reveal the dreamer's immediate concerns. French and Fromm's (1964) problem-solving efforts; Fairbairn's (1944) object relational processes; Kohut's (1977) self-state dreams; Erikson's (1954) individualized ego modes of experiencing and relating; and the developmental, organizational, and regulatory functions that we posit here, are all viewed as directly (manifestly) observable in dreams. Nancy's dreams—for example, her struggles with the molester, her attraction to happy women, and her feeling more like Betty, who remained calm while delivering a new baby—all convey directly through affects, metaphor, and images of self, other, and self-with-other what Nancy is thinking about.

Defenses—what we refer to as aversiveness (Lichtenberg, Lachmann, and Fosshage, 1992)—appear in dreams. Yet, the appearance of aversiveness does not require a transforming or a disguising of latent into manifest content. Aversiveness appears directly in dream scenarios. Nancy's aversiveness to the molester (90:1:3), and to her brother's not letting her go (85:3:5), appeared directly in the dream.

We therefore refer to the dream content (Fosshage, 1983, 1987). We do not maintain a differentiation between latent and manifest content, for that distinction assumes a transforming or disguising process in dream formation. Even though dream content has not been disguised, dream content is, nevertheless, often elusive and difficult to understand. Its elusiveness is related to a variety of factors, including poor recall of the dream, lack of clarity of the dream mentation itself, difficulty in understanding the meaning of images from a waking perspective, and the problem of finding a suitable match when juxtaposing two different mentational states.

Not to assume that the dream content has been defensively transformed has profound implications for working with and understanding dreams. Rather than viewing dream images as disguised stand-ins for something else, dream images are chosen, we believe, as the best imagistic language available to the dreamer at that moment to express and facilitate what the dreamer is thinking about. In Nancy's dream about the molester, for example, why was the molester not Father Rocco, whose telephone message had apparently triggered her dream, but a black man who hated her for being both a woman and white? Was the black man a displacement, a disguised stand-in for Father Rocco, which would have protected the dreamer's sleep? Did the use of the black man image, rather than Father Rocco, diminish her terror in her dream? We think not. Nancy fully experienced her terror in her dream. We suspect (needing, of course, more associations from Nancy) that for Nancy the image of a black man who had two reasons to hate her more powerfully captured imagistically her experience of Father Rocco than Father Rocco himself would have. In Nancy's experience, her image defrocked Father Rocco and showed his underside.

To understand a dream's themes and metaphors requires the dreamer's associations and resonance with the dream's affect, and the analyst's exploratory questions both to the dream and to its waking connection. Dream images and scenarios, however, need to be assessed clinically for what they reveal, metaphorically and thematically, not for what they conceal. With this emphasis, the use of each dream image within the context of the dream can be better appreciated for what it conveys (Fosshage, 1994). For example, the "I" in the dream identifies the dreamer. The object images represent the dreamer's images of the other. Not assuming that these object images are projections of the dreamer's self gives us access to the dreamer's images of others, self-with-others, and important relational patterns. In Nancy's dream of the molester, for example, was the black man a figure who carried the projection of her own anger, translating the object image into a self image? Again, we think not. We believe that this more convoluted understanding belies the thematic structure of the dream and, in so doing, would miss the important dream scenario of self in relationship to the other. Moreover, in this dream, Nancy was able to experience and express her anger and aversiveness directly in the dream.

### Significance of a Dream

Like waking mentation, dream mentation varies in significance. A dream, for example, may be a comparatively simple thought—for example, mowing the lawn, completing a paper, or doing other tasks of the day—without further significance. Or a dream may provide imagistically a sweeping rendition of the dreamer's life, including thematic trauma, changes, and current state (for an example, see Fosshage, 1989). Nancy's last dream of "climbing up a big hill to see the sunset across the lake" (90:4:1), for example, dramatically portrays a changing and enhanced perspective. Preparing to leave treatment, she dreams that the lake of the analysis is drying up, and she reminds herself of the need to remain vigilant of her brother, who might attempt to destroy her gains.

Research supports this view that dreams vary in significance. The more imagistically dominated REM dreams typically involve more affect-loaded scenarios. In contrast, dreams that occur during non-

REM states are more dominated by secondary process and therefore correspond more closely to waking secondary process thought. Research has demonstrated that REM dreams are more important than NREM dreams in consolidating memory and in dealing with emotional issues (for examples, see Fiss and Litchman, 1976, and Cartwright, Tipton, and Wicklund, 1980).

The notion that dreams vary in significance is a radical departure from the classical model, in which a deeper latent meaning is always assumed to be present. Clinically, we feel that it frees the analyst and analysand from a burdensome and often failure-inducing agenda of having to find an important latent meaning in every dream. On occasion, a patient will report a dream to the analyst, knowing that the analyst values dreams, and add a commentary that the dream seemed to be of little significance. Although the patient may not yet have become aware of the dream's significance, the patient may also be correct in his or her assessment.

## TECHNICAL PRINCIPLES FOR WORKING WITH DREAMS

Our first technical principle is to listen as closely as possible to the patient's experience within the dream (the use of the empathic mode of perception). Analytic inquiry is initially aimed at filling out the dreamer's experience within the dream—what we refer to as filling the dream narrative envelope, our second technical principle. For example, what were you feeling when that happened in the dream? What were you experiencing? (See Bonime, 1962, for emphasis on affects.) The combination of empathic listening and inquiry about the dreamer's experience facilitates the patient's involvement and affective connection to the dream experience and fills it out for the process of understanding its meaning. To focus closely on the dreaming experience itself can counter a patient's waking construal and interpretation of a dream, which may be sharply discrepant with the metaphorical and thematic structure of the dream. In turn, empathic inquiry implicitly validates the dream experience, increasing the patient's conviction about the meaningfulness of her dream experience.

A patient may tell a dream; yet, the dreamer's experience within the dream may be unclear. In Nancy's dream that was described at the beginning of this chapter, she said, "In a dream I had last night I was on the floor picking up something" (85:3:5). Was it clear what she was picking up? What was the context? What was she feeling? The analyst inquired about this dream image, for it was a "puzzlement" to him. His inquiry facilitated Nancy's "getting into" and filling out the dream.

To view dreams as revealing organizing processes positions the analyst and patient to trust dream imagery, its metaphors and themes, as directly communicative. Our third technical principle for dreams, as for expressed waking thoughts and feelings, is that "the message contains the message."

Traditionally the analytic task is to get behind the "manifest" imagery via "free" associations to individual dream elements. The request for associations to individual dream elements a, b, c, and d through z is heuristic only if the dream is seen as full of loosely connected elements that simultaneously conceal and express something underneath. Dreams, in our view, are synthetic mentational efforts, and are not comprised of loosely connected elements. In addition, we feel that requesting associations to individual dream elements at the expense of the overall context can easily fragment the dream experience as well as lead far away from the imagery itself.

When dreaming is viewed as an integrative and synthetic mentational process, the task is to illuminate more fully, through the dreamer's associations and elaborations, the particular meaning of an image as it is used within the context of the dreaming experience. Each image is like a word within a sentence, and sequences of images are like sentences and paragraphs that tell a story. Waking amplification as to the meaning of a dream image—for example, a particular person—is facilitative of understanding; yet, an image can only be understood fully as it is used within the dream context, for the context shapes its meaning. (The similarly or dissimilarity of the dream's image to the waking view conveys important meaning. For example, a patient's view of a person may be undergoing a change in the dream.) The patient's spontaneous associations and more focused associations to dream images (Whitmont, 1978; Fosshage, 1987; Whitmont and Perera, 1990) flush out the various meanings of a dream.

To return to Nancy's last reported dream, in which she was climbing up a big hill to find that the lake was "almost dry like a crater" (90:4:1), Nancy, fully connected to her dream experience, spontaneously connects it to the impending termination of her analysis, "The work with you is drying up. The winds of change . . . It's hard to see now how the lake can be filled again" (90:4:1). A boy in the dream who was "stomping around, collapsing the side of the bank," she immediately saw as her brother. If she had not, her analyst would have needed to inquire about this boy—Who was he? What was he like? Did he remind her of anyone? As she "scuttle[d] for safer ground," she warned herself that "I have to be careful and not let him or anyone destroy the work we've done, to put it down" (90:4:1). Nancy spells out the meaning of the dream through her spontaneous elaboration of and associations to the dream images within the context of the dream. She has understood the dream metaphorically and has not altered the thematic structure of the dream. Her understanding of the dream was informed by her waking concerns of dealing with the anticipated termination. If Nancy had not connected her dream experience with her waking life, her analyst would be needed to inquire, "Where in your life are you feeling that a lake is drying up?" Or, "What is drying up in your life?" In this instance, Nancy, through her dreaming, continued her waking efforts to deal with the coming end of her analysis.

This clinical example brings us to a fourth principle, namely, once the dream experience has been elaborated, it needs to be connected to waking life. Often, as with Nancy's dream of climbing the big hill, the elaboration of the dream experience and its connection to waking life are simultaneous processes. At other times, they occur more separately. Waking mentation can enhance our understanding of a dream, and vice versa. To understand a dream and its function usually requires consideration of the waking context. For example, a positive dream that is affirming of the dreamer's intellectual capacities could be functioning to further consolidate recent waking feelings or could be providing a restorative function in the face of self-doubt. Congruence and incongruence between waking and dream mentation provides additional leverage for understanding the patient. As an example of congruence, Nancy's last dream continued and furthered her waking thoughts about the termination of her analysis. Incongruence between waking and dreaming states can have a variety of meanings. For example, a patient who feels trusting and calm in his or her waking state could return to a previous anxiety state in the dream, or vice versa. Or, a patient could conceive of a new angle or resolution not yet thought of in waking life, which furthers developmental efforts. Nancy's expression of aversiveness toward the molester, and her consequent sense of power, were relatively new experiences for her that were imaged in the dream. Assessing the correspondence between waking and dream states and bringing both states into focus in an analytic process can increase understanding and integration of a person's mentational efforts.

Whereas the meaning of some dreams is quite clear to the dreamer, dreams frequently require additional inquiry for understanding. In the latter instance, the interpretation of the dream, our fifth technical principle, is variably shaped by the patient and the analyst. The traditional requirement that manifest content be translated into latent content can open the door to interpretations that more easily deviate from the metaphorical and thematic dream content, increasing the potential influence of the analyst. Our guidelines of empathic listening to the dreamer's experience, of amplifying the dreamer's experience, and of viewing the thematic and metaphorical structure of the dream to be revelatory are methods for maximizing the patient's influence during the *jointly* constructed understanding of the personal meaning of the dream.

What about transference and dreams? The notion that all the analysand's communications are transferential gave rise to the prevalent idea that every dream communicated to the analyst involves the transference. The manifest-latent content distinction potentiates translations of dream imagery that, in turn, enable analysts and psychoanalytic psychotherapists to translate dream figures to be disguised transferential stand-ins. These translations may pick up elements that are alive in the analytic relationship, and may not. Understanding, confusion, compliance, and aversiveness are all possible outcomes.

What are the implications of our dream model for transference? All dreams reported to an analyst have transferential meaning, in that either the content of the dream is applicable or the process of communicating the dream carries the primary meaning for the analytic relationship (see our discussion of content and process in understanding transference in Chapter 6). We feel that the traditional tendency of assuming that the content of a dream must refer to a transference conflict can easily undermine and divert attention away from the patient's dream experience. Moreover, when a repetitive relational pattern in the dream is not active in the analytic relationship but is active elsewhere, interpreting it as ongoing in the analytic relationship tends to reinforce the pattern rather than aid in its gradual suspension. We therefore never assume that the content of the dream directly relates to a problematic transference dynamic unless an analyst or an obvious metaphoric representative appears in the dream or the dreamer immediately associates to the analyst. In analyzing a dream, the relational pattern emergent in the dream is first identified and then subsequently connected by the patient to his or her waking life. If the analyst senses that this pattern is occurring in the analytic relationship as well, even though the patient has not mentioned it, the analyst can simply inquire, "I wonder if you are experiencing that here too?" The transference thus can be addressed without translating the dream imagery and without minimizing the patient's experience outside the analytic relationship in which the particular relational pattern was emergent.

In Chapter 4 we described a type of intervention that we call "disciplined spontaneous engagement" between analyst and patient. In working with dreams, spontaneous associations may come to the analyst and may be used in an analytically productive manner. The following is an example.

Ms. E began psychoanalytic treatment in her early 50s. She came from an aristocratic background, was very bright, and was an accomplished editor. She was exceedingly constricted in manner and lifestyle, and had never been involved in an intimate, sexual relationship. Approximately three months into treatment, the patient reported a brief dream. She was driving her red Porsche into her circular driveway. When Ms. E said "my red Porsche," her analyst's face spontaneously communicated surprise. After telling him how good she had felt in the dream, she noted his surprise and asked him, "What would you have had me driving?" An association immediately sprang forward in his mind. The question was, should he share it or not? To prepare both of them, and to offer a choice, he said, "Do you really want to know?" Undaunted, she replied affirmatively. He answered, "an Edsel." She was not pleased, but seemed to comprehend that his association captured something about her. In the ensuing discussion, the patient and her analyst clarified that the Edsel was the outmoded, constricted place she found herself in; the red Porsche was the vital, sporty side of the patient that was emerging. As her analyst was listening to the dream, he reacted to the contrast between the constricted aspect of her and the unexpected emergence in her dream of a vital, sporty side of her. The analyst's sharing of his spontaneous association captured the contrast between her waking and dreaming states, and served to deepen their understanding of both states as well as of her need to integrate and develop her more vital, sporty self. As it turned out, the Porsche became a potent symbol of the needed transformation that served as the overall guide for treatment. At the end of a fairly successful 5-year analysis, it seemed most fitting that Ms. E presented her analyst with a model of a Porsche to remember her by.

To summarize, the first task in approaching the dream is to clarify and amplify the dreamer's experience within the dream. The events of the dream will be told; yet, the dreamer's experience within the dream frequently is unclear. Or the patient will approach the dream from a waking perspective. General questions—like "What do you associate to the dream?" or "What does the dream mean to you?"— tend to be too open ended, often fostering an affectless, intellectualized approach to the dream. To facilitate the patient's reentering, and the analyst's entering, the dream experience, inquiry can take the form of questions like "What were you experiencing when that happened in the dream?" or "What were you feeling when this occurred?" The analyst's inquiry, remaining close to the dreamer's experience, affectively reconnects the dreamer to the experience for the purpose of amplifying and understanding the dream.

Inquiry is more focused on those dream persons or images that are in need of clarification. Object relational themes, affect-laden images of self, other, and self-with-other can be identified. The overall drama from beginning to end has immense communicative power about the dreamer's innermost struggles and strivings. Once the dreamer's scenarios are identified, the analytic task shifts to identifying (if unclear) if, where, and when these themes have emerged in the patient's waking life. The function of the dream often can only be understood when juxtaposing the patient's waking and dreaming states. When a dream expresses an exuberant mood of effectiveness and success, for example, it could either reflect a current waking state and serve to further its consolidation, or it could have served to restore self-esteem in the face of a shame-producing waking experience of failure.

This phenomenologically grounded approach also validates the dreamer's experience and increases conviction as to the meaning of the dream. Dream images are not translated as defensive stand-ins, but are appreciated for their communicative value within the structure of the dream drama. Most importantly, the dreamer can begin or continue to rely on his or her own experience (rather than on what traditionally has been the analyst's interpretive translation) to understand the dream, which facilitates self-cohesion.

# 8 Sexuality, Affection, and Erotization

## *Implications for the Treatment of Sexual Abuse*

The analysis of Nancy provides a detailed look at the effect child-hood sexual abuse has on the need for and expression of affection, the inhibition of sensuality and sexuality, and the proliferation of guilt and shame about sensual pleasure and sexual excitement. The common pathway for these needs, fears, and inhibitions to be expressed and analyzed was found in the eroticized transference that Nancy organized with her analyst. This transference opened a window into the vicissitudes of erotization derived from Nancy's sexual abuse and associated experiences that reinforced the abuse.

### THE EROTICIZED TRANSFERENCE

In *Erotic Transference: Contemporary Perspectives* (Gould and Rosenberger, 1994), a historical overview as well as different current views of erotic transference reveal the extensive disagreement among analysts as to what constitutes "erotic" and what is understood by "transference." In Chapter 5, we spelled out our understanding of transference as constructed out of both the patient's representational configurations (Lachmann and Beebe, 1992a, b, 1993) and the ongoing interchange between analyst and patient. The patient's specific contributions to the analyst–patient interaction uniquely shape each therapeutic dyad. The contribution of the analyst's countertransference is not confined to the analyst's "reactions" to the patient or to the patient's transference "demands." All aspects of the analyst—including his or her theoretical preferences, which inevitably influence both the process and content of the analysis—are included. It is crucial, therefore, that the analyst's countertransference and theoretical bias be consistently examined within the treatment. This task is of special importance in the treatment of sexually abused patients and in the analysis of an eroticized transference.

In reviewing the literature on the eroticized transference, Bergmann (1994) was "struck" that it was "written mostly in the language of one-person psychology. . . . It is never indicated what the analyst did or did not do, either to provoke this love or to return it to workable channels" (p. 514). In referring to his book, *The Anatomy of Love*, Bergmann cited the role of infantile prototypes in love, specifically emphasizing "the wish that the lover cure the wounds the infantile objects have inflicted" (p. 504). In the analytic situation, wishes to refind a lost or unrequited love, and the yearning for the healer, become powerful. Bergmann also referred to Blum's (1973) suggestion that the eroticized transference is a form of transference neurosis in which the analysand tries to actively seduce the analyst and is thereby actively repeating what happened to him or her passively in childhood. In his detailed case report, Dewald (1972) regarded the eroticized transference of his patient as a paradigmatic transference neurosis leading to a very successful analytic outcome.

We concur with the important place of the analyst's contributions in the erotic transference. In the discussion of Nancy's eroticized transference, we illustrate her attempt to find the cuddling, nestling, and nurturance that she felt she failed to receive from her mother. These longings for a maternal figure were assimilated into her shame and guilt-ridden sexual experiences with her father and brother. These initially nonerotic longings became eroticized and could be worked through in the analysis of the eroticized dimension of the transference. We include those instances where the analyst acknowledged to himself that he had participated in an enactment of the seducer–seduced (83:1:12) experiences of Nancy's childhood. The analyst's effort to "wear the attributions" is a further attempt to keep the repetition of childhood sexual experiences within analyzable proportions.

Any discussion of erotic or eroticized transference must recognize the contributions of George Klein. In his (1969) discussion of the plasticity of sexuality, he paved the way for many of the nuances of erotic manifestations that are recognized in analytic practice. Klein argued that Freud conceived of two vastly different theories of sexuality. One is the metapsychological theory of drives, which is a proposal for a general theory of human nature using quantities of energic discharge. Klein identified the other theory as the clinical theory. This theory "centers upon the properties peculiar to sexuality, upon the values and meanings associated with sensual experiences in the motivational history of a person from birth to adulthood, upon how nonsexual motives and activities are altered when they acquire a sensual aspect, and vice versa" (1969, p. 15). Klein discussed nonsexual motives being "sexualized" (p. 37) and contended that only the clinical theory recognized sexualization or erotization as salient phenomena in the clinical situation. He argued that the meaning and the "plasticity" (p. 29) of *sensuality* accounts for the phenomenology and the dynamics of sexuality.

Klein distinguished between sexuality as a drive to be discharged and as a meaningful experience to be savored, avoided, desired, feared, imposed on others, or fled from. Klein's work contributed to the analysis of the complex meanings encompassed in Nancy's eroticized transference, her expression of longings to be nurtured in sexual imagery.

Wolf (1994) understands the eroticized transference as a way in which a patient may retain a necessary connection with the analyst, that is, by eroticizing this tie. Though historically clinicians have been alert to the possible resistive aspects of the erotic transference, Wolf and others (for example, Gould, 1994) now also focus on the restorative, vitalizing, and self-enhancing function served by eroticized transferences. This line of interpretation builds on the contributions of Ferenczi (1933) and Schafer (1977).

An analyst's discomfort with sexual overtures by patients contributes to the transference–countertransference stalemates that are often ascribed solely to the psychopathology of patients who form eroticized transferences. In addition to the analyst's failure to address the sources of the transference, the analytic dialogue is diverted from the therapeutic gain that the erotic transference offers. In the analysis of Nancy, the eroticized transference carried the treatment for a considerable time. Only toward termination did Nancy clearly come to differentiate between her eroticized transference experience and her desire (and anxiety) for a satisfying sexual relationship in her everyday life. Wolf (1994) indicated that the emergence of an eroticized transference should be welcomed into the analysis as an expression of thwarted, longed-for needs that are no longer suppressed out of fear of disappointment or rebuff. By "welcoming," we do not propose that the analyst "do something" to invite the patient to eroticize him or her. Rather, we mean that eroticized feelings, such as expressions of affection and sexual imagery, are accepted, as any other expressions would be. That is, these "erotic" attributions are "worn" by the analyst, just as any other attributions of the patient would be.

We prefer the term "eroticized transference" to "erotic transference," which may more simply involve motivations of the sensual-sexual system alone. For example, Nancy's eroticized transference was derived to a significant degree from unrequited longings for physical and emotional affection from her "stiff" mother. These attachment longings, replete with sexual imagery, "curiosity about women—about breasts, bottoms, legs and comparing" (83:1:13), appeared throughout the analysis until its termination. They were then absorbed into the affectionate feelings that characterized Nancy's relationship to her analyst. In characterizing Nancy's transference feelings as "eroticized," we refer to a dynamic sequence. Nancy's nonsexual longings for nurturance from her mother were thwarted. To maintain her attachments, Nancy turned passively endured rebuffs into actively sought sexual contact (through exploration and curiosity), amalgamated these longings with her experiences of sexual molestation, and accepted the accusation that she was the powerful instigator of the "seductions" of her father and brother. Nancy's sexual feelings, albeit guilty and shame ridden, coalesced with nonsexual longings and emerged as an eroticized transference.

### ATTACHMENT, SEPARATIONS, AFFECTION, AND AVERSION

In a session in the second year of her analysis (83:1), Nancy said, "Over the weekend I was feeling a lot better, but Saturday I felt enormously depressed. I don't know if I hate the weekend because I'm away from you" (83:1:1). Later in the session, Nancy connected her "bone-crushing depression" to "fantasies of being close and making love" (83:1:3–9) to her analyst. This interpretive sequence clarified the connection between Nancy's unrequited longings, initially evoked in relation to her mother, and an anxiety-arousing, eroticized affectionate attachment.

Nancy expressed her longings for her analyst and her attachment to him as she felt his absence. She elaborated, "I find myself not wanting to be separated from you. Whatever you are, it's better than being alone. I hate myself for that" (83:3:17) and "I hate you for going away and doing that ... The same way I hated my mother. I have a vision of getting up and throwing everything in this room at you" (83:3:23). Nancy is describing the terrible dilemma caring and loving places her in. Caring makes her ashamed of herself for desiring someone who has abandoned or neglected her. Two years later, Nancy directly connected her eroticized experience of the analysis— "mental masturbation" (85:1:11)—with not having been nurtured by her mother— "I get back to Mother and not being able to cuddle, nestle, or nurse as a baby" (85:2:13).

In a session during the termination phase, when her analyst did not utter his usual "Hmm hmms," Nancy commented, "Maybe you're weaning me" (90:1:7). Subsequently, she reported a dream "about this mother giving birth and relating it so clearly to you" (90:3:23), to which the analyst responded, "After you think about how you'll miss me" (90:3:24).

The analyst's continued acceptance of Nancy's affectionate attachment (89:1), and the anger and hatred it often triggered, led to the increasing differentiation among Nancy's masturbatory experiences and her attraction to women. Now women were attractive to her "because of their being happy, not because of their having big breasts or being angry and aloof" (89:1:18).

Throughout the analysis, the analyst's attention is directed toward what occupies motivational and experiential salience at any given moment. Because the transference may be organized by any motivational system, no one system holds a privileged position. The eroticized transference may only come to occupy an unyielding dominance when the clinician experiences difficulty in accepting, understanding, and working with the responses these passions of the patient arouse. To this extent, the erotic demands, or rage-filled reactions to their nonfulfillment, are codetermined by patient and analyst. When Nancy elaborated that "in a strange way it's okay to have sexual fantasies about Christ. He represents perfection and is immaterial so there's no way to act. It's safe" (83:2:7), the analyst responded, "As compared to my physical presence so near?" (83:2:8). The responses conveyed the analyst's comfort with being the recipient of Nancy's sexual feelings. He enabled her to continue to speak freely about them. Later, she added, "I want you to take out some part of you and share it with me" (83:2:23) and continued with "I want to kiss you. No, castrate you—that would be worse" (83:2:27). Here Nancy makes clear that imbedded in her affectionate-sexual desires are intense feelings of aversion for the neglect, sexual exploitation, and failed protection she has endured. To the extent that the analyst viewed these sexual and aversive expressions as free associations, like any other communication by the patient, the eroticized transference was maintained within manageable levels without producing a therapeutic stalemate.

As the analyst tracked Nancy's longings for nurturance from her mother, and accepted and explored her sexual feelings and fantasies toward him, she increasingly trusted him with more detailed revelations about the sexual molestations by her brother, and her sexual play with her girlfriend, Margaret (85:2). In contrast to Bak (1973), who considered the erotic transference a defense against melancholia or an impending breakdown of the self, in Nancy's case we understood her eroticized transference as fulfilling needs that embodied facilitating, restorative, and invigorating potentials. Most importantly, it presaged new ways of relating sensually, sexually, affectionately, with men and women.

The careful tracking of Nancy's complex transference gradually distinguished among Nancy's sensual-affectionate feelings, longings for maternal affection, sexual-seductive intentions, and aversive retaliatory responses. In her associations to a dream (85:3), she described how her attempt to show affection was misconstrued as a sexual seduction, an illustration of a "confusion of tongues" (Ferenczi, 1933). The assumption that affection is a variant of sexuality, and the failure to distinguish between the two, may inadvertently replicate the very experiences that may have prompted a patient to seek treatment. Analysts, too, have been wary of accepting or expressing affection toward patients, lest they gratify incestuous wishes. The playful interchange between Nancy and her analyst (87:2) maintains a spirit of affection that leads increasingly to Nancy's ability to articulate her desire for a sexually attractive man (87:2:5) and to her insight, "I turn everything off" (87:2:12).

During the final months of the analysis, Nancy could speak directly about her sexual feelings for her analyst without the shame and sense of "badness" that had encrusted sexuality for her. She said, "When you came in I heard you fumbling with your keys. There was something erotic about it" (90:1:1). Later in the session, she reported a dream in which she fought against a potential molester. She emerged from the dream feeling that she was able to make a clear, forceful response to a sexual molester (90:1:3 to 90:1:11), that she could be effectively assertive and confrontative rather than thrashing about with impotent rage.

## CONSOLIDATING AN AFFECTIONATE ATTACHMENT

The feeling of mutual affection that was prominent during the final phase of the analysis came about gradually. A number of factors mitigated against Nancy expressing and feeling herself entitled to be the recipient of affection. In wearing the attributions with respect to Nancy's sexual wishes and fears, and her rage-filled reactions when she felt thwarted, rebuffed, or misunderstood, the analyst enabled Nancy to experience her sensual-sexual motives as "adult passions" rather than as the residues of her past. Furthermore, where previously any attempt at humor by the analyst had triggered Nancy's feeling that she was being teased and humiliated, a spirit of playfulness began to occur quite naturally in their interactions. Such "play" conveyed to each that the other could be trusted to join in sustaining a light mood without rejection or hurtful intent. Parallel to the analyst wearing the patient's attributions, Nancy now accepted the analyst's expectation that she could engage in adult, playful banter with him. Nancy's capacity for symbolic play blossomed during her prepubescent relationship with Margaret. Analytic play could be built on this solid but narrow base from her past. As Nancy's feelings of badness, her guilt, and her shame-ridden sexuality were explored and reexperienced in the eroticized transference, their constriction of her life diminished. She could express affection for her analyst without fearing that she or he would be placed in danger of recreating the seducer-seduced sequences of her childhood. In the past, these sequences had eventuated in her conviction that all the "sex stuff" in the family was her doing or that she would be blamed for it even if she rejected their self-serving view. Affectionate attachments had been preempted by Nancy's fear of repeating experiences of being a powerful seducer who had to keep her sexual feelings under wraps lest they threaten important attachments.

The most potent contributions to Nancy's having relinquished sensual pleasure and sexual excitement came from the experiences of sexual molestation. Their discussion and working through provides entree into the wider sphere of the treatment of sexual abuse.

## TREATING SEXUAL ABUSE

Especially in the treatment of patients who have lived through sexual abuse (Herman, 1992), retraumatizing can be triggered inadvertently when an aspect of the analyst's theory, manner, or interpretive approach is experienced as similar to the patient's trauma. For example, an analyst's theory could lead him or her to believe that prime significance must be given to interpreting that the sexual abuse fulfilled a universal fantasy and thus, at its base, whatever its cost, was a form of wish fulfillment. Such a view completely overlooks the child's absolutely appropriate needs for secure attachment, regulation in each motivational system, and protection against predatory intrusion. These are ways Nancy's caretakers failed her. For the analyst to have sought to demonstrate her oedipal or preoedipal fantasies as essential sources of her abuse experiences would have promoted a new form of the same trauma.

In our discussion of the ten principles of technique (Chapter 4), we spelled out the general procedures that we believe can minimize the likelihood that a patient's analytic experience will resemble an early pathogenic experience. By continuous investigation of the analytic relationship, and by tracking the sequence of patient–analyst interactions, we remain alert to the ruptures, empathic breaks, mismatches, and misattunements that indicate a retraumatization in the sensual-sexual area. The analyst's failure to acknowledge and investigate the patient's experience of having felt traumatized during the treatment often constitutes a danger of greater significance to the potentiality for recovery than the disruptive event itself.

In several ways, the analytic situation can be plausibly experienced (Gill, 1982) as similar to past traumatic pathogenic experiences. An analyst's misunderstanding and misapplication (Lipton, 1977) of Freud's technical recommendations, which contributes to a patient's experiencing the analyst as "cold," impersonal, or detached, has long been recognized as having a negative effect (Stone, 1961). For patients who have been abused, such an ambience can't relieve the patient's expectation of exposure to danger and may actively contribute to a re-creation of feelings of being objectified and dehumanized.

When an analyst follows a theory that stresses disclosing to an abused patient the patient's concealed deceptiveness, seductiveness, sadism or seeking of hurt, then guilt and shaming become an actual experience for the patient, whatever its resemblance to the past. Whenever Nancy experienced this, it was as if the analyst were pointing an accusing finger at her—the equivalent of blaming the victim. In contrast, when Nancy experienced the emergence within a *shared* exploration of motives to conceal, to have her femininity responded to, to want vengeance, or to be roughly handled by a decisive, potent man, she could recognize the motive as her own. Even then, shame and guilt often were triggered, but her pride in recognizing and acknowledging them as originating from herself with the analyst as participant helped ameliorate the injury to her self-worth.

A further problem may arise when a patient expresses hurt or anger and objects to the analyst's formulations as blaming the patient. Rather than accepting the patient's experience, an analyst can easily become defensive and interpret the patient's attribution as distortion-induced resistance. A vicious circle is established between two people who feel misunderstood and, in words or silently, point an accusatory finger at each other. This vicious circle is nowhere more pernicious than when evoked in the treatment of patients who have already experienced with caregivers a similar inability to negotiate the sources and effects of trauma.

## STRATEGIES IN TREATING SEXUAL ABUSE

### Abreaction and Catharsis

The role of sexuality as a basis for all trauma, and abreaction as a theory of cure, has a long and convoluted history in psychoanalysis, and continues to influence the treatment of trauma victims. Abreaction of the affects that accompany or are derived from a trauma makes sense on the face of it. However, the idea that one can rid oneself of bad feelings assumes that these feelings are finite, that they are present in specific quantity in the traumatized person, and that once discharged they will not be recreated. The experiential basis for the cathartic theory rests on the subjective feeling of relief that often occurs after the release of any strong affect.

We view affects as processes that are integral aspects of motivational systems. The investigation of the relationship among motivational systems simultaneously addresses the extent to which affectivity is restricted, affect states are experienced as overwhelming, or moods color subjective experience. These affects cannot be handled independently of the motivational systems of which they are an integral part.

We recognize that on the subjective basis of temporary relief, trauma victims are often attracted to group, cult, or individual programs that encourage working themselves up into affect states of screaming, crying, or raging. The fabrication of events may also be encouraged to fill in gaps in memory or failures in symbolic representation. We believe that having been a victim of sexual abuse should not disqualify a person from an opportunity to engage in an experience in which his or her subjective world is expressed and analyzed. Thus, in line with our user-friendly principles, we focus on the validation of self-experience, the analyst's resonance with the affective communications of the analysand, and the provision of an ambience of safety. In addition, when the material presented by the patient deals with sexual abuse and molestation, we are alert to the ways in which the analytic situation can resemble or be experienced as resembling the original traumatic experience. Alert to these similarities, we track the way in which the patient may plausibly experience the analysis as "just like my childhood trauma." The individual treatment, as a modality, thus recognizes the patient's unique reaction and unique path toward recovery. The analyst's recognition of those features a patient shares with other traumatized people is not precluded, but the particular way in which a particular person is affected by a particular trauma is accented. We are careful to avoid becoming preoccupied with the sexual abuse (see Kiersky, 1993) to the exclusion of other salient experiences, including other feelings the patient may have toward the abuser. Not until a patient feels certain that an analyst is interested in him or her as a person, not just as an incest or abuse victim, will the patient be able to investigate the traumatic experience.

We lack the empirical experience or research documentation of the efficacy of other approaches. We recognize that at times exposing or confronting an abuser and participating in a group experience with other victims may have beneficial results, but are skeptical of these approaches if a sense of individual differences is lost. The essential message conveyed in these approaches can be "don't feel helpless, you can challenge your abuser and maybe help others" or "don't feel like an outcast, you have a community to which you can belong." The therapeutic intent is to combat shame, isolation, and powerlessness. However, we hold that central to the recovery from traumatic experiences for patients who, like Nancy, have a capacity for self-reflection and symbolic representation, is analytic recognition of the unique meaning that such a patient has organized around the traumatic experience, as well as the co-construction between analyst and patient of an individualized treatment plan.

## THE ANALYSIS OF NANCY

In trauma, such as incest and sexual abuse, the loss in childhood of responsive selfobject experiences may damage the developing sense of self so that an exploratory therapeutic exchange may be difficult to initiate and sustain. In the treatment situation, establishing and maintaining a trust-filled attachment (selfobject tie) is a primary concern. In the analysis of Nancy, recognition of her need to reestablish confidence in her self-regulatory capacity was paramount to her experiencing the analyst with trusting faith and respect (an idealizing transference). Included within the reestablishment of selfobject ties in the transference is the unique manner in which each patient reacquires a capacity for self-regulation. Treatment is sometimes stalemated as the patient maintains a precarious balance between a readiness to examine past traumatic experience and a need to retain a tie to the traumatogenic objects. In maintaining this balance, the capacity for self-regulation may be sacrificed or at least in jeopardy. Nancy regarded her mother's premature turning of bowel and bladder control over to her (sending the three-year-old up the stairs with her potty to put herself to sleep) as an abandonment. In contrast, Nancy regarded her mother's giving her enemas as a desired form of attention, despite the cost in discomfort and loss of autonomy. Thus to self-regulate was to feel abandoned. To be incompetent and incontinent (enuresis, letting money dribble away) and to be withholding and retentive (constipated) was to invite hands-on, sensualized care.

When self-regulation has been heavily compromised, as in the case of Nancy, classical "resistances" (for example, mishandling of finances and psychic paralysis in making necessary practical decisions, both of which can impact on the continuity of the analysis) may represent both a retention of an old, painful autonomy-sacrificing tie and a step toward reacquiring control over one's body and one's destiny (self-regulation). In this process, a patient may at first depict the analyst as having "total control" and struggle to wrest this control away from the analyst-parent. Many traumas, especially those in which an intense affect state is triggered (Chapter 5) and the person is startled, even stunned by its unexpectedness, can limit the extent to which the experiences are subject to symbolization and reflection. Thus, "enactments" in the analysis of trauma and incest victims may be a consequence of the concrete manner in which the trauma has been retained. For Nancy, the problem of trauma took different forms. One form was the potential for intensifying affect states of depression, anxiety, and anger. Another was the absence of any memory of sensation during her brother's masturbation against and on top of her, concretized in a symptom of anaesthesia. A third form was the condensation of multiple meanings in her symptom of enuresis and its current derivatives. Enactments during which the analyst is pulled into a role response may be necessary to facilitate the process of transforming restrictive self-states of emotional constraint and hopeless despair.

In the beginning of the analysis, Nancy's analyst, aware that an "enactment" with her in response to subtle or overt sexual material could be experienced by her as a repeat of her incestuous relationships, stiffened in an enactment of its opposite—what they came to call his "diffidence." This diffidence, or possibly unnecessary caution, may have delayed the working through of the sexual trauma. In any case, quasi enactments with respect to the payment of the analytic fee and quitting her job were to proceed and intermix with the analysis of sensual-sexual motivation.

Each time the fee issue emerged, the analyst felt pulled between his basic inclination to encourage and trust Nancy's sense of fairness and responsibility and his fear of inadvertently contributing to her feeling of chaos in self-regulation through a sense of neglect.

With her attempts to both lower the fee and raise it, the analyst mainly tried to investigate the meaning. When he did not acquiesce to a lower fee, the analyst established a boundary based on his own self-interest and his faith that she could do the same through her self-regulation. Setting this boundary eventually permitted a more detailed analysis of a valid balance between altruism and self-interest as compared to Nancy's and her mother's "saintliness."

### Model Scenes

In the treatment of Nancy, we trace the working through process of model scenes, based on her past experience, that were jointly constructed during the analysis (see Chapter 4):

1. sitting on her father's lap and then suddenly being banished. This scene depicts Nancy as seductive and her father as helpless responder. His arousal is Nancy's fault; men bear no responsibility for their animal nature.

Recall that until she was five years old, Nancy ate her meals sitting on her father's lap, and then she was suddenly "banished." In the course of her analysis, she and her analyst inferred that the basis for her "banishment" may have been her father's erection while she sat or wiggled on his lap. Feeling his erection would have prompted Nancy to concur with her family's accusations that she was too seductive.

2. the brother using Nancy to masturbate against and on, and his insistence that she make herself available to him, first by threatening her to continue and then by bribing her. This scene combines with her sense of being accused of seductiveness by her father. Nancy's sense of guilt is extended to a wider range of peers. An aspect of this scene is her sadistic elaboration that "her brother would examine things—pull the wings off a fly and watch it squirm and get pleasure" (83:3:1). He assured her that their mother would not believe her if she told on him and that she should be ashamed of thinking he would do anything to harm her. In this view of the "scientist" as both a sadist and a clever deceptor, the sadism is turned around and she is the one who is accused of doing the hurting. A family collusion is illustrated in these two scenes, in which Nancy is placed in conflicted, no-win circumstances. She is left on her own to regulate these heightened affects (Pine, 1986; Beebe and Lachmann, 1995) associated with the need for sensual pleasure and sexual excitement. The groundwork for states of feeling overwhelmed and depressed

is thus laid. Explicit in the model scene is the unavailability of parental figures to provide a context, a reliable background (selfobject) support.

3. tugging at her mother's leg and sensing the stiffening of her mother's body as she resisted Nancy's importuning. In an association, Nancy recalled her mother lifting up Nancy's brother and asking him to sing to her. When Nancy climbed up as well, her mother told her that she couldn't sing even though her teacher had selected her for a solo. These scenes establish a sense that Nancy was with a caretaker who was capable of reaching for, lifting up, affirming, and praising her brother, but who would not only fail to confirm her capacities but deny them.

A fourth model scene developed in the course of the clinical exchange. In the consultation interviews, Nancy reported that Dan, another graduate student, was interested in her and that his pursuit and her responsiveness made this a promising love affair. Although Nancy continued to advance this view of their connection, the analyst inferred from her associations that Dan was far from seriously involved but rather was teasing and flirting with Nancy behind a screen of ambiguity. The essential features of this model scene were that Nancy was drawn to situations of ambiguity in her love relationships and that she herself practiced a similar form of obfuscating with the analyst.

**The Clinical Exchange**

In the second year of her analysis (83:1:1), Nancy opened a session by recounting her disappointment in a priest. She had expected him to be more responsive to her, to treat her as special because he had taken part in her conversion. She continued by stating that she had become aware of being depressed when she was away from her analyst, an indication that the treatment relationship had permitted a reliable attachment to form. Being away from her analyst momentarily disrupted her selfobject experience.

With some embarrassment, Nancy commented about "the explicit sex stuff" (83:1:3) that she had expressed toward her analyst. He could get out of control. She had read a newspaper article about a psychiatrist who raped his patient. She summarized, angrily, that if there is a sexual response to her, from her analyst or from her father, it's her fault and it becomes her responsibility. She linked her feelings to her current experience on the couch. Lying on the analyst's couch was equated with sitting on her father's lap. Even if she turned her head back, or rolled her eyes, it became an "analytical issue" (83:1:15). She said, "I remember the first time I rolled my head back and saw you, how reassuring it was. I do it to be reassured ... That you are there. Not gone. I want to put the spotlight on you. Not only me" (83:1:17).

The foregoing sequence illuminates both the trauma and Nancy's "curative fantasy." The sequence began with Nancy's failure to feel attended to and a concurrent sense of betrayal. She began to follow her usual course of blaming herself for her isolation and specifically attributed her "banishment" to having been sexually seductive. To counter her pervasive feeling of abandonment, she required her analyst's presence and suffered over the weekends. Finally, she turned the spotlight on him—he could get out of control like the rapist psychiatrist.

Nancy's attempt to reverse the spotlight was prompted, in part, by the pressure she had felt to comply with her family and accept their critical shaming spotlight shining on her. According to them, it was she who started all this "sex stuff," she was a girl and girls are responsible. Her overt compliance and the impotence of her attempts to stop Matt served as confirmations of this for her. Nancy used the opportunity provided by the story of the psychiatrist to turn a passively endured experience into an active response, a particularly important occurrence in the analysis of trauma victims. We understand it as a beginning transformation, an attempt to regain mastery and self-regulatory control. Although he recognized that her momentary affect was angry and spiteful, Nancy's analyst did not interpret her spotlighting him as a defense, a denial of responsibility, or a primary expression of hostility. Though these motives may have been involved, such interpretations would have failed to recognize her strivings to wrest herself free from the shackles of past fears, guilt, and shame. At that moment, interpreting her turning the tables on him as defensive would have failed to acknowledge Nancy's self-restorative, self-curative efforts. He believed that shining the spotlight on him represented Nancy's spontaneously emerging attempt to counter her propensity to protect her abusers through self-blame. The analyst participated in this process by tactfully "wearing the attribution" of accepting the spotlight. He questioned her about what way she wanted to be reassured (83:1:16).

Nancy continued to feel angry toward her analyst in the session that followed. She felt that she had been trapped in a situation in which the spotlight was only on her (83:2). The analyst summarized her feeling as "manifestly unfair" (83:2:24) and the theme of wanting to turn the tables on the analyst continued. The subsequent interchange covered both the transference and the "unfairness" of the accusations leveled against her by her family in making her the cause of all the sexual stuff (83:2:21–28).

At this time in the analysis, the model scene of being banished from her father's lap had not yet been fully coconstructed. But intimations of it were being noted. To the extent that Nancy was dimly aware of her father's arousal, she held herself to be its cause. Depicting her situation as unfair, and her use of the "spotlight" image to illuminate something in darkness, was most apt.

Nancy feared, angrily, that her analyst, like the psychiatrist in the article she had read, and like her father, would also lose control. Whatever followed then would be her fault. Because sitting on her father's lap and lying on her analyst's couch were condensed, lying on "his" couch was uncomfortable (83:2:9). She dreaded where it might lead. The unfairness of the accusations heaped on her by her family motivated her angry reaction toward them. She expected a similar course of events in the analysis.

After two years of analysis, the question of who is to blame and who is responsible had been directly engaged. The model scenes, "sitting on her father's lap" and "molested by her brother" no longer so rigidly constricted her experience and affectivity. Though they exercised a less inhibiting influence on her sexuality, aversive and aggressive reactions were still triggered by feelings of intimacy and attachment. The sessions two years later continue the working through of these scenes.

The fourth year of Nancy's analysis continues the working through of encumbered motivations based on the need for sensual pleasure and sexual excitement. Nancy had increased her self-assuredness. Her self-reflection was less burdened by self-blame, so she could investigate her reactions with more discrimination and objectivity: "When I left yesterday I thought it was a good hour, but still something is wrong in the background . . . I haven't paid my bills. I spent $100 for Thanksgiving dinner . . . I don't know what's going on" (85:1:1).

The theme of taking responsibility for herself lost its rigid, adversarial quality, but "responsibility" and "self-blame" were still intimately connected. The extent of Nancy's self-blame was partially derived from her experience of abuse, that was depicted in the first two model scenes. Assuming responsibility for herself thus meant accepting "blame." The model scenes "on her father's lap" and "the brother masturbating on her" contained the accusation that Nancy was the enticer. The analytic work had succeeded in exploring her ambiguous sense of herself as seductive and reticent, brazen and innocent, forward and avoidant.

The themes that dominate these sessions, wanting to be special, guilt, blame, shame, and responsibility, are similar to themes that often have been ascribed to a child's unconscious belief that she has been an "oedipal winner" whose incestuous wishes were gratified. To hold the view that the sexual molestation of a child gratifies universal unconscious incestuous wishes and that this is the central cause of its pathological effect is to ignore or depreciate the deleterious effect on each motivational system and on the patient's sense of self as a whole (Chapter 2).

The analyst and Nancy regarded Nancy's broad-based regulatory difficulties, her states of depressive affect, guilt, shame, and rage, as the result of the overlapping effects of disturbance of attachment, exploratory, aversive, and physiological motivational pressures. They came to understand these affect states as far more complex than reactions to the sexual trauma, reinforcements of oedipal guilt, or pseudogratifications in therapy. To view Nancy as an oedipal winner who unconsciously orchestrated the seduction of her brother and father and who, out of oedipal rage and competitiveness, depicted her mother as a "rejector," would not only be an incorrect interpretation of her experience but would replay the trauma she experienced in her family. Once again, Nancy would have been labeled "the seductress," only this time seen as "unconsciously" motivated. She would be retraumatized in analysis by being told that her guilt was a consequence of having gotten what she was not entitled to, and she has only herself to blame if, in the process, she lost the mutual regulatory help she required from her family.

Nancy's anxiety about intimacy and her awareness of how she had avoided a man's sexual interest in her (85:1:9) signaled her increased self-reflection and decreased affective inhibition. With somewhat less self-blame and shame, she was able to acknowledge that she felt helped by her analyst (85:1:14). In addition, she could acknowledge that she needed something from both men and women. She felt uneasy and "decadent" (85:1:9).

Nonetheless, she realized that she enjoyed talking with her analyst. Her conviction that her pleasure in speaking with him was "decadent" began to shift. She said, "So it's not decadent! But it seems decadent in contrast to what I'm used to" (85:1:15). The experiences of sitting on her father's lap and lying on her analyst's couch became increasingly differentiated. The dominance of the model scene, "sitting on her father's lap," that had cast a pall over her sensual experiences, had diminished somewhat. Her dread of being banished for seductiveness had consequently also diminished. As the condensation of father's lap and analyst's couch receded ever further into the background, she could begin to experience her analyst as a "nurturer" and herself as "nurtured." The model scene of yearning for her "stiff" mother that had led to her sexual preoccupation about women and contributed to the erotization of the transference was reworked simultaneously. Nancy began to experience her analyst as a somewhat distant mother, "the nipple on the ceiling" (85:1:13), yet nurturing without infantilizing.

Nancy's feeling of "decadence" in talking with her analyst (85:1:10) indicated a residue of guilt. She spoke of "mental masturbation" that felt both "self-arousing and self-satisfying" (85:1:11). The analyst intervened to maintain an atmosphere of safety as Nancy courageously explored feelings and memories that were painful, shameful, and embarrassing to her. As Nancy delved further into her experience, she became aware of previously unreported aspects of herself. The analyst responded by reflecting her, mirroring her, and encouraging her to continue. She did so, deepening the material without undue pressure or specific interpretations. It is at that point that her associations moved to the "bump on the ceiling—like a nipple    (and) woman's soft bottoms, I get back to mother and not being able to cuddle, nestle, or nurse as a baby. . . . It comes up because of what happens here in a decadent way. Without your nurturing me, you're helping me to grow up" (85:2:13).

As the session (85:1) continued, Nancy spoke about a friend, who helped her despite the end of the school year "terror" when her washing machine overflowed. The analyst commented, "You could speak of that as an "old-fashioned virtue" (85:1:16). That term was unusual for him. The odd phrasing popped out spontaneously, perhaps his association to Nancy's use of "decadent."

The sense of surprise and spontaneity associated with the phrase "old-fashioned virtue" signaled a transference shift instigated by the analyst. This shift would affect model scenes derived from both the need for sensual pleasure and sexual excitement. Specifically, these model scenes contained Nancy's nurturant longings, which had been ignored by her "stiff" mother and her burgeoning sexuality, which had been squelched by her rejecting and blaming father and brother. Having organized self-experience to avoid further retraumatization, she sought to protect herself against having her nurturant longings and sexual needs activated and frustrated.

We infer that Nancy could not straddle the impact of both the maternal failures in nurturing and the paternal failures in acknowledging her developing sexuality. As Nancy expressed satisfaction in her experience of the analyst as (maternally) gratifying and (paternally) responsive, his slightly jarring comment "old-fashioned virtue" appeared to ease her gently off his lap.

In the session that followed (85:2), Nancy offered a remarkably organized summation of her early sexual experiences and abuse, and for the first time presented in detail her sexual play with her female friend. Several factors may account for the information being revealed at that time. First, the empathic mode of perception and the maintenance of an ambience of safety helped pave Nancy's pathways to awareness. Second, the consistent attention to Nancy's affect states and the selfobject experience she was seeking kept iatrogenic aversive reactions to a minimum. Third, the use of model scenes to link past experience and current transference organizations maintained an emotional immediacy in the analysis. Fourth, as a consequence of the continuing working through of the model scenes, Nancy's sense of agency and self-determination gradually increased. Her greater sense of efficacy made it more likely that additional material, previously kept out of awareness, would become accessible. That is, she recalled and investigated sexual material without arousing the same intense aversive, searing shame. Fifth, in recollecting the period of play with Margaret, she recalled a time when she was 9 or 10 years old with age-appropriate sexual activities and curiosity (85:2:5). She remembered the analyst's comment, that she and Margaret were equals (85:2:5). He affirmed her membership in a community of appropriately sexually curious and assertive 10-year-old girls. Her sense of herself as a receptacle for Matt, as banished by her father, as shamed by her mother, or as viewed as provocative or seductive by her analyst, was challenged. Sixth, the analyst's slightly off-key comment, "old-fashioned virtue," spoke to her as a literate "adult." The comment added to a perspective she was deriving from her analysis that offered some distance from her father's depreciation of her intellect—girls don't need to go to college—and wholeheartedly encouraged her to explore the world of adult sexuality as a joint endeavor. Finally, the analyst maintained a stance of optimal empathic contact with Nancy's affectivity. In so doing, filling the narrative envelope could remain in the background. It was only used sparingly when a better understanding of her feelings and needs was necessary. The envelope was spontaneously filled by Nancy when she was ready to fill it with her experience—affect and all.

The recollections about the play with Margaret provided an important contrast to the preceding material. In her play, the motivational systems based on the need for assertion and exploration, attachment, and sensual pleasure and sexual excitement reinforced each other. Aversive motivations, triggered by anxiety, guilt, or shame, appeared as the dread of cancer, but were benignly incorporated into the play (85:2:5).

The recovery of this phase of Nancy's childhood and its recognition by the analyst as signaling her "equality" connected her with the resources of her past, strengthened her self-esteem, and provided a counterpoint to the self-depreciation that was part and parcel of the model scenes. The motivational systems that had been restricted in the dominating model scenes became more flexible with the addition of a newly constructed model scene of playing doctor with Margaret. Its recall contributed to the transformation of the feelings of decadence that were a carryover from Nancy's experiences of abuse. The sense of equality derived from this phase of her life also made itself known in the treatment. With her increased sense of efficacy, Nancy reconsidered the sexual abuse by her brother and the variety of reactions engendered by it. She even began to feel some compassion for her brother, who also did not receive adequate parental guidance.

Initially, the stiff and rejecting mother and the demanding child were two sides of the same coin. Nancy could not feel comfortable about her analyst's nurturance because incestuous feelings and accusations by "the men" were stirred up. Thus, sensual longings that had been blocked through her rejection by her mother and sexual excitement that had been blocked by the accusations and abuse from "the men" had been combined. Being able to experience her analyst as "nurturing" had a doubly beneficial effect. Gradually distinguishing between her father's lap and her analyst's couch, and between her mother's rejections and her analyst's restraint, Nancy simultaneously evolved a sense of herself as a less demanding and therefore less "bad" person. She also began to distinguish between her sexual feelings, for which she could take responsibility and from which she could derive pleasure, and the sexual responses of others to her. Nancy did not need to take responsibility for their inability to control their actions toward her.

The link between the rejecting mother and overly demanding child had been broken. Nancy evaluated both her need to be told what she needed to know, and her ability to acquire understanding on her own (85:3). She told her analyst to enlighten her about what was going on. Even though she recognized that she was aware of the sexual implications of her associations, she wanted her analyst to lead. In recognizing her "message" as the "message," he affirmed her growth from child to adult and acknowledged her sexual enlightenment. To have searched for concealed motivations behind the "message" would, in this instance, have conveyed to Nancy that she still was not ready to be viewed on a par with adults and that her sexual curiosity was suspect or "not healthy." Thus, she experienced the analyst as attentively nurturant without the dangers of being shamed, infantilized, or catapulted into an overstimulating adultlike sexuality. Specifically, the analyst accepted her idealization when she observed that she understands what she says *after* he says it back to her. Furthermore, he remained a distinctly idealized figure who was neither ashamed of his sexuality nor angered by her sexual curiosity. He neither concealed sexually loaded words, nor shamed her about her interests. Even Nancy's argumentative tone could be welcomed as a reflection of her growing self-assuredness.

We have centered our depiction of the work with the three model scenes constructed from the past—her brother's sexual exploitation of Nancy from ages 5 to 11; her father's covert sexual involvement with her, primarily at age 5, with verbal threats later; and her mother's failure to provide sensual nurturance throughout her life. The fourth model scene recognized during the clinical exchange was Nancy's attraction to men who practicized ambiguity and her use of uncertainty and obfuscation in these affairs, with herself and with the analyst. Nancy's attraction to and employment of ambiguity acted as an undertow pulling against the effectiveness of the analytic work.[3] We believe her use of ambiguity was both a part of the eroticization of the transference and a more broadly based aversiveness expression. We will consider the effect of this on Nancy's choice of a love object, on her other attachments, and on her regulations in general.

As the analyst discerned that Nancy's portrayal of Dan's interest and promise of a deepening relationship was not confirmed by her rendering of the details of their interactions, he encouraged her to consider the meaning and impact on her of Dan's shilly-shallying. She was unwilling to do so in any direct way. In her associations she did recognize that her most lasting affair had had these same

---

[3] In this way, Nancy's use of ambiguity was similar to the use of dissociation, disremembering, and suggestibility of many victims of sexual abuse.

manifestations of indecision and irresoluteness on both sides. Throughout the analysis this pattern continued with a long series of men. As we noted in Chapter 6, the arena in which these issues came to the foreground was in relation to her questions about the analyst "What kind of person are you?" (83:1:3). "You look benign" (83:3:1)—a source of interest and curiosity (83:3:4). By 1985 she was ready to take up the issues with Karl, who asked her to dinner "so diffidently as if he were merely paying me back for having him over. It was weird. Then I got weird too, saying well the only time I'm free is next week. I didn't want to be too enthusiastic. He was acting as if he was unsure. I'd want to, although I think I made it clear. He was being cool so not to make it a 'date'" (85:1:1). Nancy then takes up one of the sources of her resorting to "being weird." Her mother had assured her that people's interest in her "means nothing," they are only being polite (85:1:9). Mother's casting doubt became for Nancy a necessity—don't get excited and enthusiastic, "fly off into fantasyland," and you won't be disappointed—and a resource to deal with her sexual abuse—my brother doesn't mean to hurt me, he loves me. At this time, Nancy and the analyst returned to the theme of his diffidence as a comparable obfuscating compliance. This freed her to discuss in subsequent months her sensual and sexual sensations, largely as they related to masturbation. The result was a restoration (from her prior total anaesthesia) of sensation. We believe the dual analytic exploration of her use of ambiguity in male–female relationships and of body sexual experience provided the leverage for her first orgastic experience. She had a brief intense affair with a man who brushed aside her vacillations and made an unequivocal sexual advance in which intercourse was the clear goal. This experience, which occurred somewhat after the midpoint in her analysis, was as though encapsulated. It had the effect of providing a powerful reassurance to her that she could experience a full range of sexual feelings, but it did little to deal with the broader issues associated with ambiguity. Nancy's eroticized affection remained tightly bound to her love for her brother. Her contact with him had provided the principal moments of exhilaration in her often desperately lonely life. To separate the threads of affection from the sexual abuse and sadistic torment she suffered at his hands required a long analysis of who was responsible for what. We have already noted the analytic exploration of her dream of reaching for her housemate's leg as an affectionate contact and its turning into crotch touching (85:4). In this hour, the analyst noted "In your dream you do parcel (responsibility) out in a clear fashion" (85:4:26). Nancy responded in a manner that characterized the work ahead: "I start thinking, 'It takes two to tango.' Then I lose it and I'm back to 'It's all my problem.' Then I think, 'Kids need adults to learn.' It's a real problem for that to not be available" (85:4:31). Then two years later, "With any hint of sexual attraction, I say turn everything off, turn the other way" (87:2:11) Analyst: "Lest?" (87:2:12) Nancy: "Lest I lose control. Become so attracted, I seduce them. As I say that it's not just an issue of Brian and Anthony [priests]. It was with my brother and dad . . . you—because it's inappropriate. If I act seductively it's an attempt to break that down" (87:2:13). However, in the dream of being molested by the technician and fighting back vigorously (90:1:3), the analyst noted "What was helpful was the clarity with which you could see that the abuser was out of line" (90:1:10). Nancy replied, "And the clarity of my response. I was clear and increasingly forceful . . . I'm not letting myself get muddled . . . I have to respond clearly and calmly and set the limits. My new slogan on the bathroom mirror from our discussion is *My happiness is my responsibility*" (90:1:11). And in her final dream: The boy stamping around, collapsing the side of the bank "was my brother. I have to be careful and not let him or anyone destroy the work we've done, to put it down" (90:4:1).

The same ambiguity applied to her protective muddling of her feelings about all the other family members: her father, her mother, and her aunt. On one side was her need based on her loyalty to maintain the illusions each sought—her father's denial of responsibility for his sexual arousal by her and her mother's and aunt's claims for saintliness. On the other side was her need to obscure her angry, vengeful, and vindictive responses to their often gross insensitivity. Some of the aversiveness was analyzed in relation to her phobic conviction that she had harmed patients through lab errors when she felt exploited by fellow workers as she had by her mother in housework duties and in nursing Mother during migraine headaches that were blamed on her. But the key element in the discovery of the source of her use of ambiguity lay in the analysis of her enuresis. Nancy's statement, "the problem with ambiguity is while I said I didn't like it, I tolerated it all too easily and didn't make a real effort to get things clear" (89:3:31) applies, we believe, to both cognitive unclarity and bed-wetting. As Nancy said just before this, "You're encouraging me to talk about, to think about it. I'm going back to a world where sex has old destructive ugly facets to it" (89:3:27).

Based on discrete memories and inferences, Nancy believed her bed-wetting began around the age of three or four, after she had been toilet trained and continent, and ended at age 11 with her mother's money bribe—"She finally gave me something I wanted." Nancy saw herself as banished from her parents' bedroom where her crib had been until she reached the age of three. She assumed this occurred because of something she had done wrong rather than her age. In fact, she viewed her age as a liability in that she was told to take her potty and carry it upstairs alone and put herself to bed. Her bed-wetting thus began in an atmosphere of strong resentment for "banishment" and unwanted responsibility for self-regulating. Throughout her analysis, the mutual regulation derived from the analyst's presence helped Nancy to sustain herself. During weekends she had a sense of "losing it," of her time and plans drifting away, as an unspoken message to the analyst that she needed him and that he could and should feel guilty for abandoning her. All of this became abundantly clear, but what was less easily demonstrated and more theoretical was the role enuresis played in her sexual life. Nancy had begun life absorbing the erotic-argumentative atmosphere of the parental bedroom, and then the sexual excitement of wriggling on her father's lap (as she did on the analyst's couch), and the repeated excitement of Matt's masturbation against her leg and body. She shielded herself from awareness by an assortment of defensive measures and we believe her bed-wetting facilitated both the absence of conscious recognition and an outlet for the excitement. In hours not reported in the text, during states of excitement, she feared a sphincter release on the couch. She remembered or probably reconstructed the pleasure of nocturnal release with dreams that she was in the bathroom. She had experienced a warm sensation as well as the latent satisfaction of her mother's cleaning up, remonstrations, and distress. The theme of vengeance against her mother by failing, that is, continuing to be incontinent, letting success with her dissertation slip away, came to full exploration in the 90:2 hour. That her enuresis was a manifestation of her aversive motivation is easily proven. The role her bed-wetting played in her sexual life, although less easily confirmed, seems to us a valuable link between her general tendency to ambiguity, her childhood anaesthesia, and her choice of men with whom she could maintain a facade of pursuit and sexual arousal clouded in responsibility on either side. We note that she ended her sexual activity with Matt by refusing his bribe at the same time she ended her enuresis as she accepted her mother's bribe. It is at this time that she began her symbolic play with Margaret. We conjecture that Nancy's enuresis symptom helped her to contain her sexual overstimulation without a damaging loss of self-cohesion.

After six years of analysis, the impact of the four model scenes diminished. She became painfully aware of how alone and vulnerable she had been as a child. Her self-blame from childhood onward had contained the implicit hope that if she could change, and be "not bad," not involved in ugly sexual activity or incontinence, then her life would be better. The diminution of self-blame was coupled with a sense of vulnerability, aloneness, and depression. She now became aware of a state that she had tried desperately to ward off: without the ambiguous seductive relationships and the vengeance of failure, she felt she was not special to anyone. Simultaneously, Nancy engaged a widening range of affects with more variations as she explicated her self-experience. She described the "tilt" in relation to her analyst with a sense of parity and with no apparent resentment. She moved beyond enacting her fear that he would rape her like the psychiatrist who raped his patient that was reported in an early session. She could now reflect upon and analyze her fear of seducing the analyst and her fear that he could be seduced. She could equally well reflect on and analyze her belief that by failure and lack of clarity she could bind the analyst to her through guilty concern.

Having initially felt "special" on her father's lap, specialness carried ominous connotations. Yet Nancy was able to raise the issue of her desire to feel "special" and her pleasure in feeling that her analyst was "special" to her.

The continued reworking of the model scenes (banished from her father's lap, used for masturbation by her brother, rejected by her mother and drawn to situations of ambiguity with men) enabled Nancy to acquire a capacity to feel pleasurably seductive. The motivational system based on her need for sensual pleasure and sexual excitement had become less encumbered by aversiveness. Specifically, Nancy's dread that her sexuality would lead to loss of attachments diminished.

The shame associated with sexuality also gave way, as did the requirement that she surrender aspects of her self. Initially, based on her experiences of abuse by her brother and the covert seductiveness by her father, sexuality conjured up incestuous implications. In working through the various model scenes, various past figures, such as her father, mother, brother, priest, and analyst became distinct. Differentiated feelings on Nancy's part were associated with each one. Thus, the analyst was not placed on the same level of inappropriateness as her father, and she permitted herself to flirt with him. She could do so because she was confident that he could restrain himself reasonably well, and that he was committed to her welfare.

He could enjoy her developing sexuality rather than be overwhelmed by it. The range of her tolerable feelings had broadened.

The eighth year of analysis signaled its termination. The rigidly restraining aspects of the model scenes had yielded. Although their contents could still be noted, these themes were now interspersed in newly organized elaborations derived from the therapeutic relationship. Neither being seductive nor being seduced carried the onus it once did and ambiguity was no longer necessary to blur responsibility for sexual and vengeance desires and to preserve the illusion of positive love attachments. Recognizing sexual interest, her own and that of others, became an acceptable resource in her relational repertoire. Nancy's dreams during the termination phase of the analysis retained some of the imagery of her sexual preoccupations. However, these dreams signaled that her experiences of abuse had not been forgotten, but had been "demystified."

## CONCLUDING REMARKS

Four model scenes captured Nancy's experience of sexual abuse in childhood. She was explicitly used by her brother for masturbation, her father presumably was sexually aroused by her and blamed and rejected her as a seductress, her mother's "stiffness" toward her provided a double loss and she was drawn only to men with whom she could experience blurring of intention and responsibility. Nancy felt directly rejected as well as deprived of maternal protection in that her mother implicitly sanctioned the behavior of her brother and father. Based on these experiences, Nancy's analysis required the concurrent working through of her sexual abuse and the eroticized transference that was, in part, an outgrowth of her abuse.

We place Nancy's analysis in a context in which we have argued that the thorny issues encountered when sexual abuse has occurred are best worked through by individual treatment in which the patient is understood from the vantage point of the five motivational systems. Our user-friendly principles protect the patient from a therapeutic retraumatization, while analysis of the five motivational systems maintains a steady focus on the patient as a complex person rather than as simply an "incest survivor." Finally, a self-psychological treatment mode insures continuous attention to the analyst–patient interaction, and to the analyst's awareness of his or her contribution to the therapeutic exchange.

# 9 Modes of Therapeutic Action and How Our Technical Recommendations Promote Them

Meissner (1991) wrote, "The nature of change in psychoanalysis and the explanation for the effectiveness of psychoanalytic interventions has been one of the perennial problems in the understanding of the psychoanalytic process" (p. 4). Meissner traced the trend from a strict adherence to the concept of mutative (transference) interpretations (Strachey, 1934) to the current emphasis on relational factors that began with Loewald (1960) and received greater impetus in the postulates of many object relations and self psychology theorists. Modell (1984, 1986) contributed a valuable suggestion of one way to avoid being trapped in the insight versus relationship polarization. He suggested that the content of an interpretation is not mutative in itself. Rather, the implementation of the symbolic actualization of a holding environment provides the basis for the effectiveness of transference interpretations. In addition, the complex nature of therapeutic action was debated by eight analysts (Fischer and Fischer, 1996) with respect to the centrality or balance among three factors: the attainment of insight, the intensity of the emotions evoked, and the interpersonal nature of the experience. Adding to the complexity, the "insight" cited as most relevant varied with the theoretical base: ego psychology, Kleinian, Lacanian, self psychology, Mahlerian, and social constructivist. Fischer and Fischer pose two possibilities to explain the enigma of positive results despite such clinical and theoretical differences. One explanation is "Like a broad spectrum antibiotic, the treatment approaches, though different, would nevertheless have a sufficient spectrum of 'curative' qualities to promote growth and therapeutic change." The second possibility is: "the commonalities of the treatment approaches . . . would allow the patient to take from the treatment experience that which was most useful for him or to mold the treatment situation to best suit his conflict resolution and/or growth promoting needs" (pp. 309–310).

We approach the mode of therapeutic effectiveness of psychotherapy and psychoanalysis differently. We begin with the hypothesis that a strong correspondence must exist between techniques empirically found to be effective in facilitating positive change and processes that ensure or stimulate growth. We cast our net more broadly than trying to identify from the treatment experience itself whether insight, affective experience, or relational experience is central. Because growth can be recognized in many domains, we look for correlations between biological, neurophysiological, and psychological development. We identify three processes of growth that can be identified in each of these domains and that can be described in the clinical exchanges we have presented. The three processes are self-righting, shared expanding awareness, and the rearrangement (recategorization) of symbolic representational schemas or configurations (Lachmann and Beebe, 1992). If these three modes of therapeutic action are substantiated by further investigation, then principles of technique derived empirically from the various psychoanalytic theories can be examined to see to what extent each promoted the growth inherent in each mode.

## SELF-RIGHTING

Clinically, self-righting refers to an intrinsic tendency during psychoanalysis to rebound from an altered (lower level) state of functioning to a more adaptive state. The phenomenon of rebounding to a more adaptive state is often referred to as "resilience" (Fajardo, 1988, 1991). The innate potential for self-righting is measured by the category of "soothability" in the Brazelton examination of infants. As analysts and therapists, we depend on the capacity for self-righting to enable a patient (and ourselves), after an hour of intense affective involvement, to resume the state of adaptive functioning needed to leave and return to other occupations (and to prepare our receptivity for the next hour).

Throughout our clinical account, we have emphasized the significance of the disruptions in the clinical exchange that follow a perception of empathic failure by either or both participants. Self-righting is crucial to the recovery that enables the restoration of attachment and exploratory motivations. "These highly affectively charged episodes represent 'central moments' in the therapy. They are points of potential stress, yet at the same time potential episodes of growth" (Schore, personal communication, 1995).

In the second hour (83:2) of the initial week presented, Nancy and the analyst were exploring her aversive state. When the analyst had "unconsciously been drawn into an enactment in which seducer-seduced roles became confused" (83:2:19–26), a disruption occurred. Then, with the analyst's sensing into her affect state of anger and the fear aroused by her being so angry at him, she was able to self-right. Her self-righting took the form of her being able to be fully and freely expressive of her antagonism and its source in the present and past. For the analyst to have made his contribution to Nancy's self-righting, he too had to self-right. He first had to recognize that a disruption had occurred, and that he had been responsible by his intervention. A second step was required in that he had to recognize not only that his original intervention had been perceived by Nancy as an empathic failure but that he had been manipulative, and, in saying "seems," further indicated he was reluctant to face it. Her refusal to accept his partial evasion forced him to complete his own restorative effort. He then placed himself more fully in consonance with Nancy's experience (although he did not verbalize it). He was therefore able to enter her experience of anger in a manner that she experienced as facilitative.

As a factor in development, "self-righting" refers to an inherent tendency to rebound from a state of disequilibrium, of impairment, in growth with a developmental advance when a positive change occurs in a previously inhibiting condition. The term "self-righting" was coined by Waddington (1947), an embryologist who observed that a genetic program in surrounding cells will turn off a developing tendency toward abnormal growth, allowing a rebound toward normal cell structure. In normal development, steps in physiological regulation, attachment, exploration, and assertion, control of aversion, and sensual-sexual seeking that had not been taken become possible under favorable circumstances.

A dramatic example of this is that of infants raised in the Guatemalan highlands (Kagan et al., 1978). These babies, although always close to their mothers, are restricted for over a year inside a windowless hut, often in a back sling with no toys and little human interaction. At one year of age they are quiet, unsmiling, minimally alert, and physically passive. They are far behind American children in cognitive development. In the middle of the second year, however, when they become mobile and are allowed to leave the hut, their development leaps forward dramatically. When the children were tested at 10 to 11 years of age, their cognitive and perceptual abilities were at the same level as American urban middle-class children.

Within the clinical exchange, self-righting occurs in response to many nonexploratory aspects of the treatment. The analyst's reliability and willingness to accept responsibility, to listen with care and concern, to be tactful, and to communicate affective involvement and interest, individually and together, may constitute a positive change in an inhibiting experience for patients who have experienced an absence of these relational experiences. In the 85:3 session, Nancy was depressed, limp, still and silent. At first the analyst intervened by demonstrating in his interventions his interest in her feelings—he made a direct request that she describe what she was experiencing. She said, "Fog. I feel I'm in a fog when I try to think about my sexual problems" (85:3:1). Then, with the analyst's invitation to penetrate the fog or describe it further (85:3:2), she responded by gradually self-righting and offering a very productive sequence of associations. The self-righting that ensues in such examples can be considered to be a corrective emotional experience (Marohn and Wolf, 1990). As a result of many comparable experiences, patients often learn to supply themselves with what they need for self-righting. Nancy begins the 85:4 hour by saying, "I'll spend five minutes complaining about the process and then get to work," indicating her belief that the analyst, unlike her parents, will accept her aversiveness to what he asks of her. With that acceptance, she can self-right with no further intervention required.

Commonly, self-righting can be demonstrated as it occurs in response to specific endeavors of the analyst. In the example of the 83:2 hour already presented, the analyst responded directly to the disruptions in the treatment process that followed Nancy's experience of an empathic failure. The analyst helps in the recognition of the altered self-state and, if possible, in identifying the triggering source of the disruption, including the analyst's participation and contribution. "The reliable and apt recall of details from the patient's previous discourse is part of what convinces him that we hear, think, and care about him; he can now begin to experience himself as worth paying attention to, understanding, and caring about" (Levin, 1991, p. 6). The continuity of the effort to recognize, understand, and identify will often in itself lead to self-righting.

We believe that self-righting to a restored state facilitates the expanded awareness of the meaning of the disruption rather than the reverse, that understanding leads to self-righting. Schore (personal communication) proposes an intriguing source for both disruptions and restorations. Both result from affective transactions between therapist and patient involving spontaneous right hemisphere to right hemisphere communications that occur below the level of awareness. The analyst's loss of empathic perception of the patient's state of mind, especially if the analyst's aversiveness is triggered, becomes communicated to the patient by tone, gesture, facial expression, breathing rate, and so on. The change in the analyst, possibly not realized by him or her reflectively, contributes to the patient's altered state of engagement. The patient's changed state is then communicated, often nonverbally, to the therapist. Once perceived, the analyst must deal with the aversiveness triggered by the patient's withdrawal or antagonism. Schore believes that the analyst's capacity to regulate his or her own aversive affect, especially shame and humiliation, constitutes the decisive factor in whether self-righting occurs. Following Schore's reasoning, the direct right hemisphere to right hemisphere communication provides an interactive repair with recognition and exploration as consequences, not causes.

Weiss and Sampson (1986) explain the state change we call self-righting through their postulate of a largely unconscious plan of patients to change their pathogenic beliefs by testing them in their experience with their analyst. "If the analyst's responses to the tests are experienced by the patient as disconfirming the pathogenic beliefs, the patient is likely to become less anxious, more relaxed, more confident in the analyst, and bolder in tackling his problems" (p. 223). Weiss and Sampson note that generally analysts do not set out specifically to disconfirm the pathogenic beliefs since often they only become aware of them after the test has been passed via the analysts' empathically directed responses. As the danger anticipated in the pathogenic belief is disconfirmed, the patient's inherent inclination to reduce anxiety and move forward [self-right] is activated. *After* no longer feeling endangered, the patient "was able to experience the contents fully, think about them, and use them therapeutically" (p. 185). In our terms, the analyst's successful employment of the empathic mode of perception led to self-righting. In turn, the state change of self-righting permitted greater access to inner experience and the ability to communicate, and thus to the expanded awareness of both analyst and patient. The expanded awareness is then confirmed by the interpretive sequence that *follows*.

An adult's capacity for self-righting is an outgrowth of intersubjective experiences from birth on. In the first year, caregiver responsiveness to the infant's needs in each of the motivational systems facilitates the repeated transition from aversive states to positive affects of intimacy, interest, physiological regulation, and sensual enjoyment. In the second year, as caregiver and toddler become increasingly involved in controversy over agendas, the ability of each to activate a degree of altruistic responsiveness serves to promote the restoration of intimacy. These state-transforming experiences are critical to the formation of the child's brain systems that come to autoregulate switches in affective states in response to the appraisal of environmental stressors (Schore, 1994). The burgeoning of internal coping mechanisms involves the limbic system (Hadley, 1989), the autonomic nervous system, and the orbitofrontal cortex, the hierachical apex of the limbic system that is expanded in the early developing right hemisphere (see Schore, 1994, for an extensive explanation of these seminal developments). The progressive development of the brain's regulatory functions occurs in continuous mutual regulation with intersubjective experience. Looking at the brain, the limbic system and its cortical connections are involved; looking at experience, affective transitions are central to the recovery capacity that we refer to as self-righting.

What guides self-righting? Waddington (1947) suggests that for cells self-righting is guided by the genetic plan and the influence of the existing structure. In broader biological terms, if, for example, puberty is delayed because of illness or malnutrition, when the illness or malnutrition is reversed the genetic design will guide the self-righting recovery. But what guides the adult to a restoration of sleep, or friendliness and trust, or the willingness to explore, or a renewed interest in sexuality after a wounding rebuff? We suggest that the form of the self-righting is oriented to approximate an optimal prior state. As each motivational system organizes and stabilizes, state changes occur. The state changes that self psychology refers to as selfobject experiences of maximum cohesion and vitalization (Lichtenberg, Lachmann, and Fosshage, 1992) become an intrinsically valued goal for re-creation. These states of physiological regulation, attachment intimacy, exploratory-assertive efficacy and competence, and sensual satisfaction, when re-created, become hallmarks of desired self-experience. During analysis, we can expect the forms of self-righting to be guided both by the prior optimal states of each motivational system and the self (even if fleeting) and by the optimal states guided by genetic potential that have been achieved because of the especially favorable conditions during the analysis itself. The disconfirmation of pathogenic beliefs represents one example of the especially favorable conditions that occur during analysis (and other psychotherapies).

We consider self-righting to be a powerful growth process that facilitates positive change across the spectrum of supportive, expressive, exploratory psychotherapies as well as in psychoanalysis. When we consider our ten principles of technique in this context, we believe the ones most facilitative of self-righting are (1) establishing arrangements that work to create a frame of friendliness, consistency, reliability, and an ambience of safety; (2) the systematic application of the empathic mode of perception; (3) discerning affects to appreciate the patient's experience; (4) intervening to communicate comprehension, express affective attunement, and illuminate recognizable patterns *from the patient's point of view*; and (5) following the sequence of interventions to recognize the occurrence of disruptive affect states and perceived empathic failures, and accepting responsibility for the effect regardless of the intent.

## SHARED EXPANDING AWARENESS

"Expanding awareness" refers to the growth of knowledge about the self. Traditionally, the focus of analytic theoreticians has been centered on insight into specific complexes, conflicts, or compromise formations that were regarded as causes of the illness. The traditional focus portrays one person, the analyst, who points out to another person information about that person's psyche. The view we hold is that two people are concurrently developing an expanding awareness of self with and apart from the other. And because of the need to discover the nature of a transference configuration (a new creation influenced by a prior experience), each is seeking to find the self as experienced by the other. The model for this conception of expanding awareness is based on the ordinary attachment experiences of caregivers and developing children. A parent tries to discover who his or her baby is and a baby tries to seek and confirm an identity through and with his or her parents. This mutuality of search impels the acquisition of information. The most significant information sought for is the unconscious and conscious sensing of the subjectivity of the other, organized as emotion-laden perceptions and memories of events and procedures. In analysis, in contrast to ordinary life, a consistent effort is made to bring into conscious awareness the impact of procedural and event interchanges and to struggle against collusions in deception and denial. To quote Pulver (1992) about psychic change in analysis, *"an understanding relationship cannot be maintained without insight into the dynamics of the relationship itself"* (p. 204). Although this searching is joint, what is searched for is uneven. Analyst and patient seek to find the *patient* through the *long axis* of the patient's life (and maybe one or two generations back) as a narrative construction in the minds of both. Analyst and patient seek to find the *analyst* principally through the *restricted axis* of their shared experience as an intersubjective construction in the minds of both. Expanding awareness must work against and learn about the motives for using the vulnerability of the patient or the privileged position of the analyst to restrict recognition and revelation. An example of the latter from Nancy's analysis is when the analyst had to face up to his ingenuous denial of responsibility for his participation in a role enactment (83:2:24–26).

The 87:2 hour with Nancy illustrates a successful quest for shared expanding awareness. Nancy sets the tone with a playful exchange about the payment, and the analyst responds accordingly. She then introduces the theme of the hour that leads into an area of exploration of central interest to both: "It's come up before that I'm attracted to men who are not available." Then, puzzled and stymied, she asks the analyst to help. The analyst believes she is asking more for confirmation of his presence and responsiveness than for definitive assistance, so he asks, "Give you a lead to follow?" (87:2:6). Confirmation that they "know" each other follows when Nancy restates the problem, "I need to set limits" (87:2:7). The hour then proceeds in a manner that could only occur with two people who share both an enormous amount of information about the life experience of one—the patient—and way of being together as two—the patient and the analyst. A rapid shift begins between the people in Nancy's life—Sean, Brian, Anthony, her father, her brother, the analyst, the dean, and her grandfather—and between time lines—distant past, recent past, and present. Her motives shift from being liked, looked after, and approved of (attachment motives), to being warmed (a sensual motive), to being aroused (a sexual motive). By the end of the hour, they arrive at an issue that we believe neither could have anticipated. A source of her conflict about liking men derived from the grossly confused guidance of her mother, who saw sexual threats coming from reliable, caring men and overlooked, denied, and disavowed the sexual abuse from Nancy's brother, who in her mother's eyes could do no wrong. "[*with rising angry indignation*] Why in the name of Hell didn't she pay the same attention to my brother! . . . She saw it [sexual abuse] where it wasn't and didn't where it was" (87:2:25).

Our understanding of the nature of expanding awareness derives from studies of cognitive and memory organization and of neural networks. Lived experiences are abstracted and categorized in the form of discrete events—eating, going to the store, playing with Mommy, playing with toys, going to sleep. The salient features by which categories are formed are extremely simple at first: the hunger-satiety cycle, Mother's face and voice during play, the actions in a sequence. Asked to talk about making cookies, a child of three responds, "Well, you bake them and eat them" (Nelson, 1986, p. 27). The current understanding of memory is that a "memory" or a "trace" does not exist in a single brain locus. Rather, maps or networks are formed based on one or another criterion for categorization. Perceptual stimuli alone are insufficient to activate categorization. An affective dimension is essential for creating and categorizing memories. These perceptual-affective action maps have a continuous relationship with external stimuli, the differing nuances of which activate other maps. As the maps interact with one another, information is constantly recategorized (Rosenfield, 1988). When a stimulus is repeated, such as the recognition of a pattern of an experience of mild empathic failure, the strengths of the connections that produce pattern awareness are increased, making recognition easier to arrive at on subsequent exposures. Because each pattern varies somewhat in context and texture, no response will be exactly the same, thus *each recollection is a new creation* (Poland, 1992). What is stored is not a replication of the category or event, but the capacity to generalize associatively and then to narrow consequential behavior to achieve a motivational goal. Studies of brain mapping indicate that the capacity to categorize perceptually and generalize associatively is more complex in infancy than previously thought, involving the brain stem and cerebellum (Levin, 1991). Even at this level, generalization can involve commonality of feature, response, or history, any one of which can act independently of the other—"small biases in internal states can lead to large changes in responses" (Edelman, 1987, pp. 258–259).

Still further complexity occurs with the addition of simultaneous alternative modes of processing as the frontal hemispheres become myelinated and "come on line." The influence of language and other symbol systems, mediated by a complex sense of self, multiple changing motivations, and the influence of culture, gives to exchanges during analysis a dynamic transformational quality. "At the level of concepts, categorization, is carried out neither by rigorous, nor by logical, nor by universal criteria. Indeed, there may be no single general means by which categories are formed at this level" (Edelman, 1987, p. 246).

We believe that the dynamic transformational quality of the expanding awareness that takes place during analysis is the result of the facilitation of *two* individuals sharing affective experiences triggered by event descriptions and gestural and linguistic renderings of self-experience. Hadley (personal communication, 1995) states that expanding awareness requires "the arousal of affect, at least to the level of interest and the deployment of high levels of focused attention. The highest levels of interest/attention/affect are aroused from birth by the presence of another human being. These levels can be enhanced even further if the communicator and recipient share enough common experience over a period of time." The networks that mediate the relevant experience of analyst and patient expand in conjunction with the affective arousal.

At moments, analyst and analysand experience affect attunement and shared comprehension of meaning. However, moments of coincident perspective, although confirming, informative, and intimate, are responsible for only part of the momentum of analytic change. A dialectic tension exists as analyst and patient become convergent and divergent in their sense of knowing the subjectivity of each other. Boesky (1990) observes that "if the analyst does not get emotionally involved sooner or later in a manner he had not intended the analysis will not proceed to a successful conclusion" (p. 573). Benefit to the patient is not limited to receiving "correct final answers. The patient benefits from the process of the mutually attempted, partly successful, and partly failed efforts to understand. The way in which we, as analysts, misunderstand, and we always misunderstand a lot, is highly communicative to the patient, and this misunderstanding is by no means only or always regrettable" (pp. 577–578) (see also Poland, 1988). Preoccupied with concerns about the analyst's serious errors "we have failed to appreciate that the conflict of the analyst can lead to . . . useful outcomes" (p. 578). Throughout the treatment protocol, the clinical exchanges surrounding the analyst's falling into role enactments, then recognizing his or her participation and opening the sequence for joint consideration, illustrates Boesky's point.

Most attention has been focused on the analysand's developing self-awareness, insight, and narrative continuity. Less attention has been focused on the analyst's ability to form an associative generalized network about each individual patient. These two ever-changing, somewhat parallel schemas or networks are the source of the rich, deep (sometimes seemingly uncanny) perceptive sensitivities that grow in analyses (Major and Miller, 1984; Simon, 1984). Two explanations (Levin, 1991) have been offered for the impact of joint awareness of transference configurations. One is that the relevant network or map becomes enlarged through a linkage between higher cortical levels and the affect-rich limbic system and cerebellar memory system. The enlarging of the map is achieved because the gated brain-stem nuclei "no longer block out specific limbic and/or cerebellar or other inputs" (p. 51). "A second possibility is that the patient's style of coordinating his hemispheres . . . has been altered by his awareness of the analyst's style" (p. 52) of being open to playful integrations of right and left brain processed information (Lichtenberg and Meares, 1996).

Levin (1991) implicated language, including nonverbal communication, as the carrier of dynamic affective information sharing. Exchanges with metaphoric potential "tap multiple levels of experience" (p. 12) in analyst and analysand. Levin speculates that "one's natural language, once assimilated, permanently and decisively alters brain organization. Language may not only facilitate the development of the genetic plan for psychological organization, but it may also allow for adaptive reorganization as a solution to problems requiring novelty and for the manipulation of modules of knowledge . . . it is possible that our natural language also contains recurrent hierarchical elements that can be decoded as instructions to the brain's operating system" allowing the brain to "communicate with itself" (p. 117).

We have tended to believe that understanding during analysis follows a linear path—an interpretation leads to the patient's insight, which in turn leads to change. Brain studies confirm the view that communication is both linear and nonlinear. Communication during clinical exchanges involves nonlinear gestural, verbal, and affective features and, moreover, is governed by the richness of the context created by the two participants. The microanalysis of clinical exchanges compels us to think in nonlinear conceptualizations. We begin to see how the smallest tilt in the affective state of one participant can create a pronounced shift in his or her response and often imperceptibly alter the whole intersubjective context. Similarly, the wiggle-room for activating alternative associative paths that result from the ambiguity of language (e.g., Nancy's father, Father, dad, Christ, analyst) requires a nonlinear (predominantly right-hemisphere) mode of thought. Levin states: "At least three systems are critical for the kind of discriminate learning that we associate with human behavior at its most complex level; the system of the right hemisphere, with its preferential attachments to the limbic system; the left hemisphere, with its motor system dominance; and the vestibulocerebellar system . . . critical brain-stem nuclei can either glue together or unglue these major subsystems" (p. 80). *"When the arousal level is below a certain threshold*

*of excitement, the patient's cortical activity appears to be limited to only
one cortical (sensory) association area at a time* . . . [I]f a threshold
of interest is exceeded, the brain becomes activated *as a whole*, and . . . the
various associative cortical (and presumably also the subcortical)
parts of the brain come into communication with each other" (p.
12).

Many of our principles of technique combine to promote joint
expanding awareness. In addition to promoting self-righting, the
ambience created by the empathic mode of perception is critical for
establishing the spirit of an inquiry carried on by two seekers, rather
than by an expert knower and a supplicant learner. Each needs optimal
information for the inquiry, thus we attempt to fill the narrative
envelope to learn the who, what, where, when, and how of any event
or exchange under examination. Further, we respect the message as
delivered in its richest context as *containing* the needed information
rather than obscuring it. Similarly, regarding manifestations of the
aversive system as sources of motivations to be investigated in their
own right expands awareness rather than obscures it. Discerning
affects to appreciate the patient's experience and discerning the affective experience being sought gives focus to the aim of the exploration.
The joint construction of model scenes provides a method for furthering
the exploration at a broader integrative level. Along with the analyst's
interventions, which communicate his or her comprehension of the
patient's point of view, the analyst's reflecting his or her own feelings, appraisals, and intentions adds to the substantive basis for a
joint expanding awareness of the clinical exchanges. The analyst's
wearing of the patient's attributions adds to this process. Finally,
joint expanding awareness gains immeasurably from the consistent
effort to monitor the interpretive sequence. Through the monitoring
of the patient's responses to interventions made or not made, we
are able to evaluate and explore the effect of interventions in the
prior exchanges.

Like self-righting, shared expanding awareness occurs across the
full spectrum of psychotherapies. In supportive and expressive or
cognitive therapies, the extent and depth of awareness is likely to
be more restricted. Shared expanding awareness is central to the
design of both exploratory psychotherapy and psychoanalysis. In
addition, a rearrangement of symbolic representational schemas occurs
frequently during exploratory psychotherapy. However, as we will
describe, the *systematic* attentional focus on transference configurations distinguishes psychoanalysis as the therapy par excellence for
facilitating this particular type of positive change.

## THE REARRANGEMENT OF SYMBOLIC
## REPRESENTATIONAL SCHEMAS

The *rearrangement of symbolic representational schemas* during successful psychoanalysis, results, we believe, from particular experiences that increase arousal to a level that activates the brain as a whole. By rearrangement of symbolic representational schemas, we refer to a change in the manner in which the self or a significant person (or situation) is represented (categorized). Especially when the categorization is rigidly held, the changes at first may be imperceptible, requiring many repetitions and variations of the transference configuration in order to achieve flexibility of representation and plasticity of responsiveness.

The rearrangement of representational configurations that occurs during treatment has as its precursor the changes that take place at the transition point of every stage of development. The big boy who can use the potty and wear training pants, the big girl who can sleep in a bed, the youngster who can go off to school without Mother and the mother who no longer watches over him so carefully, the adolescent who can decide when to go to bed and the parent who can leave her in the house alone at night—all of these represent transitions in the manner in which the self and significant others are experienced and represented. In this process, the sense of self and the sense of others are categorized differently, making new generalizations possible. In this way, later versions of self alone and self with others are built into representational networks while early versions remain.

During psychoanalysis, we identify two processes involving transference that lead to the reorganization of symbolic representations. The first is the analyst's assisting the analysand to recognize the manner of his or her response to the analyst's perceived benevolence or malevolence. The second is the patient's edge of awareness of unconscious appreciation of contrasting perceptions of the analyst. One perception of the analyst arises when an affect-laden transference fantasy, belief, or interaction dominates the analysis. The patient's other perception of the analyst derives from the analyst as empathic listener-observer-interpreter of the transference [Lachmann, 1990].

One perception may involve the full affective sense of being especially preferred and loved by the analyst. The other perception recognizes that the analyst interprets the meaning of being special, ends the session at a prearranged time, and charges a fee. One perception may involve the full affective sense of the analyst as hated and hating, blamed and blaming, deprived and depriver. The other perception recognizes that the analyst listens to and interprets what he or she can identify as triggering acts involving hate, blame, or deprivation, thus making the experience open to shared consideration and reflection. The one representation involving self and analyst is largely organized in a primary process mode, the other largely in a secondary process mode, the discrepancy probably appreciated largely unconsciously in both modes for full effectiveness [Lichtenberg, Lachmann, and Fosshage, 1992, p. 146].

In hours during 1989 that were not recorded in the protocol, Nancy, citing the impending ending date, was extremely angry with the analyst for taking a longer than usual time away during the fall. During the hour after his return she stated that his being away for three weeks confirmed her in her belief that he didn't care about her. In this way, he was felt to be similar to her mother in only wanting to be rid of her. In order to arouse guilt and hold his interest on his return, she felt she had to tell him she had been miserable the whole time and had hardly completed any of her dissertation. As she became more calm and self-righted she acknowledged that, actually, things hadn't gone that badly but that she was slowed down. Even going slowly could be considered a gain from the analysis. As they had worked out many times, for Nancy, fast meant being reckless like her brother Matt. Slow, careful, and thorough meant choosing to be like the analyst, but she didn't feel that closeness now.

During the next hour, she noted that even though she hadn't finished the number of pages she had intended to, she was pleased with what she had done since yesterday's hour. (In the analyst's view, the patient had continued to self-right from her paralyzing depressive affect and had restored a positive schema of herself and him that had been lost in her aversive response to feeling he had abandoned her during his absence). She had received a disturbing phone call about her brother's sons, who were doing poorly in school and getting into trouble. She had advised psychological testing and treatment, but her brother refused to follow her advice, claiming lack of funds. She was frustrated. She was also disappointed with the dean's effort to help her get a job. No one seemed to want to help—the dean with his recommendation or the analyst in providing the time she needed. The analyst acknowledged her sense of hurt, but wondered about it in the light of her prior conviction that the dean had been actively supportive in his letter. She agreed, but concluded she couldn't believe that his letter of recommendation was authentic and thought it was only a pat on the head. Why should anyone want to help her? The analyst stated that she seemed to discount the possibility that, besides fondness for her, it would be in the dean's and his (the analyst's) self-interest to have her succeed. She answered that she knew that intellectually, but couldn't believe it—although she didn't know why. She had had two dreams. In one someone said "they are not our kind of people." In the other, because of money, the analyst had had to move out of his office and was seeing her in a parking lot behind a garage. It was strange and upsetting. She was puzzled because she knew she had paid her bill.

In the next hour she began wondering about the snobbery in her dream of "not our kind of people." She recognized in it her mother's attitude toward her father's family. The analyst added, and in her brother's attitude about therapists—hers and someone for his children. She said that it wasn't his snobbish attitude about people who are weak and dependent that stopped her brother, but his lack of money. He wasn't really snobbish. Actually, he lived in a run-down working-class neighborhood and was friendly with the people there. (This was the first time she had mentioned this information.) Highly interested, the analyst invited further details. She stated that the people in her brother's area had been badly affected by the recession. Because he and his wife hadn't moved when they could have, the property values had dropped and they were stuck where the schools and all of the services were underfunded and inadequate. The analyst said that was like in her dream where he saw her in a parking lot behind a garage. He asked if he had lost his money and couldn't provide properly for her to be able to progress. No, she stated, my brother didn't lose his money—in fact, he is one of the few people there who has kept his job. The reason they don't have any money for treatment is because they spent their money on pleasures as soon as it came in. The analyst then "corrected" the view of himself portrayed in her dream: he hadn't lost his money, rather, he had been spending it for his pleasure. Angrily, she retorted, you take my money and spend it to go away! The analyst added: no wonder she couldn't believe he would regard it as in his interest as well as hers to see her progress—he's busy spending her money for his pleasure. The patient on leaving looked angry and sheepish.

In this example, analyst and analysand are engaged in exploring an unconsciously determined pathogenic belief (Weiss and Sampson, 1986) that the analyst, like her brother with his children, and her parents with her, was an impoverished, inadequate, unmotivated provider of care. The awareness of each is expanded as they explore the reappearance of the negative schema of the analyst and Nancy—first he is the familiar abandoner, then he is the failed sponsor of her future, and, finally, in a new version, he is a selfish spender. We believe that the expanding awareness of the motivations, meaning, and causal linkages of these shared experiences move the treatment forward. But the key to the specific power for positive change lay in the simultaneous experiencing of two contrasting subjective realms. In one, the analysand fully experienced the analyst as implicated in her distress. In the other, he is the person she is talking to, being open with, and having her view acknowledged and affirmed by. In the words of Atwood and Stolorow (1984), "Every transference interpretation that successfully illuminates for the patient his unconscious past simultaneously crystallizes an illusive present—the novelty of the therapist as an understanding presence" (p. 60). We believe that previously fixed expectations based on pathogenic representational schemas that tilt perceptions and inferences in the direction of negative transference configurations may be derigidified by the consistent alternative sense of the analyst as empathic coexplorer.

Looked at from the standpoint of the brain, we believe that the intensity to activate the whole brain does not derive from affect alone. An affect state might trigger only right hemisphere–limbic system processing and an absence of cognition. We believe whole brain activation results from the vitality of the joint exploration and assertion of analysand and analyst working in tandem. Reviewing suggestions of Galin (1974) and Basch (1983), Levin (1991) notes that mental events in either hemisphere can become disconnected functionally from those in the other. Affect states might block out left hemisphere logical categorization and when an affective self-experience is aversive, right hemisphere responses might be disconnected. But with the whole brain activated, communication can take place between hemispheres and with the vestibulocerebellar system as well, bringing in past experience (e.g., with Nancy—mother as abandoner and brother as idealized, successful favorite). The special quality of an energetic transference interpretive experience creates a tension between the more logical categorization of the analyst by the left hemisphere and the representation by the right hemisphere linked to the vestibulocerebellar input that draws on related past experience. The discrepant categorizations require reconciliation (hierarchical rearrangement) as part of the continuous problem-solving effort of the brain. Levin believes the functioning of the prefrontal cortex creates "meaningful relationships between complex input and output variables, even when these relationships are not obvious or do not appear logical" (1991, p. 90). The prefrontal cortex makes use of motivationally relevant experiences of self and others to compare possible future states with current goals in order to test out the sufficiency of proposed solutions—what Kent (1981) calls a "forward search" strategy. In matching possible future states with goals, the prior automatic expectation of a symbolic representational configuration of self with an abandoning or selfish other, may begin to coincide with a potentially plausible expectation of self with an available or empathic other. That is, in the recategorization of experience that follows the intense transference attribution of abandoner or self-server, a hierarchical rearrangement may allow the next categorization to be one of being with someone who is available or empathic. Of course, as we know about transferences, a renewed context of a perceived empathic failure might trigger a reactivation of the aversive representational schema, but hopefully it would be less "etched in stone."

These assumptions are based on the existence of comparator functioning capable of discriminating between discrepant experiences. Stuss (1992) described comparators that operate at three hierarchical levels. Each comparator uses values developed from previous experience, modeling, and training. The lowest level compares sensory perceptual input with set expectations. The operations of this level are virtually automatic, out of awareness, and provide facilitation for daily ongoing behavior of a repetitive nature. The second level comparator facilitates selection of responses that give conscious direction to functioning toward a selected goal. At this level, anticipation, goal selection, plan formulation, evaluation and monitoring of behavior, attentional focus, and persistence are coordinated. Comparator feedback is slow, deliberate, and effortful, especially where new or complex responses are called for. The third level comparator involves "the ability to be aware of oneself and the relation of self to the environment. This prefrontal self-awareness appears to be similar to the concept of metacognition, the ability to reflect on any process itself. This level implies a self-reflectiveness of all levels, including its own. Inputs are presumably the abstract mental representations of the executive's [second level] alternative choices" and necessitate "involvement of all functionally lower levels [of the brain]" (p. 12).

To summarize, unlike the early psychoanalytic assumption of recovering fixed memories from repression, current brain research and recent analytic studies indicate that all perceptions are to some degree creations, all memories are part of an ongoing process of recategorization and imagination. Psychoanalysis leads not simply to knowing more but to reworking, recategorizing, and rearranging what is known. When this process is successful, symbolic representational schemas and all other information are generalized and recast in new, freer, and more imaginative ways. Both analyst and patient will continue to color (categorize) perceptions and draw inferences based on expectations from prior lived experience, especially those experiences they have shared during clinical exchanges. The change lies in the potentiality to uncouple an expectation from its automatically (and generally unconsciously) being triggered and, once more free, to activate a neural network of a different representational schema. To paraphrase General Douglas MacArthur: old transferences never die, they just fade away. More accurately, we can state that intense transference experiences can always be re-created; the representational schema on which they are based remain as neural networks. The success of the analytic effort lies in the reduced probability that they will be re-created—especially automatically. Instead, an alternative network will be activated and a different experience will be created.

We believe that the clinical exchanges that take place during psychoanalysis are likely to create optimal possibilities for the rearrangement of representational configurations. The frequency; commonly, the use of the couch (as with Nancy) (Lichtenberg, 1995); and the structured pattern of listening and responding all contribute to experiences of the essential reliability of each partner to the other when both are struggling with the impact of affect-loaded expressions of needs, wishes, and desires derived from each motivational system. All of the ten principles of technique come to bear most fully during formal psychoanalysis, making the clinical exchanges rich in contextual texture and nuance and open to reflective reconsideration. Musing on the difference between psychoanalytic therapy and psychoanalysis proper, Friedman (personal communication, 1995) states "it's a matter of degree: At a certain point of fineness and subtlety of reaction, at some measure of intensity of patient involvement, at some degree of consistency of therapist evasiveness, and at some level of analyst mobility and leisure it's analysis." We believe these points of subtlety of reaction are moments during which the duality of troubled expectations and the actualized empathic responsiveness confront the patient (and sometimes the analyst) most effectively with a dissonance calling for a small but meaningful shift in categorization of the experience. Although all the technical principles are important in bringing about these moments in the clinical exchange, two seem to us particularly powerful: the analyst's wearing the attributions of the patient, and the potential for and appropriately timed occurrences of disciplined spontaneous engagements. Wearing the patient's attributions holds open the moment of experiencing the representational configuration and reflecting about it, thus providing the intensity of involvement, leisure, and mobility Friedman mentions. The analyst is present in the narrative created on the basis of the schema, thereby allowing both patient and analyst to consider the experience and its meaning. The analyst is present in his or her own mind to see how he or she may have actualized the expectation. The analyst is present also in both of their experiences as an empathic perceiver of the patient's point of view. Parenthetically, the analyst at such moments is equally confronted with the duality of the patient as demander, nag, provoker, accuser, and seducer and as participant in the clinical exchange revealing his or her motivational needs and wishes. This duality presses the analyst to create new representational configurations of the patient alone and in relation to him or her in a fashion similar to the patient's revisions in representational configuration.

Disciplined spontaneous engagements are in many ways the opposite of moments of leisure and reflection. They are part of the mix that breaks the inhuman (and unbelievable) "consistency of evasiveness" that Friedman notes. They provide contrast to the empathic perceiver as Olympian benevolent altruist. Consequently, by providing a sharp contrast, they highlight the usual empathic observer position of the analyst. In addition, they provide actualized moments of role enactments for reflective reconsideration by both patient and analyst. The clinical exchanges between Nancy and her analyst reveal frequent opportunities for the analyst to wear Nancy's attributions. As we demonstrated, they led to many fruitful discoveries and opportunities for recategorization of the views each held consciously and unconsciously about the other. Although a few disciplined spontaneous engagements were noted, they were not of the more dramatic kind that often occur when analyst and patient are individually or together inclined to activate and require immediate, affectively intense communication. Nonetheless, the spontaneous engagements we have noted had the effect of providing intense moments that opened the way for examination of the role enactments into which the analyst had fallen unconsciously. First the analyst must self-right from an unexpected moment when his feelings "had grown very near that point of unmanageable strength when thoughts are apt to take wing out of their secret nest in a startling manner" (George Eliot, *Adam Bede,* 1859, p. 469). Then the conditions become optimal for a tension between an experience of an actualized transference interaction and an experience of the analyst as listener-interpreter. Disciplined spontaneous engagements provide an optimal contrast only when the fundamental mode of communication is that of repetitive empathic clinical exchanges. Without the background of a basically empathic ambience to provide contrasting experiences, repeated high tension interactions are apt to result in the exchanges degenerating into mutually traumatizing disruptions. Then negative pathogenic expectations are re-created and reconfirmed. Such reconfirmations are the opposite of the contrasting juxtapositions of engagements and reflectively shaped expanding awareness that we believe demands reconciliation by the brain's upper-level comparator functioning. Only when this contrast dominates experience are rearrangements of symbolic representational configurations apt to occur.

# 10 Challenging Questions and Our Responses

Reviewers and audiences have asked us many thought-provoking questions about our concepts of the clinical exchange. Some of the questioners requested clarifications, some raised objections. Obviously, in some instances our explanations have not been clear. In this chapter, we attempt to address this problem by offering further answers to some of the questions raised.

## DISTINGUISHING AMONG MOTIVATIONAL SYSTEMS

1. Friedman (1995) asks if it is possible to distinguish between motivational systems. In a particular clinical exchange, can the therapist recognize which system has preeminent significance? Friedman takes a clinical example (Lichtenberg, 1989) from Nancy's treatment and demonstrates how easily another reading can be made. At a point in the fifth year of her analysis (not reported in the protocol), Nancy was experiencing apprehension as she faced a series of interruptions for holidays. She reported a dream in which she was leaning against the leg of a woman from her university, straddling it in a strange way, while she felt aroused. In the dream, she experienced confusion about whether she was being sinful and whether what she was doing would be noticed. She admired and envied the attractiveness and intelligence of the woman in her dream, as she had her mother's. She asked herself why she had the dream the night before and thought it had to do with missing the next hour and the separations coming up. She then expressed her frustration over the analyst's control over her life. Her mother had had that kind of control, but hadn't exercised it properly. She hadn't protected Nancy from sexual play with Matt. The analyst reflected to himself that Nancy's anger at her mother for ignoring the sexual seductions of Matt were familiar to them both, but that the imagery in her dream suggested she was breaking new ground. He suggested to Nancy that what struck him was that in her dream she was portraying her mother's "innocent" not noticing in a new light—one in which her mother herself was involved. The analyst drew her attention to her picturing in the dream that the sexual straddling and exciting rubbing were going on right under the woman's nose. Moreover, the woman, who seemed

215

clearly to represent her mother, left her leg there. He added that
Nancy seemed to be indicating that her mother and the analyst were
directly implicated in her confusion about sin and about whether
notice was taken of the sexual sensations and contact she sought in
response to her loneliness.

Nancy responded to the analyst's comments with a noticeable stiffening of her body. Then, after a pause, in a pained tone of voice,
she asked: Was what he suggested patently obvious? After he had
spoken, she had felt tight and tense. She had thought she was doing
so well in associating to and understanding her dream. At that point,
the analyst experienced surprise and puzzlement. Before, Nancy had
been actively and comfortably confiding her sadness about missing
him and her interest in sharing her dream. His response had been
to listen with relaxed attention while he sensed her lonely feeling
and her turning to sexual excitement in response to the impending
loss of intimacy triggered by the interruptions to come. He was
unprepared for the dominance of wishes and feelings expressive of
the attachment motivational system to be so suddenly shifted to the
dominance of motives related to exploration and assertion, that is,
to concern about her intellectual competence, her feeling that she
was caught not knowing something that was "patently obvious." As
she talked on, he reoriented himself to the role in which she had
cast him. He wondered if he might have spoken in a know-it-all
tone, conveying a superior stance of "I see through the denial and
disavowal deceptions you and your mother practiced." He could not
be certain if he had done so or not, but in any case that was what
she had experienced in the intersubjective field of their work. The
dominance had shifted from one motivational system to another.
With this shift, the focus changed to the analyst's role as the source
of Nancy's feeling of incompetence in the enactment that was taking
place.

To move back from an aversive enactment to conceptual sharing
about the immediate experience, the analyst inquired whether he
understood the situation as she construed it. He asked if she experienced him as criticizing her, as saying or implying that she should
see what he sees. Nancy blurted out angrily, "Not what you see, but
*before* you see it in order to prevent your criticism. Otherwise I get
whapped," by which she meant suddenly being transported from
feeling close and doing okay to feeling dense and dumb. After more
clarifying exposition of her view of the analyst as critical and demanding,
and of her anger, Nancy paused and returned to describing her feelings of impending loneliness and her strong inclination to replace

her closeness with the analyst during his absence by any means of soothing (cigarettes, food, sex) at her disposal.

In the analyst's after-the-hour notes, he reflected that the first cue that enabled him to identify the role enactment in which Nancy had engaged him was the unexpected change in her self-state and the corresponding change in his own. They were both "whapped" by the other, but by following her verbal associations he was able to recognize himself from her perspective as the "whapper." He was experienced by her as exposing her naivete and supposed denseness. The analyst regarded the "whapping" scene as condensing many painful episodes of empathic failures in response to her childhood efforts to receive affirmation and praise for her attempts at exploration and assertion. In this hour, an immediate exploration in depth was not required for attunement to be restored, and for the principal original theme of attachment and its loss to regain dominance. Recognition and acknowledgment of her subjective experience were sufficient to bring the disruption to an end and to enable self-righting to occur. At other times, particularly when Nancy was facing examinations (and later in the analysis when struggling with her dissertation), exploratory and assertive motives did require more extensive exploration.

This clinical vignette prompted Friedman's probing critique. The same experience that we believe constituted an abrupt shift from an attachment motive to aversive motives, related to a sense of failure in exploration and assertion, was conceptualized by Friedman as Nancy's feeling "I have been defeated in an attempt to get close to the analyst and the insult to my competence now carries overtones of estrangement from the man I thought of as my partner." We believe that this alternative formulation is accurate in that attachment motives remained active throughout the sequence. Our claim of a shift in dominance by one system over the other is based on our attempt to understand what happened when the attachment-based experience was disrupted. The evidence from Nancy's associations indicates that she felt "You caused me to feel dumb and that leaves me feeling disorganized" rather than "You pushed me away and that leaves me all alone." Stated differently, loss of closeness and sadness are neither the triggering experience for the disruption nor dominant in Nancy's associations to it. "Was what you suggested patently obvious?" and "not what you see, but *before* you see it" are statements that present enough ambiguity to warrant two readings. Nancy might be emphasizing the pain and humiliation of replacing the analyst's closeness with his criticism. Or she might be emphasizing the pain and humiliation of feeling dense and dumb in both her eyes and his because she has failed to live up to an intellectual (exploratory) goal. The analyst subscribed to the latter reading then and we continue on further reflection to do so.

As he tried out a number of variations, each of which is plausible, Friedman concluded that deciding is not easy. Thus, in offering our reading of the exchange we cannot be definitive. We can only identify the basis for our conviction. The patient's reaction and our understanding of it is embedded in a matrix of prior experience the analyst and Nancy have had with each other. The analyst knew from past exchanges that Nancy could draw pride from performing an intellectual task *well*, but under pressure she easily shifts to a competitive *better than*. And "better than" ultimately means similar to Matt, who in their mother's eyes was both intellectually brilliant and *quick*. The analyst was surprised that Nancy's reaction occurred when it did, but as he recovered from being startled he felt certain that he recognized the signs that she was experiencing a humiliating loss of pride in her brain power. To not be *quicker* than the analyst led her to feel dense and dumb, *and* subject to criticism rather than praise by the analyst, *and* less loved and thereby lost to him. With these three interrelated responses to conjure with, the analyst already had a complex mix, and the clinical problem at hand added complexity: what to do to restore the working closeness (attachment) in order to explore the motivation that was the source of the disruption. Thus, although the loss of closeness may be the immediate problem, her vulnerability to a "whapping" loss of pride, a terrible overwhelming shame and humiliation that paralyzed her efforts, was the affect that was exposed for further analysis. As the analysis proceeded, her vulnerability in respect to intellectual exploratory-assertive endeavors placed her at considerable risk of failure in her effort to earn her doctorate. Friedman (1995) clearly comprehends our position: "the patient's sequence of reactions shows that one particular vulnerability, *together with* its relationship to other vulnerabilities, predisposes the patient to a certain potential order of urgency" (pp. 450–451).

Thus, in trying to recognize or categorize what motivational system may be dominant, we can orient ourselves by the functioning called for under different circumstances and the vulnerabilities that trigger urgency. When Nancy was under the stress of preparing for and taking her orals, exploratory-assertive motives were definitively dominant. When confronted by the analyst's impending absence, attachment motives, usually heavily tinged with aversive affect, became dominant. Sometimes the shifts appeared to be dramatic—like "programs" switching on and off. Frequently, however, motivational systems interact with subtle shifts in the mix. For Nancy, intimacy pleasure, sensual enjoyment, and competence pleasure were often intertwined, with disturbances in each readily evoking aversive responses. Therefore, the question can reasonably be asked: if motives derived from several systems are often intertwined and dominance shifts are subtle, what advantage does the theory have for the ordinary course of treatment? Friedman offers an answer we appreciate: what the motivational systems "schema might do for us is to provide a provisional focus of attention even if not a certifiable, minute-to-minute, motivational diagnosis" (pp. 452–453).

### THE SIGNIFICANCE OF INFERENCE AND ATTACHMENT

2. Building on the extensive research of the Mount Zion group, Weiss (1995) asks two interrelated questions: first, does our formulation understate the significance of the inferences the patient has drawn from prior experience; and, second, in giving each motivational system equal importance as organizers of experience, do we understate the significance of the attachment motives that Weiss considers primary? We are in full agreement with the findings (Weiss and Sampson, 1986) that the recognition of inferences drawn from events helps to explain the formation of pathological beliefs and that patients enter treatment with an unconscious plan to disconfirm these crippling beliefs. For example, Nancy inferred from her mother's preference for the effortlessly quick-witted Matt and her put-downs of Nancy that Nancy would have to dazzle by her intellectual prowess to win the approval of her mother, Matt, her professors, the analyst, and at some moments, most importantly, herself. Looking back at the protocol notes, we agree that we often leaped from rendering an experience and its outcome without acknowledging the inference either the patient or the analyst had made to arrive at a conscious or unconscious explanation of its meaning. This "slippage" is likely at times to lessen the clarity of our shared expanding awareness.

We are less in agreement with Weiss's second critique. We do not share Weiss's (1995) opinion that while the motivational systems "are all important, the attachment system has a special place . . . because the infant and the young child's wish to maintain ties to his or her parents is paramount. If he or she develops problems in another system it is because pursuing the goals of that system brings him or her into conflict with his or her parents" (p. 467). As an example, Weiss writes, "A person who sees his or her parents as fragile, and so weakens himself or herself to protect their authority, may not permit himself or herself to be comfortable either in sexual or in exploratory activities" (p. 468). Or, Weiss adds, the patient may not allow himself control over his physiological functions or to be appropriately aversive. We argue against regarding all problematic effects as radiating out of conflicts of attachment. Holding to such a restrictive theory may close our minds to the consideration that problems may *arise* in any system and then secondarily affect any other system. For example, a learning disability such as dyslexia disrupts developments in the exploratory-assertive system. The child is apt to infer that he or she is out of step with others and this inference alone may be a primary source for a shame-ridden sense of self. The ties to the parent may be adversely affected by their disappointment, adding a sense of a failing self as hurting and humiliating not only him or her but others as well. Alternatively, the patients may be drawn closer by their concern and efforts to help, leading the child to infer that he or she is a person who can overcome difficulties in exploration and that when needed others will be available to help. Or, the inability of a child to experience sensual pleasure and proprioceptive activity because of tactile sensitivity may disrupt developments in both sensual and physiological regulation. These disruptions may have a consequent effect on attachment and the inferences that the child draws depending on caregivers' responses. For an understanding of the absence or presence of the effect on each motivational system we need to have a theory that informs us of those developments that are critical to each. Possibly Weiss would agree with that. The difference lies in our assumption that dominance among systems shifts from moment to moment and that no system has a special place. Problems in one system may or may not be reflected in its impact on another and the inferences drawn from that impact. Each instance must be investigated in its particulars.

We recognize that since object relations in one form or another (Bowlby, Klein, Winnicott, Sullivan) is increasingly influential, Weiss's point of view will find broad agreement. We recommend caution in accepting the prevailing view of object-relational dominance. The history of psychoanalysis reveals how easily one broad conception such as sexuality or aggression or separation-individuation or narcissism or oral envy can be convincingly regarded as superordinate. We must consider the power of certain ambiguous metaphors to stimulate creative minds to fold somewhat unrelated representations under single rubrics. Our minds have the capacity to bend ideas into single focal entities the way a lens can bend the whole spectrum of colors into a single focal glow. Moreover, in the therapeutic situation the attachment system does have a special place in the dyadic relationship and modes of communication. We can easily mistake the medium (the intersubjectivity of the clinical exchange) for the message (the complex motivations that comprise the patient's *whole* lived experience).

Following Kohut, we recognize the significance of mirroring, alter ego sharing, and idealization experiences for the quality of the clinical exchange. Sometimes these powerful attachment phenomena are in the foreground, requiring the exploration of the effect of their presence or absence on the immediate clinical exchange. At other times, these foundational experiences of attachment are in the background, making exploration of other motivational areas possible. When the background therapeutic tie is disrupted, exploration as such ceases until restoration can take place. In these ways relational (attachment) experiences are significant. However, as we explore moment-to-moment shifts in affects and associations, we believe our concept of five motivational systems expands our ability to use the clinical exchange to understand the diverse qualities of human experience. For example, success or failure in regulating physiological requirements can be recognized by particular contents, sensations, and affects that give to bodily experience its characteristic, unique quality. If we simply fold hunger into attachment, we will be less able to understand the permutations of the many physiological states involved in the regulation and dysregulation of the hunger-satiety cycle.

Let us consider a patient describing an asthma attack. The patient relates the mounting sensation of wheezing and gasping for breath mixed with his increasing fear of death. The patient describes further the feeling of waking each morning for weeks after an attack with the thought of where his medicine and spray are. When the patient feels anxiety about almost anything, he reaches for his pocket atomizer for reassurance. At this point, we might conjecture that he has inferred an unconscious belief that he has a vulnerable body, or bad fortune that he has asthma, or good fortune that he has a treatment that helps. Then he begins to remember how he would hold his mother's hand with desperation and how in his mind he has started to hold the analyst's hand to help him forestall a rise in fear that could trigger an attack. The analyst might now conjecture that he has formed the conscious or unconscious belief that being in contact with his mother enhances his sense of security. Another analyst could read the situation in reverse: The patient has inferred that he needs to be submissive or clinging or ill to gain access to his mother or to forestall guilt over aggression. All are possibilities, but why prejudge?

We believe that the most parsimonious and reasonable interpretation is that this vignette exemplifies the dominance of experiences of a physiological dysregulation. For the analyst, the task is to sense into the internal state of sensation and affect, and let inferences emerge guided by the associative flow. Primed with an empathic appreciation of the terror of feeling unprotected, the analyst can then comprehend the patient's morning arousal apprehension and its target, the medicine that reduces his sense of helplessness. Then a further shift brings the patient from a central preoccupation with physiological disruption to the place attachment experiences have in his attempts at reassurance and the restoration of physiological equilibrium. Motives derived from the system developed in response to the psychic regulation of physiological requirements remain dominant throughout the patient's associations, with motives of exploration and assertion (having and using the medicine) and motives of attachment coming into focus. The aversive aspects of the disruptions, painful chest sensations and intensifying fear, are powerful determinants of the motives for restoration of a regulated physiological state.

## THE PLACE OF THEORY IN THE HEAT OF AN IMMEDIATE CLINICAL CHALLENGE

3. How does a practicing analyst or psychotherapist use the motivational systems when confronted with the immediacy of the clinical encounter? This is one of the most frequent questions we are asked, and it is difficult to answer. Partly our difficulty arises from the simplicity of one answer: you hold the schema of the systems in the back of your mind as an orientation. Then when you need to orient yourself as to "what's going on" you bring it to the foreground of your mind momentarily. You use the five systems as you would a road map. When you are unsure where you are, you momentarily orient yourself with the map and then return to your journey.

We recognize that that answer is as unsatisfactory as saying "it's easy, all you have to do is read the directions when trying to find the right place for all the nuts, bolts, and pieces of your child's swing set." For an answer more in keeping with the complexity of the task, we need to review our essential claims. First, we believe the five motivational systems encompass a full range of human motivations and that all other schemas do so less well. Second, knowledge of the five systems assists the analyst in his or her quest for empathic access to the patient's state of mind. They provide a theoretical schema broad enough and experience-near enough to be where both patient and therapist can sense the patient's feelings, thoughts, and intentions as the patient can recognize and sense them. These are indeed large claims and we don't make them lightly. In fact, two prior books (Lichtenberg, 1989; Lichtenberg, Lachmann, and Fosshage, 1992) were written to present the evidence for the first claim, and the case of Nancy presented here is offered in support of the second claim (see also Lichtenberg and Kindler, 1994; Ringstrom, 1995).

The essential elements of the five systems and their component elements are, we believe, easily learned cognitively. Central to the use of the theory is the role of affects, those that are triggered in each experience, those that are re-created as reaffirmations of the sense of self, and those that are sought for their lasting or temporary soothing or vitalization. Our conception of affects is the orienting guide we ourselves follow as we participate in clinical exchanges. We address affects as our first way to establish with the patient our empathic comprehension of the patient's message. Thus, the affects that are triggered in each motivational system, in conjunction with identifying the aims of the patient, are our way to verify our identification of the dominant system and our way to use our theory to be experience-near. We have trained ourselves and those who have learned from us to appreciate affects and goals without conscious "obsessing" during an hour. Once the general ideas have been mastered, we believe they can be applied intuitively as a comfortable means of orientation and the language of the patient and analyst can flow easily toward and from this orientation. We also believe that when therapists become aware of repeated failures in comprehension and communication, they can benefit from a moment's reflective consideration of the motivational system they believe they are interpreting and whether the patient may be expressing the dominance of another system. To summarize, we offer the motivational systems so that a therapist holding them in the back of his or her mind (preconsciously) may intuitively have greater empathic success. In addition, in the inevitable instances of empathic failure, identifying the dominant motivational system of both therapist and patient, especially mismatches between them, provides a means to "diagnose" a possible source of the failure (Lichtenberg and Kindler, 1994).

THE SIGNIFICANCE OF EARLY EXPERIENCE
AND THE USE OF MODEL SCENES

4. Arlow (1990) challenges the significance we place on early lived experience and our use of model scenes. He points to theories that use infant research as the source of the phenomenological error in which the analyst foists on the patient's associations an interpretation based on a model concept of pathogenesis. (See Ellman, 1991, for a detailed review of this critique.) Arlow takes up our claim that research and direct observation provide us with model scenes closer to the lived experiences of the child and that these normal and pathological prototypes facilitate the analytic process. In making his charge of "foisting," Arlow (1979) implies that we would not use the same criteria as he for evidence that a supposition is worthy of consideration: "Material in context appearing in related sequence, multiple representations of the same theme, repetition in similarity, and a convergence of the data to one comprehensible hypothesis constitute the specific methodological approach in psychoanalysis used to validate insights obtained in an immediate, intuitive fashion in the analytic interchange" (p. 203). Two examples from Nancy's treatment might serve as "tests." Viewing Nancy's history through the filter of the analyst's theory of normal and pathological development and motivational systems, he hypothesized that Nancy and her mother had a fundamental disturbance in their attachment experience with each other. The infant's care by her father and grandfather during the first months would be suggestive but not conclusive even at a theoretical level because on reunion a positively motivated mother could woo her baby into establishing a strong attachment bond. So the theory leaves it open.

What can we say about the analytic experience? We believe that anyone reading the verbatim exchanges would conclude that following "the guidelines of context, contiguity and convergence" (Ellman, 1991, p. 279), Nancy's longing, clinging, and seeking for affectionate, nurturant responses were intense throughout the treatment. These affective markers of attachment needs, desires, and wishes were reinforced in the analyst's mind by associations to breasts, to bottoms, to soft, rounded female body parts. A model scene that analyst and patient developed together was of her pulling on and clinging to the analyst for caring responses while he, like her mother, stiffened as she pulled on a leg for support and attention. Pulling on and leaning against legs reappeared in dreams, shifting, as did Nancy's quest, from the desire for intimacy to sensual and sexual desires.

The second example is more open to doubt. Nancy's memory was that she had continued to eat while sitting on her father's lap until the age of five, and then suddenly was expelled. She had no explanation for this hurtful dismissal. During an hour in which Nancy talked about this experience, the analyst became aware of sexual arousal. He wondered about the source because Nancy's tone was mournful and resigned. Then he noticed her body movements on the couch, which struck him as an unusual amount of wriggling. The analyst then had a spontaneous image of Nancy as a little girl wriggling around on her father's lap, with her father becoming aroused. Consciously or unconsciously, father and daughter knew what was happening—probably not for the first time. Her father possibly in fear of his arousal, ejected the child without explanation of the actual cause. This construction was solely the analyst's, based on his conception of the sensual-sexual system of both father and daughter.

Although Arlow and others could regard the subsequent interpretations to Nancy of the analyst's conjecture as "foisting" a model scene from childhood, the source of the information fulfills Arlow's criteria of having been "obtained in an immediate fashion in the analytic interchange." Moreover, in keeping with our concept of the joint construction of model scenes, the analyst offered his speculation in the spirit of an open-minded inquiry. For Nancy, at the time and subsequently throughout the analysis, this construction made eminent sense. She did not have direct confirmatory memories. She did provide many associations of what she regarded as her father's duplicity in walking around exposed, observing her interest, and chastising her for it. This often-repeated theme was the basis for the analyst's interpretation (83:2:8) of his presence as a trigger for her excitement. In a still more generalized form, the core ambiguity of nurturant "asexual" men and their actual or fantasized sexual interest in her was a repetition of similarities to her experience on her father's lap as she wiggled about. This constituted a central theme of the criteria for her choice of the men to whom she most commonly responded. Again, we subscribe to the criteria Arlow clearly articulates. We believe we are documenting "a convergence of the data into one comprehensible hypothesis . . . obtained in an immediate, intuitive fashion in the analytic interchange" (Arlow, 1979, p. 203).

## THE AVERSIVE MOTIVATIONAL SYSTEM

5. Jones (1995) disagrees with our concept of an aversive system comprising responses of antagonism or withdrawal. In Jones's view,

"fear and rage represent two very different motivational systems" (p. 49). The affect of fear acts as a signal of a system designed to protect physical safety, whereas rage serves as a monitor of what Jones calls the "competitive/territorial" system. Thus aggression "serves the very specific adaptive function of allocating scarce resources, such as food, mates, and territory" often "through the establishment of dominance hierarchies" (p. 50). We believe that Jones makes a good case for the significance of competitive/territorial strivings and their organizing influence, especially in latency children. We might view Nancy and Matt as competing for the territorial possession of their mother, a competition Nancy felt Matt won from the very beginning. Rather than territoriality, we have referred to agenda choices and demands and the inevitability of clashes of agenda between child and parent, between siblings, and between patient and therapist. We can benefit from being more aware of and sensitive to issues of competition of territorial nature. Nevertheless, we prefer to retain our conception of a single aversive system. Our infant and clinical observation suggests that an experience to which a person responds as aversive will trigger individual variations and combinations of fear, anger, shame, and sadness with subsequent combinations of antagonism and withdrawal. Activities that involve competition need not be aversive at all. They need not arouse rage, shame, or fear. Rather, competition may fall in the area of exploration and assertion evoking interest, efficacy, and competence. Or competitive rivalry may fall in the area of attachment and enhance the joy of intimacy with the invigoration of winning a loved one's positive response. Moreover, aversive responses are a necessary prelude to the use of judicious combinations of antagonism and withdrawal that permit one to be effective in managing controversy, in experiencing power and the confidence it builds, and in setting internal limits that guard against guilt- and shame-inducing excesses.

## THE EMPATHIC MODE OF PERCEPTION

6. Josephs (1995) questioned our employment of the empathic mode of perception: "To speak of empathic *perception* rather than of empathic *understanding* seems to imply something that approximates direct access to the patient's subjective experience" (p. xiv). Josephs sees us as indicating that through our attempt to understand from within the perspective of the analysand, we "imply that this situation is something over which the analyst has some degree of control rather than consider the possibility that the analyst's perception of reality saturates the clinical encounter" (p. xiv). In our delineation of the

empathic mode of perception, we do not believe we have implied that we have direct assess to the patient's subjective experience. Josephs's critique makes us wonder if we have been unclear in the significance we ascribe to empathic perception in the clinical exchange. In our view, the empathic mode of perception demarcates a listening stance that is aimed at understanding the patient's experiential world from within the frame of reference of the patient. Rather than representing an easy route to direct access, empathic listening is a difficult endeavor requiring considerable training and extensive experience with each patient. The closest an analyst can claim to a direct assessment of the subjective experience of a patient lies in the recognition of and attunement to some common overt emotional expressions. Joy at a welcomed success, sadness at a death, and anger at an insult offer immediate entry into the affective state of a patient. The work of expanding our joint understanding must follow.

We are uncertain what Josephs means by the analyst's reality saturating his perception. In all our statements we have emphasized that all perception is guided by expectations based on prior experience. Thus, we speak of the *influence* any observer, including a trained empathic listener, brings to bear on what is being observed. We believe, however, that "saturation" of the clinical encounter by the analyst's preconception represents a failure of empathic perception, not a constituent or outcome of it. The patient's influence on the coconstructed meaning arrived at during the clinical exchange is inevitably enhanced by our primary focus on understanding from within the patient's perspective. We see the analyst as able to shift between an empathic mode of perception and another source of information, that of an external observer (Lichtenberg, 1983) or what Fosshage (1995a) has called an "other-centered" perspective. When an analyst views the patient as attempting to control, seduce, or amuse him or her, the analyst is regarding the patient from an other-centered perspective. The therapist then needs to return to the empathic mode and inquire about the patient's intent from the patient's point of view. A further source of information (and a major safeguard against "saturation" by the analyst's reality) lies in the inward directed (introspective) focus analysts maintain on their own state of mind—their feelings, attitudes, experiences, and motives.

Rather than regarding the issue of the analyst's influence on his or her perceptions as a weakness of the empathic mode of perception, we consider the search by patient and analyst for evidence of the inevitable occurrence of influence to be a source of valuable information about the workings of the intersubjective context. The controlled setting within which the clinical exchanges occur provides propitious opportunity for therapist and patient to sort out, as best they can, the influence each may feel is exerted by the preconceptions of the other.

## THE ANALYST'S INFLUENCE ON TRANSFERENCE

7. Another question about influence arises from our contention that a patient's transference experience is variably codetermined by patient and analyst. How do we assess the extent of the influence on a patient of the analyst's verbal and non-verbal activity? At times the patient's expectations based on past experience are so intense that the patient will require little more of the analyst than his or her presence to re-create a particular experience. On the other end of the continuum, the analyst's comments, attitudes, affects, and actions can speak so loudly that virtually no patient could ignore them. An analyst's sarcasm, despair, or seductiveness will immediately and directly influence the patient's view of the analyst and the safety of the setting. In between are the many experiences of greater subtlety that derive from the particularities and susceptibilities of each partner. Many factors come into play in sorting out these mutual interactive influences. When a patient's influence on the analyst is not intense the analyst is freer to investigate his or her influence on a patient's here-and-now transference experience. The analyst can track closely the patient's experience during their exchanges to understand the genesis of the way he or she is being experienced. If a patient feels distraught, the analyst will inquire when and how the patient's experience began. The analyst can surmise his or her possible contribution and inquire about it. This inquiry, including the analyst's acknowledgment of his or her activities, invites the patient to confirm or disconfirm the analyst's view. Each may help to validate the experience of the other. Moreover, the spirit of inquiry invites the patient to feel safer in bringing forth perceptions of the analyst that the patient had been afraid or ashamed to acknowledge.

A complicating factor in determining the factors in a subtle, mutually altering intersubjective context is the changes made by each of the partners. Traditionally, analysts have been apt to view changes in the patient as being the principal variable. Contemporary experience recognizes that this perspective was simplistic. We believe that the analyst must be sufficiently open to change (Balint, 1968, described it as "pliable") to be interactionally shaped by the patient. The analyst's openness to change influences the treatment in significant ways. On occasion, an analyst will modify his or her behavior sufficiently to prevent replicating a traumatic experience for the patient. The therapist may be conscious of his or her reasoning or may change more intuitively, sensing an impending disruptive affect state. The analyst's modification in approach enables a patient to have alternative experiences to expectations based on the patient's prior lived experience. Aware of the stiffening or refusal Nancy assumed was in the analyst based on her experiences with her mother, the analyst interpreted this assumption in a warm tone that implicitly conveyed reassurance of his responsiveness.

The analyst's openness to influence by the patient often leads the analyst to take a stance in opposition to a conscious or unconscious accommodation to a patient's needs or wishes. This occurred at a point in Nancy's analysis when the analyst refused her request-demand for a fee adjustment which she had expressed as an absolute need. The effect of the analyst's response to such verbal and especially nonverbal pressure is to experience himself or herself being pulled into a role enactment concordant with the patient's re-creation of a prior traumatic experience. Our thesis is that when we as therapists allow ourselves to be pulled into a role experience, we can then access levels of "participant" (Sullivan, 1974) sensitivity. Then, once having extracted ourselves, we regain a perspective that facilitates awareness. Through wearing the attribution made or implied in the experience, we are in an optimal position to analyze the relational scenario (Gill, 1982; Hoffman, 1983).

## PSYCHOANALYSIS AND PSYCHOTHERAPY

8. Many members of audiences who have heard us present our concepts have asked: Since you use analyst and analysand, therapist and patient interchangeably, do you make a distinction or not? If your techniques are meant for analysts practicing analysis, are they of any help to someone who sees patients or clients once or twice a week or for brief psychotherapy? We organized our book around a specific case example that we regard as "analytic." Nancy was seen three times per week lying on a couch with the analyst positioned behind her and to the side so that he could observe her facial expression. These formal aspects of the traditional analytic frame are not the criteria we use to regard a treatment as "psychoanalytic." As our title indicates, we begin with the clinical exchange. One view of the exchange is that one person describes his or her experiences to another in the expectation that the therapeutic skills and training of that

professional will facilitate a beneficial effect. Another view is that a professional hopes to facilitate a beneficial effect by encouraging a troubled person to reveal as openly as possible his or her state of mind and experiences. The therapist-analyst intends to institute an exploration of the patterns and meanings inherent in the communicative exchanges that take place between himself or herself and the patient. Using these two views, the one from the patient's motives and agenda, the other from the therapist's motives and agenda, we can say an "analytic approach" is one that works to facilitate self-righting, a joint expansion of awareness, and the rearrangement of symbolic configurations. Looked at in this way, analysis and psychoanalytic psychotherapy are essentially identical in design: establishing a clinical exchange that optimally opens a path to awareness, thereby increasing flexibility of choice and response. Our principles of technique are formulated to promote the type of clinical exchange between the particular therapist-patient pair that explores communications and elucidates the meaning of experience. We believe that we approach each clinical exchange with the same principles of technique whether the patient is seen four times or one time a week and whether it is for long-term or brief psychotherapy (Ringstrom, 1995). We hope to have established a basic functional interrelationship between the essential features of the clinical exchange, the ten principles of technique, the motivational systems, and the modes of therapeutic action we describe. The difference between a formal analytic arrangement and a more limited frequency of sessions and length of treatment lies not in the approach we take, the technique we employ, or the goal to expand awareness, but in the *opportunity* to activate each of the modes of therapeutic action.

## INTERNALIZED OBJECTS AND
## PROJECTIVE IDENTIFICATION

9. Object-relational analysts ask whether our use of model scenes is not an attempt to address the same issues they refer to as internalized objects. They further ask why we do not recognize projective identification as the primary response that influences (controls) the analytic situation of traumatized patients or that influences (controls) the analytic situation in general.

We distinguish between internalized objects and model scenes. Model scenes (see Chapters 2 and 3 of *Self and Motivational Systems* for a full discussion of this topic) are constructed by analyst and patient. In contrast to internalized objects, model scenes are coconstructed. Internalized objects are understood to have been acquired by a patient through processes of projection and introjection. These internalized objects color the patient's experience, distort interpersonal relationships, and exercise a dominating power over the patient's affective life. However, they reside within and belong to the patient. In relation to internalized objects, the analyst may be a target for their (re)projection, and observe, comment, and offer interpretations about their presence and power. The analyst thus is an observer and interpreter of the patient's internalized objects, but is a cocreator and coorganizer of model scenes.

A model scene captures important themes, transference relationships, or character styles of the patient in literary, imagistic, or metaphoric terms. Its source is coconstruction, not a process of projection and (re)internalization. Each analyst–patient dyad constructs its own model scenes. Different analysts treating the same patient might construct different model scenes in the course of an analysis.

We find the concept "projective identification" a most problematic one. We prefer to regard the analyst as being "pulled" by the patient into various "roles." Engaging in and interpreting a variety of enactments with a patient is an ever-present part of treatment. We would argue that if a therapist were to completely avoid being pulled into any enactments with the patient, the treatment would lack passion and probably never get off the ground. In wearing the patient's attributions, we address the necessity for the analyst to accept the patient's "pull" in order to be able to analyze it.

We agree with Gill (1994) that projective identification has become an interactive rather than a one-person concept. It does deal with the effect on the analyst of the ascriptions of the patient. Gill states that an "intent in projective identification is to make the other person feel that which the projector is disavowing" (p. 102). We believe that role enactments and role engagements are likely to have precisely this same effect. Implicit in projective identification is the belief that the analyst's experience vis-à-vis the patient constitutes a direct, readable projection of what the patient is disavowing. Frequently we feel that conceptualizing role enactments offers a more flexible accounting of a coconstructed fluid experience. A therapist will pick up in or out of awareness a feeling or attitude or atmosphere resonant with the patient's conscious or unconscious state. When this occurs, it provides a valuable source of information about the intersubjective context of the treatment and often leads to effective model scene constructions. However, often the therapist's comforts and discomforts, thoughts and fantasies are not resonant with the patient's overt and covert communications in the fashion of a tuning fork. To assume that they are and then to proceed on the basis of that assumption is hazardous. Doubtlessly all would agree to that statement in principle. Our concern is that the theory of projective identification may lead an analyst who is convinced by his or her emotional or physiological response to regard a patient who objects to an interpretation based on the assumed projection as resisting rather than questioning the validity of the analyst's own assumption. We readily accept the view that the analyst's experience is coconstructed with the patient, but the specific input of patient and analyst to each other needs to be investigated with a great deal of openness. To assume, a priori, that the analyst's experience equals the patient's projection assumes a degree of objectivity on the part of the analyst that we are reluctant to claim.

According to Gill, in projective identification, the patient may hope to find in the analyst a good example, someone who will be able to deal with the attributions of the patient in a mature way. From this view, the analyst is expected to provide a good example of how to deal with unjust accusations. Unfair accusations, misassigned responsibility, and other unjust attributions were issues that had to be resolved many times during Nancy's analysis, using the theoretical frame we prefer. We do not believe it is necessary or useful to single out any phenomenon of role responsiveness or role enactment with a special designation of projective identification. Throughout an analysis, the analyst provides an example of a responding reacting partner in the clinical exchange. How well the analyst accepts idealization, responds when under attack or being seduced, and maintains a rein on the analytic ambience, provides "examples" to the patient. How the analyst deals with accusations is but one subset of these examples that we have included in our discussion of wearing the attributions.

Were the analyst to be expected to provide an example of "mental health," "freedom from neurosis," or "normalcy" for the patient, the analyst would be placed in an untenable superior position. Schafer (1983) pointed out that the analyst may only be an example of greater maturity because he or she is under relatively less pressure than the patient during the analytic hour. But, Gill adds, "an analyst who is ever alert to his (or her) participation in the process may be under as much, if not more, stress than the patient" (1994, p. 103). (See also Friedman, 1988.) We totally agree with Gill and Friedman. Our hope is that the technical principles we have spelled out, while adding to the analyst's responsibilities, may also provide the analyst with guidelines that offer some relief from these pressures.

## GROUP PSYCHOTHERAPY

10. R. Segalla (personal communication, 1995) asked if group therapy might not often be a valuable addition to the diadic clinical exchanges we delineate. She believes that treatment in a group might be called for—especially when the personality of an analyst and his or her responses and interventions might not directly elicit all of a patient's primary problematic organizing patterns. Segalla suggested that group therapy would provide a broader opportunity for creating new intersubjective contexts and thereby triggering transference configurations. We agree with her point and feel that the efficacy of group therapy is related to the presence of both therapists and group members. The multiplicity of involved participants often triggers a broad range of repetitive transference configurations and provides an opportunity for psychologically reorganizing encounters.

## DREAM INTERPRETATION

11. When we have presented our organization model of dream formation and dream interpretation, the following questions consistently emerge: 1) How does our model account for nightmares? 2) Are all dreams progressive? 3) Are dreams ever disguised? 4) If dream images are not viewed as disguised stand-ins for the analyst, will the transference be missed? 5) Don't dreams have more than one meaning?

1) Nightmares are experiences during which frighteningly intense conflicts and affect reactions are insufficiently managed and modulated by dream mentation. These dream states correspond with intense anxiety states that occur during waking mentation in which affect containment fails leading to disturbed affect-cognitive states (Chapter 5).

2) While we posit that the supraordinate function of dream mentation, like waking mentation, is to develop, maintain, and restore psychological organization, any momentary dream mentational effort varies in the success of these functions. Moreover, conflict can occur between the function of developing the new organization or restoring the old. In one dream, a dreamer may restore an older, more familiar self-percept (organizing pattern), despite the percept's being devitalizing and inhibiting. In another dream, a dreamer may develop a more positive self-percept, which is vitalizing despite the fear that

the new percept could lead to a loss of connection with a significant attachment figure. Dream mentation, like waking mentation,
may indicate moves forward, static, or backward.

3) Although aversiveness (see our understanding of defenses, in
Lichtenberg et al., 1992) often emerges in dreams, we do not believe
that it results in a disguising translation of dream imagery. We subscribe
to the view that dreams are a product of the brain's continuing
mentational process of organizing experience rather than that they
serve the function of protecting sleep. Although a dreamer might
choose to use a less anxiety-inducing image to stand for another, we
believe that dreamers typically choose images on the basis of meanings that further aid them in their mentational efforts. The aversive
function may be directly apparent in the dream or it may emerge
when juxtaposing a dream with the previous waking state. For example,
in Freud's Irma dream, the dreamer's aversiveness in the form of
discrediting his critics was directly apparent in the dream. The dreamer's
efforts to discredit could only be understood from Freud's depiction
of the events of the preceding day as his effort to protect and restore
his self-esteem.

4) Therapists who view dream images as a nonlinear, metaphoric
language that conveys a working out of problems, rather than as
disguised stand-ins for something else, position themselves to explore
more effectively the choice of images and their meaning. Moreover,
to view dream images as more directly revelatory than not, validates,
rather than undermines, the patient's dream language and experience, all of which supports the dreamer's conviction about his dreaming
experience.

What about transference? A patient may relate a dream to a relational encounter outside the analysis and may not directly associate
to the analyst. If the analyst believes that the particular thematic
experience under consideration is also operative in the analytic relationship, the analyst can easily bring it into the analytic relationship
by inquiring, "Are you experiencing that here, too?" Addressing the
transference does not require translation of dream images. Moreover,
to translate a dream image as a stand-in for the analyst without
inquiry and validation creates the danger of assuming that the thematic
experience apparent in the dream is currently operative in the analytic
relationship when it may not be. To make this assumption tends to
rivet the patient to this particular thematic way of experiencing, just
at the time when the patient may be experiencing the analyst in a
different way.

5) Analysts often say that dreams have multiple meanings when they wish to resolve a debate about differing interpretations of a particular dream. The assumption that behind the manifest content of a dream there are multiple potential latent meanings contributes to the notion of multiple meanings, for it enables analysts to make endless translations of dream imagery. Although dreams can be most complex and, therefore, involve a number of concerns and meanings, we believe that dreams, like waking articulations, have "main meanings" (Friedman, 1995); that is, dominant motivational thrusts. The dreamer focuses on particular motivational concerns during sleep. The dreamer, from a waking perspective, and the analyst will be most successful in their attempt to arrive at the dream's main meaning by emphasizing in their inquiry the dreamer's emotional and interactional experience in the dream.

## THE DANGER OF ANALYTIC "INAUTHENTICITY"

12. Several respondents to ideas presented in this volume brought up similar questions. They ask if our technical principles promote a degree of analytic inauthenticity. In stating the principle that therapy must be conducted in a "frame of friendliness," are we not asking analysts to behave disingenuously? The therapist may not always feel "friendly" toward the patient. To be told to act "friendly" may put an analyst's behavior at variance with his or her subjective state or immediate experience. In a similar vein, they ask: might our suggestion that the analyst wear the attributions of the patient provide the analyst with a means to deny or dodge his or her actual feelings and actions? Further, would not an analyst's attempt to maintain "unrelenting empathy" require an unnatural suppression of self-interest to the point that the analyst would appear to remove himself or herself from the intersubjective context of the treatment?

We would be seriously troubled by these questions if we felt they indicated that we were coming across as advocating a goal of invariant friendliness, empathic perfection, and artificial restrictions of the therapist's responses during the clinical exchange. Our basic assumption is that therapists must have an essentially benevolent attitude toward the patients they treat, what Stone (1961) called a physicianly attitude. This is part of what we mean by frame, to use one metaphor, and the background holding environment to use another. We advocate the value of manifesting this basic attitude in the same form of friendliness that characterizes any invitation to sharing of

intimacy. Often, to establish relatedness, and inevitably once intimate sharing is established, therapists must grapple with aversiveness
in all its manifestations. Beginning with Gedo (1979) and London
(1983), many analysts including us have addressed both the
inevitability and the desirability of confrontative adversarial moments
in any successfully proceeding treatment.

Questions about authenticity have arisen also from therapists who
hold the view that the ongoing interpersonal relationship between
analyst and patient should be kept free from distortions and deceptions, from both the analyst's and the patient's side. The technique
espoused by these therapists requires the therapist to be clear about
his or her personal feelings about the patient. The patient may thereby
become aware of habitual interpersonal patterns on the assumption
that the analyst's experience of the patient has general applicability
for the patient. From this point of view, the analyst would place a
particular premium on maintaining not a frame of friendliness but
a frame of "authenticity." The same "authenticity" is demanded of
the patient. Achieving authenticity in itself is seen as a goal of the
treatment and the analyst's openness to personal feelings and attitudes provides a model for the patient. Thus, while we focus on
understanding the patient from within the patient's perspective, the
interpersonal focus is on conveying to the patient a disjunction between
the patient's intentions and the analyst's experience of the patient.

We regard a therapist's overall friendliness as an invitation to a
patient to join her in a spirit of cooperation and safety—that is, for
the patient to experience fully whatever he or she feels and thinks
from moment to moment, however unfriendly that might be, and
then to cooperate in exploring its meaning and derivation. And the
therapist must of necessity feel free to feel the full gamut of his or
her emotions. In speaking of a frame of friendliness, we refer to the
general ambience of the treatment, not the inevitable enormous variations in affective reactivity that take place during the clinical exchanges
(as between Nancy and the analyst). Any reaction of the analyst is
first subject to the analyst's self-scrutiny. When the therapist's reaction is deemed to be germane to the treatment, then the therapist's
openness to awareness and tactful revelation is crucial. The goal of
maintaining a frame of friendliness as an overall ambience helps
orient the analyst away from "innocently" conveying through clarifications, interpretations, and confrontations the analyst's irritation,
anxiety, hostility, or retaliation. A therapist's repeated departure from
the frame provides a clue to the therapist that personal issues may
need his or her self-reflective consideration. Responsibility then falls

on the analyst to self-right, take his or her "tone" into account in understanding the patient's associations, and use his or her recognition in further interventions.

In maintaining a frame of friendliness, we are suggesting to the analyst that this is an optimal state for both patient and analyst to access unconscious motives and construct model scenes. When the analyst veers from this frame, it is up to the analyst to discern whatever contribution to his or her affective state was triggered by the patient in their immediate therapeutic interaction.

Our advocacy of maintaining a frame of friendliness is in continuity with Stone's (1961) and Greenson's (1967) advocacy of maintaining a "human relationship." They realized that what had passed for "analytic neutrality" can plausibly be experienced by patients as anything but neutral. We recognize analytic neutrality as a fiction. Were neutrality, abstinence, and nongratification to be actualized, it would present a potential retraumatization for patients whose lived experiences were devoid of closeness and care. Alternatively, a therapist attempting to insistently superimpose a frame of friendliness on some patients might also run the risk of retraumatization. For those patients, a therapist's attempt to maintain a frame of friendliness may evoke distrust, suspicion, and a dread of being lulled into dropping vigilance only to be invaded. "Friendly" in such a situation would be a contradiction in terms.

Other questions about authenticity arose from our suggestion that the analyst wear the attributions of the patient. Here our respondents asked: to what degree are we advocating disclosures? Are eroticized transferences subject to the analyst wearing attributions, just as aggressivized transferences would call this forth?

When the analyst "wears" the attributes assigned by the patient, several processes are set in motion simultaneously. First, the therapist is alerted as to how he or she is being experienced by the patient. Privately the analyst may then reflect on the plausibility of this perception, and may even acknowledge the plausibility of the attribution. Second, the therapist is placed in a most advantageous position for exploring the meaning of the attribution. We do not require the patient to correct the attribution and be more "realistic"—at least as far as the analyst's view of reality is concerned. That is, we are clearly not advocating a technique of reality testing, to show the patient what is real or what is distorted or misperceived. Rather, we are seeking to understand the patient's world from within his or her experience. By wearing the attributions, we do not promote an adversarial stance vis-à-vis the patient that at the point of attribution would lead either to defensiveness or, worse, to compliance and capitulation. Rather, we are engaging in an exploration that is designed to increase the patient's and analyst's access to a sphere of experience that previously has not been made available for analytic scrutiny.

In wearing the attributions, the analyst neither confesses and discloses nor denies and disputes. The issue is left open. The analyst nondefensively explores the sources, meaning, and consequences of the patient's attributions. Even in these circumstances, the frame of friendliness is sustained.

Because neither confession nor disclosure is required of the analyst, the question as to the content of the attribution is moot. Whether the patient attributes hostile or seductive intent to the analyst makes little difference from a technical standpoint, except that the analyst is alerted to consider his or her role in shaping these attributions.

We can only touch on the complicated topic of self-disclosure at this point. Self-disclosures can range from an acknowledgment by the analyst of the use of a particular "tone" noted by the patient to a revelation of angry or sexual feelings toward the patient. The analyst can be expected to acknowledge that a particular disjunction, misattunement, or rupture has occurred, or that a tactless comment has been made, and to consider his or her basis for the contribution. But the analyst may or may not share the details of his or her self-reflection. Indeed, ultimately, what may be a convincing insight of the analyst may still be subject to self-serving rationalizations. No impartial, "objective" third party is present to reflect on the rupture, to ascertain the relative contributions and relevant motivations of patient and analyst to the rupture. Rather than trying to resolve the issue by assuming that the analyst "knows best," the analysis proceeds with analyst and patient assuming that the patient's experience and attribution can be "worn" by the analyst. The endpoint of this exploration is not that the patient has to accept "full" responsibility for whatever has occurred. Rather, the benefit to the therapy accrues from the opportunity the patient has to explore the experience of being with "a rejecting lover" or "sadistic competitor" or "seductive betrayer." These descriptions would not comprise a balanced characterization of the analyst in all his or her complexity. Because themes of this nature are part of human experience, they should not be alien to, disavowed by, or rejected by the analyst. Rather, analysts can entertain these themes in their minds and wear them in the investigatory exchanges because, although hopefully minuscule, they can plausibly be aspects of any person's motivations.

## AFFECTIVE TOLERANCE DISTURBANCES

13. In response to our advocating that the therapist track the patient's affects we have been asked, "What about patients with primary problems in affect tolerance, either those patients who flood the clinical exchanges or those patients in whom affects are absent, as in alexithymia?"

From a developmental standpoint, we hold that affects are an integral part of each of the motivational systems and that they are shaped in the caretaker–infant dyad as well as in processes of self-righting and self-regulation. These processes influence and are influenced by the infant–caretaker dyad.

The pathology of affect regulation and affect tolerance is often based on noncontingent mutual regulation. Without the necessary affective attunement and sensitive regulatory responses, the infant is required to develop extensive solitary self-righting and self-regulatory skills. Alternatively, intrusive excessively contingent mutual regulation interferes with opportunities to develop self-righting and self-regulatory skills. Either disturbance in caregiver–infant regulation will result in problems in affect tolerance.

We are familiar with the effects of disturbed caregiver–infant attachment, but problems in affect tolerance cut across all motivational systems. The problem of being flooded with or devoid of affect may be related to a primary disturbance in physiological regulation and noncontingent mutual regulation. Likewise, affect disturbances may be derived from inhibitions and restrictions in assertion and exploration, and from the absence of sensual enjoyment, especially in instances of early sexual overstimulation and abuse. Each of these regulatory failures can lead to a dominance of aversiveness through frustration and rage or withdrawal and apathy.

Tracking the patient's affect—whether constricted, flooded, or modulated—thus involves tracking the motivational contexts in which the affects are embedded. When affects are markedly constricted, as in alexithymia, we attempt to sense both the possible affect from small clues of facial expression, gesture, vocal tone, and somatic metaphors. and the danger the patient fears to himself and to his ties to others. When overwhelming affect states occur, we attempt to recognize the sources that trigger the affects; the extent to which the patient has been unable to manage these intense states; and the heroic measures used by the patient to avoid, deflect, and control the affect storms and their consequences. Before individual affects can be distinguished, the therapist would recognize that a variety of affectively stimulating circumstances are responded to by the patient with predominantly aversive or negative affects. For example, sexual excitement, curiosity, and attachments may all be experienced as anxiety or dread or rage. Specifically, as the patient feels responded to or "close" to the analyst in the course of the treatment, these aversive reactions may be evoked. The therapist then has an opportunity to track the patient's affective experience in the treatment sessions. At other times, affects may be experienced as bodily sensations or symptoms. As these states or symptoms (blankness, headaches, or missed sessions) are noted, the analyst can track the specific affective experience of the patient and the motivational and situational context and analyst–patient interaction that evoked the emotion.

## SELFOBJECT EXPERIENCE

14. Another question that arose from our fourth principle of technique is "What do you mean by a selfobject experience? How can someone seek an experience they don't know they are seeking?" These questions arose from our drawing attention to affective goals of vitalization and soothing that can augment the experiences of the many emotions that are triggered in each motivational system. We believe that patients seek and gain vitalization or soothing from pursuits that range from reciprocated love relations, a chess game, a work of art, music, a beautiful day, to an addiction to heroin, food, or pain. Our audiences have easily understood the motivational goal of a selfobject experience as an *attempt* at self-regulation through self-strengthening, enlivening, and affect regulation when it involves intimacy, interest, competence, assertion, power, sensual pleasure, and physical well-being. Their questions were evoked by our recognizing that the choices patients make that are maladaptive and often self-destructive are based essentially on the same affective goals. The confusion arose when we claimed that clinically patients most commonly hide from themselves and their therapist the positive experience (often short-lived) they seek and gain from repetitive maladaptive pursuits. They will often describe in great detail the pain, horror, and self-debilitation that results from the addictive behavior, but the momentary vitalization or soothing selfobject experience will be buried, often out of available awareness, by a mountain of shame, embarrassment, humiliation, and guilt.

The need for selfobject experiences is based originally on the hard-wired "needs" intrinsic to each of the motivational systems that in early interactions with caretakers become part of the hierarchy of motivations of the person. Selfobject experiences are sought with respect to each of the motivational systems. However, the content of the selfobject experience, whether it is the presence of someone experienced as idealized or affirming, or the use of a nonhuman substitute for a person (a reliance on drugs or withdrawal into the world of computers), evolves over time in response to experiences of empathy on the positive side or ruptures in important ties on the dehumanized side.

The need that is fulfilled by both adaptive and maladaptive self-object experiences is specific to each of the motivational systems. For example, assertion in the form of engaging in a fiercely competitive activity or sensual enjoyment and physiological relaxation from basking in the sun may each provide a sense of self-enlivenment or soothing, thereby strengthening the person's sense of self. In the absence of such opportunities, because of the fear of emotional or physical harm from competition or condemnation of leisure or sensuality, self-enlivening or soothing may be sought through drugs, alcohol, or aversive withdrawal into hauteur and contempt. These reactions can temporarily modify distress in the sense of self. They may thus provide a temporary selfobject experience for the person.

To the question "How can someone seek something that they don't know they are seeking?" we respond that the seeking (or fear of seeking) of selfobject experiences is a universal phenomenon. The awareness of the goal being sought is dependent on the sense of safety in reexperiencing and revealing the positive gain involved. In tracking a patient's selfobject experiences in the treatment, we are tracking the patient's (re)emerging, tentative attempts to find experiences that will provide the affirmation that has been repeatedly sought and ruptured in the patient's life.

## THE MESSAGE CONTAINS THE MESSAGE

15. Advocating that "the message contains the message" led Paul Stepansky to ask, how wide is the message? Does the message include everything in an hour or a sequence of hours? Is there one message before a disruption and a second message during the disruption? Is the message to be considered an intrapsychic expression or is it constructed intersubjectively?

In advocating that "the message contains the message" we are recommending that analysts begin their exploration by taking the patient's communications at face value before looking "beneath the manifest content." When a patient reports a dream and adds "it was not about you, the analyst," analytic wisdom has dictated that the negation is defensive, and should be so interpreted. Similarly, analysts have been taught that when patients speak about the present they are resisting remembering the past just as when patients speak about the past they are resisting addressing the transference.

We are advocating that the patient initially be taken at his or her word. First explore the conscious intent of the patient's communication. The dreamer who stated that his dream was not about the analyst may be expressing a strong need and desire to consider a relationship, conflict, or problem in his extra-analytic life and does not want to be dragged into a ritual focus on the "transference." Furthermore, the message includes not only what the patient says, but the tone, manner, affect, body language, and gestures with which the message is conveyed. The visible and auditory communications of the patient are all part of the message.

We begin at the surface before we proceed further. To infer, interpret, and plunge beneath the surface may leave the patient feeling puzzled and excluded. By responding directly to the full explicit message we are more likely to engage the patient in a joint exploration of its associative links and implications. Such joint exploration includes the patient's participation in the analytic process and enables the analyst to understand the patient from within the patient's experience. This technical recommendation is in line with our principle of gradually expanding the range of accessible material, thereby enabling the patient to access ever more previously inaccessible material. In this sense, today's concealed communication will be tomorrow's message. But, when offered as "the message," analyst and patient are in a better position to utilize, explore, and interpret this now "experience-near" communication.

By the time the analyst "gets" the message, it may already have been communicated by the patient for a number of sessions, or may just have been brought up by the patient in the preceding moments of the analytic hour. Yet, even if it is only relevant during the hour in which the analyst "gets" it, the message may have been developing over some time during previous sessions. We thus assume that the message, as understood by the analyst, has relevance for a portion of the patient's life, whether it is heard in only one session or in a series of sessions.

We are not proposing that the underlying, latent, or concealed implications of the patient's message be ignored. Rather, we want to avoid the possibility that the patient is put through an experience of having his or her communications and intentions dismissed, or worse, of surrendering his agenda and accepting the analyst's omniscience. Furthermore, preemptive analytic interpretations of "the message" run the risk of being theory driven and experience-distant. We want to be reasonably sure that the patient is not left behind as we drop in an express elevator directly to the patient's presumed repressed or disavowed unconscious.

Because we view the analytic set-up as comprised of three dimensions—the intrapsychic, the intersubjective, and the patient's affective-cognitive state—we understand the message as derived from all three dimensions. For example, the message may be that the patient is in a state of hopelessness and helplessness. However, this affective state of the patient may be derived from a traumatic past, or may be a way of warding off a currently threatening hopeful expectation that is felt to be destabilizing (an intrapsychic defense), or may be a response to the analyst's excessive optimism in the face of the patient's despair (an intersubjectively organized transference reaction). These three sources are not mutually exclusive. Derived in some proportion from all three sources, all three dimensions need to be addressed. However, in the example just cited, "the message contains the message" means that the patient's *state* as currently experienced takes precedence.

## FILLING THE NARRATIVE ENVELOPE

16. Is there an inherent contradiction between filling the narrative envelope and tracking the patient's experience? We have been asked, doesn't asking for more information or details cause interruptions in the spontaneity of associations? On the surface it does look as though filling the narrative envelope and remaining attuned to the patient's affective experience are in contradiction. But we also recognize the necessity for the analyst to orient himself or herself to the patient's experience. In so doing, the analyst may require a broader grasp of details relevant to the patient. Furthermore, not to investigate relevant details may convey to the patient the therapist's lack of interest in the specifics of the patient's life or a lack of curiosity about the patient's experience.

What we have termed "filling the narrative envelope" is sometimes referred to as "conducting a detailed inquiry" and is central to the conduct of an analysis as proposed by Levenson (1992) and Mitchell (1993). These analysts advocate asking questions such as "What happened? What was the precise sequence? Who did what, when, and to whom?" (Mitchell, 1993, p. 106). Such inquiry is based on the assumption that it is crucial to know "what people actually do with each other and the strategies they have learned for being a person with other persons" (p. 106). To these authors, the detailed inquiry serves to dispel ambiguity and omissions. It is a technique designed to expose self-deceptions and to reveal unconscious concealment—a central goal of analysis for these authors. In contrast, our goal is to facilitate our empathic perception. We fill the narrative envelope to gain the knowledge of the patient's lived experience that permits the analyst to sense into the patient's state of mind and motivation.

The place held by inquiring into the subtle details that constitute a lived event or a fantasy must be balanced against the relative importance of tracking the patient's affect and the selfobject experience sought. Judiciously filling the narrative envelope keeps the analyst aware of important circumstances of the patient's life; conveys the analyst's interest, concern, and curiosity to the patient; and maintains the ambience that is essential for analyst and patient to traverse the path to awareness.

Another group of respondents to our presentations has asked, "does not filling the narrative envelope tilt toward a linear or cognitive emphasis in treatment?" If that was the only "technique" we advocate, the concern would certainly be warranted. However, we consider filling the narrative envelope one of several ways by which treatment is best conducted. All of our principles need to be kept in balance. That is, the analyst follows the exigencies of the treatment. The techniques we propose are guides for formulating propitious interventions. Filling the narrative envelope is balanced with tracking the patient's affect, and our focus on affect is balanced by building a body of knowledge about events, cognition, and broader life experiences. Concern is warranted only when a technical procedure is carried out to an extreme, and the ambience of the total treatment relationship is thereby compromised.

## TERMINOLOGY

17. After a presentation of the motivational systems and the principles of technique, one member of the audience expressed his enthusiasm for the ideas but said he resented hearing a new vocabulary. Why, he asked, did we not retain familiar terms like id, ego, and superego that he had spent years learning to use? To fully answer we would have to reexamine each term and present our reasoning for the choice. Self, for example, reflects our continuity with the theories of Heinz Kohut, who replaced ego psychology's tripartite structural model with a model of self as the unified structure of the mind. We have moved a further step away from Kohut's modification and refer to

a sense of self. As consistently as we can, we do employ terms that are relatively easily translated into experience. Accordingly we speak of physiological regulation of hunger or the need to eliminate. We refer to attachment as both an activity and a quest for intimacy. We describe exploration and the assertion of preferences as a motive behind play, study, and work in response to interest and in the search of feelings of efficiency and competence. Although we recognize the manifold evidences of aggression (using it as a noun), we prefer to avoid its technical use because of its embeddedness in concepts of psychic energy. We prefer to describe responses of aversiveness as a general reaction and argue that both antagonism and withdrawal are equally significant innate response patterns. While we continue to use the term "sexual," we emphasize that experiences of sensual enjoyment are more characteristic of the infant's life and that sexual orgastic excitement, however significant, is not the fundamental model Freud regarded it to be. As more general terms, we employ "systems" and "regulation." These terms allow us to integrate the concepts of biology and neurophysiology into our theory. To describe our technical recommendations, we use terms we have found useful in the past, such as the "empathic mode of perception" and "model scenes." We have coined new designators we hope are both useful and evocative, such as the "wearing of attributions" and "disciplined spontaneous engagements." In both our choice of terms and our descriptions we strive to offer the reader language that is close to the words a therapist might speak to a patient. Our hope is that the technical principles we have spelled out will provide guidelines that facilitate the therapist's conscious and unconscious choices of communicative responses in the clinical exchange.

# References

Arlow, J. (1979), The genesis of interpretation. *J. Amer. Psychoanal. Assn.*, 27:193–207.
———— & Brenner, C. (1964), *Psychoanalytic Concepts and the Structural Theory*. New York: International Universities Press.
Atwood, G. & Stolorow, R. (1984), *Structures of Subjectivity: Explorations in Psychoanalytic Phenomenology*. Hillsdale, NJ: The Analytic Press.
Bacal, H. (1985), Optimal responsiveness and the therapeutic process. In: *Progress in Self Psychology, Vol. 1*, ed. A. Goldberg. Hillsdale, NJ: The Analytic Press, pp. 202–227.
———— & Thomson, P. (1996), The psychoanalyst's selfobject needs and the effect of their frustration on treatment: A new view of countertransference. *Basic Ideas Reconsidered: Progress in Self Psychology, Vol. 12*. Hillsdale, NJ: The Analytic Press, pp. 17–35.
Balint, M. (1968), *The Basic Fault*. London: Travistock.
Basch, M. (1976), The concept of affect: A re-examination. *J. Amer. Psychoanal. Assn.*, 24:759–777.
———— (1983), The perception of reality and the disavowal of meaning. *The Annual of Psychoanalysis*, 11:125–154. New York: International Universities Press.
Beebe, B. & Lachmann, F. M. (1994), Representation and internalization in infancy: Three principles of salience. *Psychoanal. Psychol.*, 11:127–165.
———— Jaffe, J. & Lachmann, F. (1992), A dyadic systems view of communication. In: *Relational Perspectives in Psychoanalysis*, ed. N. Skolnick & S. Warshaw. Hillsdale, NJ: The Analytic Press, pp. 61–81.
Blatt, S. & Behrends, R. (1987), Internalization, separation-individuation, and the nature of therapeutic action. *Internat. J. Psycho-Anal.*, 68:279–297.
Boesky, D. (1990), The psychoanalytic process and its components. *Psychoanal. Quart.*, 59:550–584.
Bonine, L. (1977), Function of dreams. *J. Abnorm. Psychol.*, 72:1–28.
Brenner, C. (1976), *Psychoanalytic Technique and Psychic Conflict*. New York: International Universities Press.
Breuer, J. & Freud, S. (1893–1895), Studies on hysteria. *Standard Edition*, 1:1–305. London: Hogarth Press, 1955.
Broucek, F. (1991), *Shame and the Self*. New York: Guilford.
Bucci, W. (1985), Dual coding: A cognitive model for psychoanalytic research. *J. Amer. Psychoanal. Assn.*, 33:571–607.
———— (1992), The development of emotional meaning of free association: A multiple code theory. In: *Hierarchical Conceptions in Psychoanalysis*, ed. A. Wilson & J. Gedo. New York: Guilford, pp. 1–66.
Cartwright, R. D., Tipton, L. W. & Wicklund, J. (1980), Focusing on dreams: A preparation program for psychotherapy. *Arch. Gen. Psychiat.*, 37:275–277.
Dahl, H., Kachele, D. & Thoma, H., eds. (1988), *Psychoanalytic Process Research Strategies*. Berlin: Springer-Verlag.
Deutsch, H. (1944), *The Psychology of Women*. New York: Grune & Stratton.
Dewald, P. (1972), *The Psychoanalytic Process: A Case Illustration*. New York: Basic Books.
Dorpat, T. (1990), The primary process revisited. *Bull. Soc. Psychoanal. Psychother.*, 5:5–22.
———— & Miller, M. (1992), *Clinical Interaction and the Analysis of Meaning*. Hillsdale, NJ: The Analytic Press.

Edelman, G. (1987), *Neural Darwinism: The Theory of Neural Group Selection.* New York: Harper & Row.

Edelson, M. (1984), *Hypothesis and Evidence in Psychoanalysis.* Chicago: University of Chicago Press.

Eissler, K. (1953), The effect of the structure of the ego on psychoanalytic technique. *J. Amer. Psychoanal. Assn.,* 1:104–143.

Eliot, G. (1859), *Adam Bede.* New York: Signet Classics, 1981.

Ellman, S. (1991), *Freud's Technique Papers.* Northvale, NJ: Aronson.

Emde, R. (1983), The prerepresentational self and its affective core. *The Psychoanalytic Study of the Child,* 38:165–192. New Haven, CT: Yale University Press.

———— (1988a), Development terminable and interminable: 1. Innate and motivational factors from infancy. *Internat. J. Psycho-Anal.,* 69:23–42.

———— (1988b), Development terminable and interminable: 2. Recent psychoanalytic theory and therapeutic considerations. *Internat. J. Psycho-Anal.,* 69:283–296.

Epstein, S. (1994), Integration of the cognitive and the psychodynamic unconscious. *Amer. Psychol.,* 8:709–724.

Erikson, E. (1954), The dream specimen of psychoanalysis. *J. Amer. Psychoanal. Assn.,* 2:5–56.

———— (1959), *Identity and the Life Cycle. Psychological Issues,* Monogr. 1. New York: International Universities Press.

Fairbairn, W. R. D. (1944), Endopsychic structure considered in terms of object-relationships. In: *Psychoanalytic Studies of the Personality.* Boston: Routledge & Kegan Paul, pp. 82–136.

Fajardo, B. (1988), Constitution in infancy: Implications for early development in psychoanalysis. In: *Learning from Kohut: Progress in Self Psychology, Vol. 4,* ed. A. Goldberg. Hillsdale, NJ: The Analytic Press, pp. 91–100.

Fenichel, O. (1941), *Problems of Psychoanalytic Technique.* New York: Psychoanalytic Quarterly.

Ferenczi, S. (1953), *The Selected Papers of Sandor Ferenczi, M.D., Vol. 2.* New York: Basic Books.

Festinger, L. (1964), *Conflict, Decision, and Dissonance.* Stanford, CA: Stanford University Press.

Fischer, N. & Fischer, R. (1996), What Cures in Psychoanalysis. *Psychoanal. Inq.,* 16:137–310.

Fiss, H. (1986), An empirical foundation for a self psychology of dreaming. *J. Mind & Behav.,* 7:161–191.

———— (1989), An experimental self psychology of dreaming: Clinical and theoretical applications. In: *Dimensions of Self Experience: Progress in Self Psychology, Vol. 5,* ed. A. Goldberg. Hillsdale, NJ: The Analytic Press, pp. 13–24.

———— & Litchman, J. (1976), Dream enhancement: An experimental approach to the adaptive function of dreams. Paper presented at meeting of the Association for the Psychophysiological Study of Sleep, Cincinnati, OH.

Fosshage, J. (1983), The psychological function of dreams: A revised psychoanalytic perspective. *Psychoanal. & Contemp. Thought,* 6:641–669.

———— (1987), A revised psychoanalytic approach. In: *Dream Interpretation: A Comparative Study,* rev. ed., ed. J. Fosshage & C. Loew. Costa Mesa, CA: PMA Publications.

———— (1989), The developmental function of dreaming mentation: Clinical implications. Reply in: *Dimensions of Self Experience: Progress in Self Psychology, Vol. 5,* ed. A. Goldberg. Hillsdale, NJ: The Analytic Press, pp. 3–11, 45–50.

—— (1990), Clinical protocol. *Psychoanal. Inq.,* 10:461–477.

—— (1994), Toward reconceptualizing transference: Theoretical and clinical considerations. *Internat. J. Psycho-Anal.,* 75:265–280.

——(in press), Interaction in psychoanalysis: A broadening horizon. *Psychoanal. Dial.*

——(in press), Countertransference as the analyst's experience of the analysand: The influence of listening perspectives. *Psychoanal. Psychol.*

French, T. & Fromm, E. (1964), *Dream Interpretation: A New Approach.* New York: Basic Books.

Freud, A. (1936), *The Ego and the Mechanisms of Defense.* New York: International Universities Press, 1966.

Freud, S. (1900), The interpretation of dreams. *Standard Edition,* 5:339–625. London: Hogarth Press, 1953.

—— (1905), Jokes and their relation to the unconscious. *Standard Edition,* 8:9–236. London: Hogarth Press, 1960.

—— (1911), The handling of dream-interpretation in psychoanalysis. *Standard Edition,* 12:89–96. London: Hogarth Press, 1958.

—— (1912a), The dynamics of transference. *Standard Edition,* 12:97–108. London: Hogarth Press, 1958.

—— (1912b), Recommendations to physicians practising psychoanalysis. *Standard Edition,* 12:109–120. London: Hogarth Press, 1958.

—— (1913), On beginning the treatment. *Standard Edition,* 12:121–144. London: Hogarth Press, 1958.

—— (1914a), Remembering, repeating and working through. *Standard Edition,* 12:145–156. London: Hogarth Press, 1958.

—— (1914b), Observations on transference love. *Standard Edition,* 12:157–171. London: Hogarth Press, 1958.

—— (1923a), Remarks on the theory and practice of dream interpretation. *Standard Edition,* 19:109–121. London: Hogarth Press, 1961.

—— (1923b), The ego and the id. *Standard Edition,* 19:1–66. London: Hogarth Press, 1961.

—— (1926), Inhibitions, symptoms, and anxiety. *Standard Edition,* 20:87–172. London: Hogarth Press, 1959.

Friedman, L. (1988), *The Anatomy of Psychotherapy.* Hillsdale, NJ: The Analytic Press.

—— (1995), Main meaning and motivation. *Psychoanal. Inq.,* 15:437–460.

Galin, D. (1974), Implications for psychiatry of left and right cerebral specialization. *Arch. Gen. Psychiat.,* 31:572–583.

Gedo, J. (1979), *Beyond Interpretation.* New York, International Universities Press.

Gerson, B. (1994), An analyst's pregnancy loss and its effects on treatment: Disruption and growth. *Psychoanal. Dial.,* 4:1–18.

Gill, M. (1963), Topography and Systems in Psychoanalytic Theory. *Psychological Issues,* Monogr. 10. New York: International Universities Press.

—— (1982), *Analysis of Transference, Vol. 1.* New York: International Universities Press.

—— (1983), The interpersonal paradigm and the degree of the therapist's involvement. *Contemp. Psychoanal.,* 19:200–237.

—— (1991), Merton Gill speaks his mind. *Amer. Psychoanal.,* 25:17–21.

—— (1994), Transference: A change in conception or only in emphasis? *Psychoanal. Inq.,* 4:489–523.

Glover, E. (1931), The therapeutic effect of inexact interpretation: A contribution to the theory of suggestion. In: *The Technique of Psychoanalysis.* New York: International Universities Press, 1955, pp. 353–366.

Goldberg, A. (1978), *The Psychology of the Self: A Casebook.* New York: International Universities Press.

Gould, E. & Rosenberger, J., eds. (1994), Erotic transference: Contemporary perspectives. *Psychoanal. Inq.,* 14:477–639.

Gray, P. (1973), Psychoanalytic technique and the ego's capacity for viewing intrapsychic activity. *J. Amer. Psychoanal. Assn.,* 21:474–494.

Greenberg, J. & Mitchell, S. A. (1983), *Object Relations in Psychoanalytic Theory.* Cambridge, MA: Harvard University Press.

Greenberg, R. (1987), The dream problem and the problem in dreams. In: *Dreams in New Perspective: The Royal Road Revisited,* ed. M. Glucksman & S. Warner. New York: Human Sciences Press, pp. 45–58.

———— (1993), An integrated approach to dream theory: Contributions from sleep research and clinical practice. In: *The Functions of Dreaming,* ed. A. Moffitt, M. Kramer & R. Hoffmann. Albany, NY: State University of New York Press, pp. 363–380.

Greenson, R. R. (1967), *The Technique and Practice of Psychoanalysis.* New York: International Universities Press.

Guntrip, H. (1969), *Schizoid Phenomena, Object Relations and the Self.* New York: International Universities Press.

Hadley, J. (1989), The neurobiology of motivational systems. In: *Psychoanalysis and Motivation,* ed. J. Lichtenberg. Hillsdale, NJ: The Analytic Press, pp. 337–372.

Hartmann, H. (1964), *Essays on Ego Psychology.* New York: International Universities Press.

Herman, J. (1992), *Trauma and Recovery.* New York: Basic Books.

Hoffman, I. (1983), The patient as interpreter of the analyst's experience. *Contemp. Psychoanal.,* 19:389–422.

———— (1991), Discussion: Toward a social-constructivist view of the psychoanalytic situation. *Psychoanal. Dial.,* 1:74–105.

———— (1992), Some practical implications of a social-constructivist view of the analytic situation. *Psychoanal. Dial.,* 1:74–105.

———— & Gill, M. (1988), Critical reflections on a coding scheme. *Internat. J. Psycho-Anal.,* 69:55–64.

Holt, R. (1967), The development of primary process. In: *Motives and Thought: Psychoanalytic Essays in Honor of David Rapaport. Psychological Issues,* Monogr. 18/19. New York: International Universities Press, pp. 344–383.

Horowitz, M. J. (1988), *Introduction to Psychodynamics.* New York: Basic Books.

Jacobs, T. (1991), *The Use of the Self.* Madison, CT: International Universities Press.

Jones, E. (1953), *The Life and Work of Sigmund Freud, Vol. 1.* London: Hogarth Press.

Jones, J. (1995), *Affects as Process.* Hillsdale, NJ: The Analytic Press.

Josephs, L. (1995), *Balancing Empathy and Interpretation.* Northvale, NJ: Aronson.

Jung, C. G. (1916), General aspects of dream psychology. In: *The Structure and Dynamics of the Psyche, Collected Works, Vol. 8.* New York: Pantheon Books, 1960, pp. 237–280.

Kagan, J., Kearsley, R. & Zelazu, P. (1978), *Infancy: Its Place in Human Development.* Cambridge, MA: Harvard University Press.

Kardiner, A. (1939), *The Individual and His Society: The Psychodynamics of Primitive Social Organization.* New York: Columbia University Press.

Kent, E. (1981), *The Brains of Men and Machines.* Peterborough, NH: BYTE.

Kernberg, O. F. (1975), *Borderline Conditions and Pathological Narcissism.* New York: Aronson.

—— (1976), *Object Relations Theory and Clinical Psychoanalysis.* New York: Aronson.

—— (1992), *Aggression in Personality Disorders and Perversions.* New Haven, CT: Yale University Press.

Klein, G. (1970), *Perception, Motives, and Personality.* New York: Knopf.

Kohut, H. (1971), *The Analysis of the Self.* New York: International Universities Press.

—— (1977), *The Restoration of the Self.* New York: International Universities Press.

—— (1984), *How Does Analysis Cure?* ed. A. Goldberg & P. Stepansky. Chicago: University of Chicago Press.

Kris, E. (1956), On some vicissitudes of insight. *Internat. J. Psycho-Anal.,* 37:445–455.

Lachmann, F. (1986), Interpretation of psychic conflict and adversarial relationships: A self-psychoanalytic perspective. *Psychoanal. Psychol.,* 3:341–355.

—— (1990), On some challenges to clinical theory in the treatment of character pathology. In: *The Realities of the Transference: Progress in Self Psychology, Vol. 6,* ed. A. Goldberg. Hillsdale, NJ: The Analytic Press, pp. 59–67.

—— & Beebe, B. (1989), Oneness fantasies revisited. *Psychoanal. Psychol.,* 6:137–149.

—— & —— (1992a), Reformulation of early development and transference: Implications for psychic structure formation. In: *Interface of Psychoanalysis and Psychology,* ed. D. Wolitzky, M. Eagle & J. Barron. Washington, DC: American Psychological Association, pp. 133–153.

—— & —— (1992b), Representational configurations and selfobject transferences: A developmental perspective. In: *New Therapeutic Visions: Progress in Self Psychology, Vol. 8,* ed. A. Goldberg. Hillsdale, NJ: The Analytic Press, pp. 3–15.

—— & —— (1993), Interpretation in a developmental perspective. In: *The Widening Scope of Self Psychology: Progress in Self Psychology, Vol. 9,* ed. A Goldberg. Hillsdale, NJ: The Analytic Press, pp. 45–52.

—— & —— (in press), Three principles of salience in the organization of the analyst-patient interaction. *Psychoanal. Psychol.,* 13.

Lazar, S. (1990), Patient's responses to pregnancy and miscarriage in the analyst. In: *Illness in the Analyst,* ed. H. Schwartz & A. Silver. Madison, CT: International University Press, pp. 199–226.

Levin, F. (1991), *Mapping the Mind.* Hillsdale, NJ: The Analytic Press.

Levin, R. (1990), Psychoanalytic theories on the function of dreaming: A review of the empirical dream research. In: *Empirical Studies of Psychoanalytic Theories, Vol. 3,* ed. J. Masling. Hillsdale, NJ: The Analytic Press, pp. 1–54.

Lichtenberg, J. (1981), The empathic mode of perception and alternative vantage points for psychoanalytic work. *Psychoanal. Inq.,* 1:329–356.

—— (1983), *Psychoanalysis and Infant Research.* Hillsdale, NJ: The Analytic Press.

—— (1989), *Psychoanalysis and Motivation.* Hillsdale, NJ: The Analytic Press.

—— (1990) Rethinking the scope of the patient's transference and the therapist's counterresponsiveness. In: *The Realities of Transference: Progress in Self Psychology, Vol. 6,* ed. A. Goldberg. Hillsdale, NJ: The Analytic Press, pp. 23–33.

—— (1991), What is a selfobject? *Psychoanal. Dial.,* 1:455–479.

——— (1994), How libido theory shaped technique (1911–1915). *J. Amer. Psychoanal. Assn.*, 42:727–739.

——— (1995), Forty-five years on, behind, and without the couch. *Psychoanal. Inq.*, 15:280–294.

——— & Kindler, A. (1994), A motivational systems approach to the clinical experience. *J. Amer. Psychoanal. Assn.*, 42:405–420.

——— & Meares, R. (1996), The role of play in things human. *Psychoanal. & Psychother.*, 13:3–16.

——— Lachmann, F. & Fosshage, J. (1992), *Self and Motivational Systems: Toward a Theory of Psychoanalytic Technique.* Hillsdale, NJ: The Analytic Press.

Lindon, J. (1994), Gratification and provision in psychoanalysis: Should we get rid of "the rule of abstinence"? *Psychoanal. Dial.*, 4:549–582.

Loewald, H. (1960), On the therapeutic action of psychoanalysis. In: *Papers on Psychoanalysis.* New Haven, CT: Yale University Press, pp. 221–256.

London, N. (1983), Confrontation and selfobject transference: A case study. In: *Reflections on Self Psychology*, ed. J. Lichtenberg & S. Kaplan. Hillsdale, NJ: The Analytic Press.

Luborsky, L. (1976), Measuring a pervasive psychic structure in psychotherapy: The core conflictural relationship theme. In: *Communicative Structures and Psychic Structures*, ed. M. Freedman & S. Grand. New York: Plenum Press.

——— & Crits-Christoph, P. (1989), A relationship pattern measure: The core conflictural relationship theme. *Psychiatry*, 52:250–259.

Mahler, M. S. (1968), *On Human Symbiosis and the Vicissitudes of Individuation.* New York: International Universities Press.

——— Pine, F. & Bergman, A. (1975), *The Psychological Birth of the Human Infant.* New York: Basic Books.

Major, R. & Miller, P. (1984), Empathy, antipathy, and telepathy in the analytic process. In: *Empathy II*, ed. J. Lichtenberg, M. Bornstein & D. Silver. Hillsdale, NJ: The Analytic Press, pp. 227–248.

Malin, A. (1993), A self psychological approach to the analysis of resistance: A case report. *Internat. J. Psycho-Anal.*, 74:505–518.

Marohn, R. & Wolf, E. (1990), Corrective emotional experience revisited. *Psychoanal. Inq.*, 10:285–456.

McKinnon, J. (1979), Two semantic forms: Neuropsychological and psychoanalytic descriptions. *Psychoanal. & Contemp. Thought*, 2:25–76.

McLaughlin, J. (1978), Primary and secondary process in the context of cerebral hemispheric specialization. *Psychoanal. Quart.*, 47:237–266.

Meissner, R. (1991), *What Is Effective in Psychoanalytic Therapy.* Northvale, NJ: Aronson.

Mitchell, S. (1988), *Relational Concepts in Psychoanalysis.* Cambridge, MA: Harvard University Press.

Modell, A. (1984), *Psychoanalysis in a New Context.* New York: International Universities Press.

——— (1986), The missing element in Kohut's cure. *Psychoanal. Inq.*, 6:367–385.

Moraitis, G. (1988), A reexamination of phobias as the fear of the unknown. *The Annual of Psychoanalysis*, 16:221–249. New York: International Universities Press.

Nelson, K. (1986), *Event Knowledge.* Hillsdale, NJ: Lawrence Erlbaum Associates.

Noy, P. (1969), A revision of the psychoanalytic theory of the primary process. *Internat. J. Psycho-Anal.*, 50:155–178.

────── (1979), The psychoanalytic theory of cognitive development. *The Psychoanalytic Study of the Child,* 34:169–216. New Haven, CT: Yale University Press.

Ogden, T. (1982), *Projective Identification and Psychotherapeutic Technique.* New York: Aronson.

Ornstein, A. (1974), The dread to repeat and the new beginning. *The Annual of Psychoanalysis,* 2:231–248. Madison, CT: International Universities Press.

Ornstein, P. (1987), On the self-state dreams in the psychoanalytic treatment process. In: *The Interpretation of Dreams in Clinical Work,* ed. A. Rothstein. Madison, CT: International Universities Press, pp. 87–104.

Palombo, S. (1978), The adaptive function of dreams. *Psychoanal. & Contemp. Thought,* 1:443–476.

Peterfreund, E. (1983), *The Process of Psychoanalytic Therapy.* Hillsdale, NJ: The Analytic Press.

Pine, F. (1981), In the beginning: Contributions to a psychoanalytic developmental psychology. *Internat. Rev. Psychoanal.,* 8:15–33.

────── (1986), The "symbiotic phase" in the light of current infancy research. *Bull. Menn. Clin.,* 50:564–569.

Poland, W. (1984), The analyst's words: Empathy and countertransference. *Psychoanal. Quart.,* 53:421–424.

────── (1988), Insight and the analytic dyad. *Psychoanal. Quart.,* 57:341–369.

────── (1992), Transference: An original creation. *Psychoanal. Quart.,* 61:185–205.

Pulver, S. (1992), Psychic change: Insight or relationship. *Internat. J. Psycho-Anal.,* 73:199–208.

Racker, H. (1968), *Transference and Countertransference.* London: Hogarth Press.

Rapaport, D. (1953), On the psychoanalytic theory of affects. In: *The Collected Papers of David Rapaport,* ed. M. Gill. New York: Basic Books, 1967, pp. 476–512.

Reik, T. (1949), *Listening With the Third Ear.* New York: Farrar, Straus.

Ringstrom, P. (1995), Exploring the model scene: Finding its focus in an intersubjective approach to brief psychotherapy. *Psychoanal. Inq.,* 15:493–573.

Rogers, C (1951), *Client-Centered Therapy.* Boston: Houghton Mifflin.

Rosenfield, I. (1988), *The Invention of Memory: A New View of the Brain.* New York: Harper & Row.

Schafer, R. (1982), *A New Language for Psychoanalysis.* New Haven, CT: Yale University Press.

────── (1983), *The Analytic Attitude.* New York: Basic Books.

Schore, A. (1994), *Affect Regulation and the Origin of the Self.* Hillsdale, NJ: Lawrence Erlbaum Associates.

Schwartz, H. & Silver, A., eds. (1990), *Illness in the Analyst.* Madison, CT: International Universities Press.

Segel, H. (1974), *An Introduction to the Work of Melanie Klein.* London: Hogarth Press.

Silverman, M. (1987), Clinical material. *Psychoanal. Inq.,* 7:147–166.

Simon, B. (1984), Confluence of visual image between patient and analyst: Communication of failed communication. In: *Empathy II,* ed. J. Lichtenberg, M. Bornstein & D. Silver. Hillsdale, NJ: The Analytic Press, pp. 261–278.

Slavin, M. & Kriegman, D. (1992), *The Adaptive Design of the Human Psyche.* New York: Guilford.

────── & ────── (1994), Why the therapist needs to change: Conflict, deception, and mutual influence in the therapeutic relationship. Unpublished manuscript.

Sloane, P. (1979), *Psychoanalytic Understanding of the Dream*. New York: Aronson.

Spence, D. (1982), *Narrative Truth and Historical Truth*. New York: Norton.

Spillius, E. (1995), Developments in Kleinian thought: Overview and personal view. *Psychoanal. Inq.,* 14:324–364.

Spitz, J. (1957), *No and Yes*. New York: International Universities Press.

Stern, D. (1985), *The Interpersonal World of the Infant*. New York: Basic Books.

Stolorow, R. & Atwood, G. (1992), *Contexts of Being: The Intersubjective Foundations of Psychological Life*. Hillsdale, NJ: The Analytic Press.

—— & Lachmann, F. (1980), *Psychoanalysis of Developmental Arrests*. New York: International Universities Press.

—— & —— (1984/1985), Transference: The future of an illusion. *The Annual of Psychoanalysis,* 12/13:19–37. New York: International Universities Press.

—— Brandchaft, B. & Atwood, G. (1987), *Psychoanalytic Treatment: An Intersubjective Approach*. Hillsdale, NJ: The Analytic Press.

Stone, L. (1961), *The Psychoanalytic Situation*. New York: International Universities Press.

Strachey, J. (1934), The fate of the ego in analytic therapy. *Internat. J. Psycho-Anal.,* 15:117–126.

Stuss, D. (1992), Biological and physiological development of executive function. *Brain & Cognition,* 20:8–23.

Sullivan, H. (1947), *Conceptions of Modern Psychiatry*. Washington, DC: The William Alanson White Psychiatric Foundation.

—— (1953), *The Interpersonal Theory of Psychiatry*. New York: Norton.

Tomkins, S. (1962), *Affect, Imagery, Consciousness, Vol. 1: The Positive Affects*. New York: Springer.

—— (1964), *Affect, Imagery, Consciousness, Vol. 2: The Negative Affects*. New York: Springer.

Wachtel, P. F. (1980), Transference, schema and assimilation: The relevance of Piaget to the psychoanalytic theory of transference. *The Annual of Psychoanalysis,* 8:59–76. New York: International Universities Press.

Waddington, C. (1947), *Organizers and Genes*. Cambridge: The University Press.

Wallerstein, R. (1984), The analysis of the transference: A matter of emphasis or of theory reformulation? *Psychoanal. Inq.,* 4:325–354.

—— (1986), *Forty-two Lives in Treatment*. New York: Guilford.

Weiss, J. (1993), *How Psychotherapy Works*. New York: Guilford.

—— & Sampson, H. (1986), *The Psychoanalytic Process*. New York: Guilford.

Whitmont, E. (1978), Jungian approach. In: *Dream Interpretation: A Comparative Study,* ed. J. Fosshage & C. Loew. New York: PMA, pp. 53–78.

—— & Perera, S. (1990), *Dreams, A Portal to the Source*. New York: Routledge, Chapman & Hall.

Winnicott, D. (1958), The capacity to be alone. In: *The Maturational Processes and the Facilitating Environment*. New York: International Universities Press, 1965, pp. 29–36.

Winson, J. (1985), *Brain and Psyche*. Garden City, NY: Doubleday.

Wolf, E. (1988), *Treating the Self*. New York: Guilford.

—— (1980), On the developmental line of selfobject relations. In: *Advances in Self Psychology,* ed. A. Goldberg. New York: International Universities Press, pp. 117–132.

# Index